— In Grateful Appreciaton To —

RUTH Q. DODGE

FOR DEDICATED SUPPORT
TO THE CAUSE OF JUSTICE
AND THE
SOUTHERN POVERTY
LAW CENTER

Also by Morris Dees with Steve Fiffer

A Season for Justice

HATE
ON TRIAL

HATE ON TRIAL

THE CASE AGAINST AMERICA'S MOST DANGEROUS NEO-NAZI

Morris Dees
and
Steve Fiffer

VILLARD BOOKS
1993

Library of Congress Cataloging-in-Publication Data
Dees, Morris.
Hate on trial
p.   cm.
ISBN 0-679-40614-X
1. Metzger, Tom—Trials, litigation, etc.
2. Wrongful death—Oregon.
3. Hate crimes—United States.
4. Hate crimes—Oregon.
5. White Aryan Resistance.
I. Fiffer, Steve.   II. Title.
KF228.M48D44   1993
364.1—dc20   92-50491

Manufactured in the United States of America

9   8   7   6   5   4   3   2

First edition

For Cathy Bennett

There could be very bad things happen to you if you carry out this exercise in futility. You are taking on too much, Morris baby, you are messing with white power. Nobody messes with white power. You go against nature.

—Anonymous letter sent to Morris Dees, September 17, 1990

ACKNOWLEDGMENTS

The same team that contributed so greatly to the legal effort against Tom Metzger and White Aryan Resistance also supplied invaluable assistance in the writing of this book. Southern Poverty Law Center legal director Richard Cohen, who guided the Metzger case through dangerous waters, again proved that he is also a remarkable editor. Counsel Elden Rosenthal and Jim McElroy read the manuscript and contributed important insights, as did our client and friend Engedaw Berhanu. Klanwatch's Danny Welch, who played such an important role in bringing the lawsuit, spent countless hours assisting in the reconstruction of events. The Center's Sara Bullard, Joe Roy, Linda Stringer, and Judy Bruno were also instrumental.

Others, too, played an important role in shaping the final product. Elizabeth Dees and Sharon Fiffer were unofficial but indispensable editors. Villard's Diane Reverand, our official editor, was equally indispensable.

Recognition is also due to our literary agent, Carol Mann; to Elden's secretary, Sally Lane; to tape transcriber Pam Parker; to Mulugeta Seraw's friend Cygnette Cherry; and to Kate, Nora, and Robert Fiffer for their support.

Special thanks must be given to several friends for their assistance before, during, and after the trial in Portland. These include the Anti-Defamation League, Margie Rosenthal, Michael Greene, Carlton Grew, and a brave contingent from the Portland Police Bureau that provided protection during the trial: Sergeant James "Gator" Hudson, Officer Ed "Edmo" Brumfield, Officer Dirk Anderson, Lieutenant Mike Cullivan, Sergeant Ken Pacheco, Officer Brian Schmautz, Officer Nate "Natimo" Shropshire, Officer Sean Pritchard, Officer Wayne Baldassare, Officer Paul Weatheroy, Officer Bill Gray, Sergeant Frank Romanagg, Sergeant Bob Wilson, Officer Brett

Smith, Officer Mike Stradley, Officer John Frater, Officer Kevin Griffey, Detective Jim Hunter, Officer Paul Fisher, and Captain Richard Tate.

Among those providing important information were three individuals whose names have been changed to protect their privacy. In the book they are identified by the pseudonyms Cody Wallis, Goggles Flynt, and Pete Gibbons.

Finally, without the financial support of the Center's many friends, the long and costly battle would not have been possible. They have our undying gratitude.

CONTENTS

CONTENTS

Prologue

In the early 1980s, a group of armed and dangerous revolutionaries called the Order carried out a series of crimes in the name of white supremacy. Their most notorious deed was the killing of Alan Berg, a Denver talk show host who had ridiculed bigotry during his radio broadcasts. At the time that Berg was gunned down in front of his home, he was the second person on a hit list compiled by the Order. I was the first person on that list.

In response to this dramatic wave of terror, the FBI launched an intensive manhunt that ended on Whidbey Island, Washington, where Robert Mathews, the Order's leader, was killed in a fiery shootout.

With his death, Mathews became a martyr in the white supremacist world. An organization called White Aryan Resistance (WAR) dedicated itself to carrying forward Mathews's goal of white revolution. The WAR youth wing launched OPERATION WARLORDS. The goal of the organization was to "create a new wave of predatory leaders among Aryan youth." WAR vowed to encourage violent racist attacks "across white America while simultaneously rebuilding the hunter-killer instincts in our youth."

This book is the story of the effort to stop OPERATION WARLORDS in the courts in Portland, Oregon.

HATE
ON TRIAL

This is Aryan Update, a production of WAR. Now to Portland, Oregon, for a report from Rick Cooper, chairman of the National Socialist Vanguard. What's new in Portland, Rick?

Well [Tom], a number of skinheads have been moving into Portland . . . to work in a relatively fertile area in that the white people in this area are basically sympathetic to white racial causes.

It all sounds great, Rick. . . . And, unofficially, the fights and attacks against the race-mixers and some of the race traitors and the racial scum has been picking up because of the new warriors moving into the area. But I'm sure there will be more on that later. When it comes out, it will be all at once.

—Tom Metzger, White Aryan Resistance telephone hotline,
October 24, 1988

CHAPTER ONE

November 13, 1988

■

Portland, Oregon

Voices from below pierced the cool, still night, waking Elizabeth Reinisch in her second-floor apartment on Southeast Thirty-first Avenue. She sat up in bed, got her bearings. Uncertain whether to go to the window or go back to sleep, she simply listened. She could not understand the words from the street, but she knew that there was trouble. Reinisch, a twenty-nine-year-old service representative for the phone company, moved to her window and opened it.

The cold air invaded the bedroom, carrying a frightening message. "Look out, he's got a gun," Reinisch thought she heard someone say. This was followed by two *pops*—similar to gunfire, she would later tell police.

Her mind raced as she stood by the window shivering, searching for clues. A car pulled into the driveway across the street. A figure hurried out and moved southbound on Thirty-first toward Pine Street. A voice cried, "Quick, get into the car! Let's get out of here!"

Reinisch rushed from the window and dialed 911.

When she returned the car was gone. She dressed quickly and ran downstairs. *Dear God!* A young man lay in the street, his body twisted, blood flowing from his crushed head.

The police arrived, followed by the fire department's Engine and

Rescue Unit 9 from Southeast Thirty-fourth and Belmont. Fire Lieutenant Dennis Mayo was prepared for a shooting, but the unconscious young man on the damp pavement had been beaten, not shot. He was still alive, though barely. Mayo gave him oxygen until Care Ambulance 74 appeared.

The ambulance crew went to work quickly. Paramedic Jerry Andrews cut off the man's shirt, tried to stabilize him, and then rushed him to Emanuel Hospital.

The ambulance passed policemen who had already found two witnesses, each a dark-skinned young man. One, Wondwosen Tesfaye, was bleeding and in need of medical attention. The other, Tilahun Antneh, was hysterical. In broken English, he gasped that the victim's name was Mulugeta Seraw.

Antneh told the police that Seraw, Tesfaye, and he were originally from Ethiopia. Earlier in the evening they had been at a party. Antneh had offered a ride home to Tesfaye and Seraw. He had just dropped Seraw at the curb in front of his apartment building when a car with several young men and women approached. At least two of the men—both with shaved heads and wearing dark leather jackets—jumped out.

One of these men was carrying "a big stick." He hit Antneh's car, smashing the rear windows and a taillight. He also hit Seraw. Others assaulted Antneh and Tesfaye, who had scrambled out to help their countryman.

By the time the police had finished talking to Antneh, the unconscious Mulugeta Seraw had arrived at Emanuel's intensive care unit. Fearing his massive brain injury would prove fatal, doctors hooked him up to a ventilator and waited. He never awoke. Six hours later he was declared dead.

Minutes after Seraw's death, his uncle, awakened earlier by a call from the authorities, arrived in Portland from the San Francisco Bay Area. Like his nephew, Engedaw Berhanu had come to the United States to get an education and to escape the war and famine in Ethiopia. Like his nephew, he had always believed in the American dream. Now, sobbing as he formally identified the body, he no longer knew what to believe.

* * *

From the description provided by eyewitness Antneh, the Portland police were certain that skinheads had beaten Mulugeta Seraw to death. Word that a black man had died, apparently at the hands of these young, radical racists, traveled quickly from the police station to the community to the wire services. Sadly, the nation was no longer shocked by such news. Skinheads, as easy to spot as robed Klansmen, had already earned a reputation for violence in Portland and other major cities.

Although details were sketchy, the death immediately mobilized Portland. Mayor Bud Clark said he was "saddened and disturbed," and urged citizens as well as public officials to develop constructive programs to combat racial violence. At Seraw's funeral, the pastor of his Seventh-Day Adventist church told the several hundred mourners, "We are ashamed and embarrassed that one who was a visitor to our city was slain like a common dog in the streets." At a community meeting in northeast Portland, 350 citizens anxious about the spread of white supremacist violence turned out to hear Police Chief Richard Walker. In a letter to the gathering, Governor Neil Goldschmidt said he was outraged by the killing.

The police launched an intense search for the killers, assigning fifteen officers to the case. Feeling the investigation's heat, two skinhead leaders who had recently moved from California to Oregon called a Portland television station and asked to be interviewed on the evening news. On November 16, Dave Mazzella and Michael Barrett appeared on Channel 12 and insisted that local skinheads had nothing to do with the killing. Outsiders must be responsible.

Twenty-four hours later, the Portland police took Mazzella into custody. The slight blond nineteen-year-old was wanted on an outstanding warrant by California authorities because he had missed a hearing on an assault charge.

Tom Nelson, one of the detectives coordinating the Seraw homicide investigation, was not interested in outstanding warrants, though. He asked Mazzella what he was doing on November 13. Suddenly, unexpectedly, the floodgates opened. Saying he was sickened by the death and wanted out of the white supremacy movement, Mazzella told the detective that his roommate, Steve Strasser, had described the beating to him on the morning of the thirteenth. Strasser, a twenty-year-old factory worker who belonged to the local skinhead gang East Side White Pride, could not contain his excitement as he repeatedly detailed how he and fellow "Pride" members Kyle Brewster and Ken Mieske did battle with the three Ethiopians.

The battle was decidedly one-sided. Brewster, a former high school homecoming king, pummeled Seraw with brass knuckles. Then Mieske, a would-be actor and singer, knocked Seraw into the gutter with a baseball bat. "Steve said the guy [Seraw] was saying he was sorry," Mazzella told Detective Nelson. "But Steve told him, 'Well, sorry's not good enough,' and started kicking him."

Mazzella had also talked with Mieske after the killing. "Ken said, 'I didn't know that nigger was going to die,' " Mazzella reported.

Before the interview ended, Mazzella related much more information about the events leading up to the beatings, the killing itself, and the aftermath. He identified Patti Copp, Brewster's girlfriend, as the driver of the skinheads' car. And he said that Mieske's girlfriend, Julie Belec, and Strasser's girlfriend, Heidi Martinson, were also in the vehicle.

Mazzella gave Nelson permission to record his statement. Knowing he had just delivered his comrades to the police, he told the detective that he hoped he wouldn't be identified as the skinheads' Judas. "I could get in a lot of trouble," he said.

While Mazzella remained in jail awaiting extradition to California, the police rounded up those he had fingered. Patti Copp, Heidi Martinson, and Julie Belec were interviewed. Acknowledging that their boyfriends had fought the Ethiopians, they spoke of extenuating circumstances: the skinheads had been provoked, they suggested. Nevertheless, Mieske was arrested on November 19. Strasser and Brewster were taken into custody the next day.

SKINHEADS ARRESTED IN KILLING read the November 21 headline in Portland's major newspaper, the *Oregonian*. Mieske and Brewster, both of whom refused to talk, stood charged with murder and were held without bond. Strasser, who had been more forthcoming, was charged with second-degree assault and held in lieu of $100,000 bail.

Portland breathed a sigh of relief. Justice had apparently been served. But, down in Fallbrook, California, Tom Metzger, the fifty-year-old charismatic leader of White Aryan Resistance (WAR), the most dangerous of America's burgeoning neo-Nazi groups, saw the killing differently. "Sounds like the skinheads did a civic duty," he announced over his telephone hotline.

You have reached WAR Hotline, White Aryan Resistance. You ask: What is WAR? We are an openly white-racist movement. . . . Skinheads, we welcome you into our ranks. . . . The federal government is the number one enemy of our race. When was the last time you heard a politician speaking out in favor of white people? . . . You say the government is too big; we can't organize. Well, by God, the SS did it in Germany, and if they did it in Germany in the thirties, we can do it right here in the streets of America. . . . We need to cleanse this nation of all nonwhite mud-races for the very survival of our own people and the generations of our children.

—Tom Metzger, White Aryan Resistance telephone hotline, June 27, 1988

CHAPTER TWO

November 29, 1988

Montgomery, Alabama

Danny Welch put a folder marked SERAW on my desk. "This might be the case we've been waiting for, Morris," he said. He took a seat and began peppering me with facts about the murder in Portland.

I didn't look up. A long-delayed trial against the Invisible Empire Knights of the Ku Klux Klan and its Klansmen who had assaulted blacks marching peacefully in Decatur, Alabama, was finally at hand. As chief trial counsel for the Southern Poverty Law Center, I was hustling to refamiliarize myself with details and witnesses lost in the paper shuffle of the last several years. There was little time to discuss a new case, especially one more than twenty-five hundred miles from home.

"The newspaper says that one of Mieske's nicknames was Batman," Danny said, holding up an article from the *Oregonian*. "He was also known as Ken Death."

"Okay," I sighed. I put down the deposition I'd been reading and picked up the Seraw file. Danny, a wiry thirty-seven-year-old with short blond hair, could wait hours for a deer without moving a muscle. But he had never been able to wait for an answer from me. He tapped his foot like he was standing in a bed of fire ants.

Distracting as it was, I could live with this nervous professional energy. I'd known and liked Danny for almost thirty years, ever since I'd frequented his daddy's country store at the crossroads near my farm about twenty miles south of Montgomery. He'd gone off to the army after high school, then returned to rise through the ranks of the Montgomery Police Department, becoming shift commander of the robbery/homicide division before he was thirty. When Klansmen angry with our efforts to fight racial discrimination and KKK terrorism burned the Southern Poverty Law Center in 1983, I offered him a job as head of security. He now served as chief investigator for Klanwatch, the Center division that monitored the Klan and brought lawsuits against the KKK and other hate groups.

We'd been through some frightening times together. It had been Danny who'd made a midnight run to guard me after the FBI called and said I was next on the hit list of the Order, the white supremacist group that had gunned down Alan Berg, a Denver radio personality who had frequently clashed with neo-Nazis and other hatemongers.

"These skinheads were brutal," Danny said as I skimmed the Seraw file. "You know that woman who thought she heard shots fired? It turned out that was the sound of a baseball bat shattering Mulugeta's skull."

I closed my eyes. *Where did the hate come from? The newspapers said Mieske hadn't even known Seraw. What was it inside this young man that caused him to act so cruelly to a fellow human being?*

I shut the folder. "Danny, if the guys who did this are found guilty, they'll probably go to jail for life. But there's no civil suit for us here. This isn't the Donald case."

Eighteen months earlier we had bankrupted the United Klans of America (UKA), the KKK group responsible for some of the most heinous crimes of the civil rights era. Our involvement had been triggered by a murder—the lynching of a nineteen-year-old black man named Michael Donald in Mobile in 1981. After one member of the UKA was convicted of the killing and a second pleaded guilty, we filed a civil lawsuit on behalf of Michael's mother against several members of the UKA and, most significantly, the organization itself.

Our theory—admittedly novel—was that the UKA, like any corporation, should be held liable for the acts of its agents when those agents were acting to further the organization's goals. By securing secret Klan documents and demonstrating that the UKA had a long history of using violence to advance its stated goal, the "God-given supremacy of the white race," we were able to persuade an all-white jury to deliver a landmark $7 million verdict for Mrs. Donald in February 1987. Unable to come up with the money, the Klan organization was forced to satisfy the judgment by turning over its national headquarters to Mrs. Donald. She sold the building and used the proceeds to move out of public housing for the first time in her adult life.

This had been my most important case in twenty-five years as a lawyer. My parents were tenant cotton farmers in Montgomery County. I had picked cotton side by side with blacks and had as many black friends as white when I was growing up. Still, it had taken a long time before I questioned the segregation that had been in place well before my birth in 1936.

Some of the UKA's past actions that we focused on at the Donald trial had special significance to me. After Imperial Wizard Bobby Shelton's thugs beat the Freedom Riders in Montgomery in 1961, I represented a neighbor with ties to the Klan who was accused of assaulting a newsman during the riot. As I left the courthouse, I was confronted by two black men, who asked me how I could work for a violent racist. I'd always thought of myself as a friend to blacks, sympathetic to their lot, but these honest inquisitors forced me to consider whether my actions reflected my thoughts. Then and there I decided that no one would ever again have to ask where I stood.

Two years later the UKA's infamous bombing of a Birmingham church moved me to take my first public stance against the violence of the civil rights era. On the Sunday after the tragedy, I asked my neighbors in our Pike Road Baptist Church to join in prayer for the families of the four black girls who had died in the blast and to send money to help rebuild the church. My fellow Christians' angry rejection of my plea caused me to leave what I saw as a hypocritical church. This started a split with old friends, who soon ostracized me and, worse, my family.

By the time of the 1965 Selma-to-Montgomery march for voting rights, I was ready to become more involved. I did not have the courage to walk the forty-nine miles with Dr. Martin Luther King, but

I did drive marchers from Montgomery to Selma so they could partici-pate. So, too, did Viola Liuzzo, a mother of five from Detroit, who was shot and killed by three UKA members.

Waiting in the shadows of the state capitol for the marchers to arrive and the speeches to begin, I encountered my uncle James Dees. My late father, Morris Dees, Sr., had never challenged segregation but had been considered a special friend of the blacks in our community because he treated them with dignity and respect. His brothers, James and Lucien, on the other hand, were among the more notorious racists in the county. As the speeches began, James pulled a gun from his waist, waved it in the air, and called me a "nigger lover" who had disgraced the family.

Shortly after graduating from law school in 1960, I had closed my practice to create a publishing company that became quite successful. Not too long after my confrontation with Uncle James, moved in part by reading lawyer Clarence Darrow's autobiography, I took a long look at my life. Despite the passage of the Civil Rights Act of 1964 and the Voting Rights Act of 1965, the blacks whom I had grown up with were still "disenfranchised." Whites held the power and showed no willingness to share it. Blacks were still excluded from good jobs, decent housing, elective office, good educations, jury service, and a host of other rights that whites took for granted.

It would take lawsuits to gain these rights. There were few black lawyers around and hardly any white ones who would touch contro-versial cases. I felt that I was a good lawyer wasting my time trying to make a few more million dollars. I sold my business and with a fellow attorney, Joe Levin, created the not-for-profit Southern Poverty Law Center to fight discrimination and poverty with innovative lawsuits and education programs.

The Donald case was effective only because we were able to bring the UKA itself into court. A civil suit against the Klansmen, all of whom were doing the organization's bidding and none of whom had any money, would not have resulted in the justice or financial remu-neration we were seeking.* In Portland, it appeared, the skinheads

---

*In bringing cases such as the one on behalf of Mrs. Donald, the Center, a not-for-profit institution, does not charge a fee or take any part of the resulting monetary judgment. We exist solely through the generous support of approximately 100,000 donors.

were destitute and there was no hate group that we could sue and try to bankrupt by winning a large judgment.

Danny frowned at my assessment and took the Seraw file. "One of the articles mentions Dave Mazzella and Mike Barrett," he said, trying to locate the clipping. "You know who they're connected to."*

I did know that Mazzella and Barrett had worked with Tom Metzger and his son, John, the head of Aryan Youth Movement (AYM), WAR's youth division. Mazzella was vice president of AYM, while Barrett led WARskins, a skinhead group closely affiliated with WAR. The two skinheads had even appeared with John on Oprah Winfrey's talk show.

There was nothing I would have liked better than to put the Metzgers and their organizations out of business. They had emerged as the most dangerous demagogues of a white supremacy movement that had been building momentum for the last ten years. That movement had started with the rebirth of the Ku Klux Klan, which had been dormant since the end of the civil rights era.

The Klan has traditionally reemerged when working-class whites feel their economic or social standing is threatened. With jobs scarce and double-digit inflation driving up prices in the late seventies, the stage was set. To many it seemed that minorities were getting all the breaks through affirmative action programs. The allegations of new Klan leaders like David Duke—that Jews controlled the economic pie and that blacks, Hispanics, and refugees were getting the biggest pieces—struck a responsive chord with an increasing number of whites hungry for a better life. Klan membership rose dramatically.

The new edition of the Klan carried on old traditions, attacking black marchers in Alabama and Georgia, terrorizing Vietnamese fishermen in Galveston Bay, lynching Michael Donald. But thanks to surprisingly vigorous criminal prosecutions by the Reagan Justice Department and several verdicts won by our Center, the Klan was on the decline again by 1988.

There was, however, no cause for celebration. New leaders had quickly picked up the Klan's torch. Their agenda, much of it derived from Nazi Germany, was more militant, more deadly, than the

*At this time, we did not know Mazzella had informed on the skinheads. It would be several months before we learned this information.

Klan's. It was no longer sufficient to burn crosses, they argued. True victory would come only with widespread indoctrination and, eventually, revolution.

The manifesto for that insurgence was an eye-opening 211-page novel published in 1978 by white supremacist William Pierce. *The Turner Diaries* detailed a fictional U.S. revolution in 1992, led by whites fed up with our "Zionist Occupational Government" (ZOG), which catered to non-Aryans. The successful uprising included assassinations, bombings, and the hanging of Jews, blacks, liberal judges, and "race traitors" from lampposts.

In 1983, Robert Mathews, a thirty-year-old radical racist, had attempted to make life imitate "art," by forming the Order. Also called Bruders Schweigen (the Silent Brotherhood), this band of men living in the Pacific Northwest signed a "declaration of war" against the federal government. Members of the Order were not paper tigers. Using *The Turner Diaries* as their guidebook, they killed several people, including Alan Berg.

The group financed its activities and the activities of white supremacists around the nation by robbing armored cars; it took $3.8 million in a Ukiah, California, holdup alone. After Mathews shot an FBI agent in November 1984, the authorities cornered him on Whidbey Island, Washington. Refusing to surrender, he died in a fiery shootout in December.

Mathews's death put an end to the Order but not to the revolutionary movement. When the Center brought a suit to stop the paramilitary activities of the White Patriot Party in North Carolina in 1985, we learned that the group's leader, Glenn Miller, gave *The Turner Diaries* to all the "elite forces" he was training for the overthrow of the government. Remarkably, the recruits included active-duty U.S. soldiers from Camp LeJeune and Fort Bragg, who provided weapons and instruction. Our efforts earned Miller a jail sentence.

With Mathews dead and Miller silenced, Tom Metzger had become the leading white supremacist revolutionary. A former John Bircher and California Klan leader, he had achieved notoriety in the seventies by leading tax protests and organizing armed border patrols to keep Mexicans from illegally entering the United States. Running for Congress in 1980, he actually won the Democratic nomination. He lost that election when the Democrats disavowed him, but he came back two years later to run for the U.S. Senate and polled an astonishing 90,000 votes although he made no excuses for his anti-black, anti-Semitic beliefs. Metzger's faith in the political system soon died, and his transformation into racist revolutionary was complete by the mid-eighties. That transformation could be seen in the name of his organization. What began as White American Political Association became White American Resistance, then finally White Aryan Resistance.

Mathews was his hero. Metzger held WAR rallies from a trailer he called Mathews Hall. He communicated regularly with imprisoned survivors of the Order, and his speeches and the literature he produced contained numerous "Hail the Order"'s and loving references to the group's martyred leader.

"The old ways are over. It's open season on niggers, kikes, cops, and capitalists—kill 'em all and let the devil sort them out," read Metzger's literature. But it was not merely this message that made Metzger a real threat. He knew how to deliver that message and who should receive it.

Looking clean-cut and sounding almost reasonable, young David Duke had successfully manipulated the media and opened the airwaves for a wide assortment of racists in the seventies. Metzger, a former Duke protégé who said he earned his living as a television repairman, also sensed the importance of mass communication. Like Duke and others, he and his son, John, and their minions often appeared on nationally syndicated talk shows—Oprah, Morton Downey, and Sally Jessy Raphael. Just a few days before the murder in Portland, John had been a guest on Geraldo Rivera's show and had initiated the highly publicized brawl that broke the host's nose.

Metzger also shrewdly grasped that he could reach millions via noncensored "public access" cable television channels across the country. In 1984, he began producing and hosting his own talk show, *Race and Reason*. Years earlier Metzger, like several other racist leaders, had been a minister in the Christian Identity "church," whose principal tenet is that the Jews are the descendants of Satan and that white Aryans are the true Chosen People. With cable his new pulpit, he preached his message and recruited followers, just as the TV evangelists did. Within a few years he was broadcasting to thirty-five cities.

The printed word supplemented the spoken. Metzger published *WAR,* a professional-looking bimonthly newspaper. To monitor the growing number of hate groups, Klanwatch obtained Metzger's paper, as well as several other racist newspapers and periodicals. The issue we received a few weeks before Seraw's death was typical Metzger fare. The bold headline, illustrated with weapons and a Jewish star, trumpeted JEWS GET AWAY WITH MURDER. The accompanying article suggested Israeli terrorists were attacking Aryan nationalists in America with impunity.

A cartoon of a bat-wielding, shaved-headed warrior headlined WHITE POWER directed the reader to an essay by Clark Martell, founder of the Chicago-based Romantic Violence, one of America's first skinhead gangs. Under a photograph of some thirty young men and women flying Confederate flags and banners with swastikas and the iron cross, Martell exhorted readers to follow him as "I join the church of war . . . behind the skinhead battering ram as it rolls . . . through the gates of power." Alongside the essay, Metzger conveniently printed the addresses of thirteen skinhead groups that interested readers could contact.

By chance this issue also included a Metzger editorial about me. Calling me the "Czar of the Southern Poverty Law Center," Metzger accused me of using the toothless Klan "as whipping boys for money-raising scams . . . fighting poverty by growing rich." Winning lawsuits against this ineffective, powerless old organization was like shooting fish in a barrel, Metzger insisted.

Metzger's multimedia approach did not stop with his television show or this newspaper. The telephone was another way to reach the public. On WAR hotlines in several cities, Metzger and his operatives offered followers the usual incendiary racist, homophobic cant, as well as advice, and information about upcoming events. Four days before the Seraw murder, the WAR-affiliated hotline in Escondido, California, had told callers:

> The white youth are rising in the streets of America, and we are going to march on to total victory and on to a new world order. Remember, America is being invaded by Mexicans, raped and deceived by Jews, and maligned and fornicated upon by the blacks. . . . Anything the white race can do to survive is moral and anything the white race does not do is immoral. . . . Remember that white revolution is the only solution.

If Metzger displayed a certain form of intelligence in recognizing that technology could be as important as ideology in building a following, he also wisely recognized a fresh pool of potential followers: impressionable, alienated youth, many of whom were skinheads. The skinhead movement, born in Britain in the early 1970s, had emerged here in the early 1980s independently of organized white supremacist groups. Young, reckless, and anxious to prove their courage, skinheads quickly became the most violent of all radical racists, attacking not only blacks and Jews but Asians, Native Americans, Hispanics, gays, and even liberal whites.

A Pied Piper of hate, Metzger quickly directed his racist tunes toward these young street warriors. "I saw their potential to drag the racialist movement out of the conservative right-wing mold and into a newer era," he explained to a magazine writer. To the skinheads themselves he piped: "You are the New Order. Skinheads are in the forefront. Do you know why Jews are worried about the skinheads? Because the skinheads kick ass."

I knew what Danny was thinking in trying to get me to consider involving the Center in the Seraw case. Two of the Metzgers' skinhead lieutenants, Dave Mazzella and Michael Barrett, had been in Portland when warriors from East Side White Pride had battled the three Ethiopians.

"I'd love to nail the Metzgers, Danny. They're evil sons of bitches, and they said some nasty things about me and the Center. But Mazzella and Barrett weren't even charged with the murder, and there's nothing to link Mieske, Brewster, and Strasser to Metzger. Until there's something to show a connection . . ." I shrugged.

Danny said nothing.

I picked up the deposition I'd been reading. The room was silent except for the tap-tap-tapping of his foot.

Do not go march-happy. Some so-called white nationalists can't wait to drag all their friends into the street for a glorious march. . . . The fact is marches accomplish nothing except to ID you. . . . Robert J. Mathews never sponsored a parade, but he and his friends made more of an impression in one year than all of the white nationalists' marches of this century. WAR . . . says: Don't play your enemy's game. Organize tight little groups. Don't react, act. . . . This is a real war. You, my friend, are behind enemy lines.

—Tom Metzger, White Aryan Resistance telephone hotline, January 23, 1989

CHAPTER THREE

March 14, 1989

■

Montgomery, Alabama

Danny was waiting in my office with a fax. The first page was a copy of an envelope addressed to Ken Death, 645 S.E. 46th, Portland, Oregon. The return address in the upper left-hand corner read "AYM"—the acronym for Aryan Youth Movement. The envelope had been postmarked in San Diego on October 6, 1988, just five weeks before the murder of Mulugeta Seraw.

I looked at Danny, who flashed an I-told-you-so smile. "Where'd this come from?" I asked, flipping to the second page.

"Larry Siewart of the Portland P.D. called and said they found it in Julie Belec's place." Ken Mieske—"Ken Death"—had been living with Belec in her parents' house at the time of the murder.

Klanwatch has long shared intelligence with law enforcement agencies. This occasionally leads to criticism of the Center by those liberals who automatically think of the police and FBI as the enemy. More often it leads to information helpful in pursuing our lawsuits. After our less-than-encouraging conversation in November, Danny had made contact with Siewart, who monitored hate crimes for the Portland police. Siewart had told Danny he greatly admired Klanwatch. To solidify the connection, Danny sent Siewart material we had concerning the skinhead movement. Now, Siewart had returned the favor.

Dear East Side White Pride:

Wanted to drop you a line and let you know we would like to open up communication with your group.

You'll get a feel of how we work when you meet Dave Mazzella and Mike Gagnon soon.

A.Y.M.'s been around for almost 10 years. We changed our name from White Student Union a few years back for the more militant A.Y.M.

Rolling Stone will be featuring an interview with A.Y.M. (Skinheads)/W.A.R. in their October issue. Also, [the TV show] "Reporters" will be doing an interview with us in a week.

We have about a 700 [name] list of supporters, members, etc. and we have 10 chapters around the U.S.

We work with any pro-White, anti-drug, White group as long as they do not talk.

Racial Regards,
John Metzger

"Damn," I said.

"A damn smoking gun is what it is," said Danny.

"Are you sure that's John Metzger's signature?" I asked.

Danny nodded. "I checked it against our files."

This was a tie to Portland that the Metzgers could not deny, and it was surely enough to begin a full-scale investigation into the connection between Tom and John and the skinheads who had murdered Mulugeta Seraw. If that investigation proved fruitful, we might, after all, be able to file a suit against the Metzgers and WAR patterned after the Donald case.

Proving the case against the UKA had been difficult. If not for our luck in coaxing critical Klan documents from Benny Hays, a Grand Titan of the UKA, and our success in persuading two ex-Klansmen to testify—both of whom were hidden in witness-protection programs—we might not have prevailed. And if Tiger Knowles, one of Michael Donald's murderers, had not made a tearful speech in the courtroom to Mrs. Donald and the jury, admitting his sins and asking for a large verdict against the Klan, we might have fallen far short of the attention-getting, bankrupting $7 million judgment.

Winning a case against the Metzgers would be even harder. First, we would have to show that the Metzgers or their lieutenant Mazzella had direct contact with the skinheads who killed Seraw and encouraged them to carry out the "business" of WAR and AYM. Next, we'd have to demonstrate that the business of WAR and AYM included committing racially motivated violence. Finally, we'd have to prove that the Metzgers or Mazzella had in some way encouraged the violence that led to the murder. This last point was particularly tricky. The skinheads, Danny had learned, were arguing that Seraw's death had nothing to do with race or ideology. Mieske and Brewster apparently insisted that before the fight they hadn't even been aware that Seraw and the occupants of the car were black. It was just an old-fashioned street rumble between two spirited groups.

We might be able to prove the facts were different. But how could we overcome an even bigger obstacle? *There was nothing linking Mazzella to the murder.* We had no idea what role, if any, he had played. But it seemed that if he had been involved in the murder, he would have been charged along with the others. He hadn't, and thus our Metzger-to-Mazzella-to-Mieske chain was missing a crucial link.

At this stage neither Danny nor I cared that the Seraw case looked tougher than the Mobile Klan lynching case. Since our November discussion, Klanwatch had published a special intelligence report on hate crime in 1988. The information was alarming. Racially motivated violence was rising dramatically. In December, three skinheads in Reno, Nevada, had shot and killed a man solely because he was black. Metzger's WAR material had been found in their room, along with a letter from John Metzger. And in the six weeks following the Seraw murder, Portland skinheads, apparently unmoved by the death and undeterred by the arrests, had committed thirteen assaults and robberies.

The Klanwatch report documented hundreds of other incidents—threats, vandalism, synagogue desecrations and cross burnings, assaults, shootings, arson, and murder. These incidents took place all over the country—in the North more often than in the South—in all sorts of places—parks, bars, naval bases, and, increasingly, on college campuses. In addition to the murders in Portland and Reno, there were skinhead-related killings in Las Vegas, San Jose, Minneapolis, Louisville, and Halifax, North Carolina.

Looking over the report, I'd had to remind myself that this was 1988—twenty-four years after the passage of the Civil Rights Act, twenty years after the death of Dr. Martin Luther King. And the outlook did not appear any brighter as we approached the last decade of the second millennium. In January white supremacists had invited skinheads to join in their annual march in Pulaski, Tennessee, protesting the Martin Luther King holiday. In 1987 there had been a total of sixty marchers. Now, just two years later, with the addition of skinheads, the total reached four hundred. Danny had shown me a picture of the rally in which marchers flashed the Nazi salute amid Confederate flags and signs reading NAACP: PLANET OF THE APES.

Four hundred marchers. A half dozen murders. The numbers do not seem overwhelming. Did anyone at the Southern Poverty Law Center really believe that Tom Metzger and the skinheads or any of the other white supremacist leaders and their followers could get very far with a revolution to create an all-Aryan state?

No.

Did we believe that Metzger was capable of orchestrating widespread terror, violence, and murder?

Absolutely. And not just with skinheads as his soldiers.

The conditions were ideal for an explosion. Racial intolerance was on the rise. Mainstream white Americans were growing angrier about affirmative action and other programs to benefit minorities and about urban ills they associated with blacks. A drawing in one of Metzger's newspapers showed a young black man with exaggerated features wearing a shirt with the legend *RAP ON,* a bottle of liquor in his back pocket. The accompanying poem read:

> *COON, COON . . .*
> *BLACK BABOON . . .*
> *BRUTAL, WORTHLESS,*
> *THIEVING GOON . . .*
> *OFTEN HIGH . . . THRIVES IN JAIL . . .*
> *HIS WELFARE CHECK IS IN THE MAIL . . .*
> *SOME 40 OFFSPRING HAVE BEEN HAD,*

NOT ONE WILL EVER CALL HIM DAD . . .
AND YET HE HOLLERS DAY AND NIGHT:
"I BLAMES DE WHITE MAN FO' MY PLIGHT,
IT'S HIM SPREADS TRASH ALL 'ROUND MY SHACK,
IT'S HIM WHAT MAKES ME SMOKE DIS CRACK.
HE PUSH MY KIND TO BURN AND LOOT,
AN SENDS DE PO-LICE DAT WE SHOOT . . .
BUT INCH BY INCH WE TAKIN' HOLD,
LIKE WHEN DE WHITE BREAD STARTS TO MOLD.
WE'LL OVERRUN YO HOMES AND SOON . . .
DEY BE ONLY FIT FOR DE BLACKASSED COON."

Crude and unsophisticated, to be sure. But how different, really, was the blatant message in this poem from the subtle message in a television spot aired by the backers of George Bush during the 1988 presidential race just weeks before the Seraw murder? The slick Bush campaign commercial telling the story of Willie Horton, a furloughed black convict who brutalized a white woman, shamelessly played on the same fears that Metzger was exploiting.

Of course, the vast majority of George Bush's backers were not candidates for Tom Metzger's WAR army. But their children belonged to the first generation in decades that would not live as comfortably as their parents had, and a growing number, looking for scapegoats, were finding the Pied Piper's music alluring.

In the last four months of 1988, the U.S. Justice Department had initiated almost as many cases for racially motivated violence as it had in all of 1987, which had been a record year. Anti-Semitic crimes were at a five-year high. A shocking 90 percent of these crimes were committed by persons under twenty-one, many of them skinheads.

Now was the time to stop the insanity. A victory against the Metzgers would not only put an end to WAR, the nation's most dangerous hate business, it would send a message to others looking to enter this growth industry: Think twice.

I told Danny to spend as much time as he needed forging the links in the chain necessary to connect Tom Metzger to Seraw's death.

You have reached Aryan Update, a production of WAR.

DATELINE—WAR OFFICE: . . . The white backlash is proceeding so well that . . . we'll go for it all in a total mobilization of white resistance nationwide. It's winner take all, comrades! The day of the Aryan counterattack has come! . . . Let's take it all back! White victory!

. . . Let's do the backlash boogie! Get mad as hell and don't take it anymore. Screw their hate laws, their anti-white hate laws, try to stop a white hurricane if they can.

—Tom Metzger, White Aryan Resistance telephone hotline,
February 6, 1989

CHAPTER FOUR

April 18, 1989
◾
Oakland, California

Engedaw Berhanu told me that both he and his nephew Mulugeta Seraw, like many of their countrymen, had come to the United States to further their education. Engedaw, who had been an editor and translator in Addis Ababa, Ethiopia, had started out in Washington State pulling weeds on a farm for $1.50 an hour and later worked in a factory to support himself while taking a full college course load. Mulugeta, also in college, had worked in a Portland fast-food restaurant before finding a better job, as janitor in a parochial elementary school. For several months, Mulugeta had slept in a bare "bachelor's quarters" adjacent to the school's boiler room. "Neither of us lived well," Engedaw said.

Mulugeta had been a short, thin man. Engedaw, now a social worker with the Mental Health Service in Alameda County, was of average height, solidly built. At first I thought it was his conservative suit and his glasses and receding hairline that made him look older than his forty years. Then I realized it was the burden of tragedy, the weight of a heart made heavy by the loss of a loved one, that had aged him. I had seen the same devastation in Michael Donald's mother.

Engedaw and I were sitting in the Oakland office of his lawyer, Tesfaye "Tess" Tsadik. Bill Hunter, who had served as U.S. Attorney for the Northern District of California and now shared office space with Tsadik, had joined us. Anita Zussman, a Los Angeles–based attorney with the Anti-Defamation League, was also present. Only three weeks had passed since I'd told Danny to move forward on the Seraw case.

A few days earlier, Hunter had phoned on behalf of Engedaw and Tsadik, who had come to him contemplating legal action. Aware of our success in the Donald case and our continuing interest in battling white supremacists, he suspected we might be interested in taking on the skinheads. After accepting his invitation to come to Oakland, I had called the ADL, a longtime foe of hate groups. The Bay Area, Portland, and Fallbrook, California—the home of WAR—are a long way from Montgomery, and unlike the ADL, the Southern Poverty Law Center has no regional offices with lawyers, administrators, or investigators. Our forty-person staff, including five lawyers, fits somewhat tightly into our only office, a two-story building across the street from the Dexter Avenue Baptist Church, where Dr. King was the preacher when the civil rights movement began.

When I asked Engedaw to tell me about himself and Mulugeta, he sat silently for some time, then wiped away a tear. "Mulugeta arrived in this country in 1980," he began. "I met him at the Portland airport. He was twenty years old. We hugged each other. He gave me a gift of dried food from back home, and then we drove to my apartment in Beaverton, a few miles southwest of the city."

The sky was blue and clear, Engedaw remembered. In the distance Mount Hood, its shoulders draped in white, stood majestically. To Mulugeta, the horizon, life itself, seemed limitless.

A year earlier, Mulugeta had written his mother's brother, then a graduate student at Portland State University: "Uncle Engedaw, I wish to follow you to the United States. I want to study business." Engedaw persuaded Portland Community College to accept Mulugeta, and, as required by law, he found an American couple, the Tuppers of Goldendale, Washington, willing to sponsor Mulugeta in the United States. Such sponsorship did not include financial assistance, so Mulugeta would have to work to support himself.

Employment opportunities were limited for an Ethiopian high school graduate who spoke English with some difficulty, but Mulugeta finally found work at the fast-food restaurant. He washed dishes and earned minimum wage. The job wasn't exactly what he had expected, but he did not complain.

The Amharas of Ethiopia, a Christian people who provided the nation with all but one of its monarchs from 1270 to 1974, were not complainers. Mulugeta grew up in the heart of Amhara country, in the highlands of the northwestern province of Gondar. He lived in a round hut with a thatched roof in a hamlet so small it had no name. The nearest town of note, Debre Tabor (population 20,000), was a five-hour walk away.

The highlands of northwest Ethiopia are dotted with settlements like the one where Mulugeta lived. Clusters of farmers, most of them related by blood or marriage, raise crops and livestock on land that had belonged to their parents, grandparents, great-grandparents. The vista is breathtaking, Engedaw told me, the climate is gentle except during the rainy season, and the land is usually kind. Come harvesttime in late fall there is enough food to feed the family and often a surplus that can be taken by mule and sold in Debre Tabor. Like other boys in the highlands, Mulugeta began helping his father on the farm when he was about six years old.

Not all the children in the hamlet received a formal education, but when he was about eight years old, Mulugeta began attending classes at a boarding school operated by Seventh-Day Adventists in Debre Tabor. On weekends he made the long walk back home.*

Engedaw had attended the same school several years earlier. An excellent student, he had gone on to high school in Addis Ababa. When he finished his secondary education, he found work as a translator and assistant editor at a Seventh-Day Adventist publishing house in the capital. The job paid fairly well, and he was able to send enough money back home to help pay for Mulugeta's tuition and board at the church school in Debre Tabor. By this time Mulugeta's mother had died giving birth to her sixth child.

When Mulugeta graduated from high school he wrote to his uncle

---

*Most Ethiopians are Coptic Christians, belonging to a church that had its origins in Egypt in the second century. Mulugeta's ancestors belonged to this church for centuries—until his great-great-uncle and others from the community questioned its orthodox teachings and journeyed several hundred miles north in search of a new faith. Seventh-Day Adventist missionaries in Asmara eventually converted the party, who then brought their new beliefs back home.

and asked to join him in the United States. Engedaw had initially planned to stay in America only long enough to get his journalism degree, but friends and family in Ethiopia advised against a return because the country was in turmoil following the military coup that had ended Emperor Haile Selassie's forty-four-year reign. The new socialist state was on the verge of war with its Somali population and with Somalia itself. So Engedaw decided to stay in the United States and changed his major to social work. Although he had been somewhat disheartened by the employment opportunities in America, he had found the people here most friendly.

Mulugeta's experience during his first years in America paralleled that of his uncle—long hours of study and long hours at work. His English was not very good at first, and after he became custodian at the Catholic elementary school he would visit the classroom of first-grade teacher Cygnette Cherry after school hours and read the books her students used. The teacher worked with Mulugeta on his reading skills. When she found out he loved music, she gave him tapes of children's songs. In his apartment, Mulugeta sang along with the tapes to improve his English.

Early in 1982, Engedaw told Mulugeta that he was moving to the San Francisco Bay Area. Despite a master's degree in social work, Engedaw, too, had been working as a janitor. "This was not a very good job considering my qualifications," he explained to me.

Engedaw had never experienced overt racial prejudice; no one had slurred him or called him names. But he could see no reason other than the color of his skin for his failure to find work in his field. He thought the situation in the Bay Area more promising. "You're welcome to come," he told Mulugeta.

Mulugeta declined. "He said, 'I have lived here almost two years. I have a job. I have friends. I'm going to school. Don't worry about me,'" Engedaw told me. Again, tears gathered in his eyes. He asked for a moment to compose himself

"I was not worried," Engedaw finally continued. Mulugeta's English had greatly improved. He was doing well at the community college. And Mulugeta had no shortage of friends from both the American and Ethiopian communities. There were perhaps one hundred Ethiopians living in the Portland area, many of them students. Gathering regularly in their homes, the local Ethiopian restaurant, or on the soccer field, they were a source of strength and stability for one another. "Mulugeta was quite popular," smiled Engedaw. "He was very sociable and a natural leader. There were people much older than he, but he somehow managed to be the hub of the community."

Over the next five years, Mulugeta remained involved in the community. Like his countrymen, he felt anguish over the famine that killed tens of thousands of Ethiopians. When he could, he sent money to his father and to his young son, Henok, born after he had left Addis Ababa.

In 1985, Mulugeta developed an intestinal parasite that kept him in the hospital for months. When he was released, he had lost a great deal of weight. His illness and the need to earn a living forced him to drop out of school periodically, but he continued to dream of getting an accounting degree and going back to help his country. He took a job at Avis, driving an airport shuttle bus.

Engedaw and Mulugeta spoke to each other on the phone frequently and visited regularly. In September 1988, Engedaw, now married and a father, came to Portland. Uncle and nephew drove to Washington State for a relative's wedding. On the way back to California, Engedaw spent the night at Mulugeta's apartment. In the morning he looked in on Mulugeta, who was sleeping peacefully. "I decided not to wake him," said Engedaw. "That was the last time I saw him."

With Engedaw's moving narrative, Mulugeta Seraw had come alive for me. No longer just "the victim," he now had a history, a rich past, a hopeful future. The thought of the Guns N' Roses lyrics, of Tom Metzger's constant denigration of blacks and immigrants, of the rising tide of racism in mainstream America, made me sad, then angry. Here was a fine young man pursuing the American dream whose life had been shattered by that most American of symbols, a baseball bat. Ken Mieske, pathetic and malleable, had been the designated hitter. I wanted to go after the coach who had put him on the field.

I explained to Engedaw that the Center would be happy to represent him free of charge. We'd probably begin by suing the three skinheads charged with the killing. We'd then use the pretrial discovery process to try to gather enough information to link the Metzgers or other leaders to the murder. If we were successful, we would add them as defendants. "Under any circumstances, even if the jury awards a big verdict, there probably won't be a lot of money to collect," I said. There was no evidence that the Metzgers were rich. By all accounts they lived rather modestly. Whether there were significant funds in the WAR treasury remained to be seen.

"I understand," Engedaw said.

"But if we can connect the Metzgers to this, we can damn well stop them from encouraging skinheads to commit racial violence. And we can send a message to other groups, too."

Engedaw's response was that of a man with deep feelings for two very different countries. "I want something positive to come from this," he said. Then he added, "Mr. Dees, I have a duty to avenge Mulugeta's death."

Anita Zussman and I flew to Portland the next day. A heavy gray mist hung over the city. I realized too late that I should have dressed for "spring" in the Northwest.

I longed for home. The Alabama countryside comes alive in April. The honeysuckle and wisteria begin to bloom, and the hummingbirds return to the courtyard outside my bedroom window. On farms where cotton is still grown, the sturdy green plants break the sandy surface swiftly, as if in a time-lapse photograph. On really warm days, the swimming holes on the Tallapoosa River are alive with kids.

I had come to Portland not for the waters but to talk to the police and to find local counsel who might assist us with the case. Anticipating that Engedaw would retain us, I had asked an old friend, Ira Glasser, to recommend lawyers in Portland. Ira, executive director of the American Civil Liberties Union (ACLU), had directed me to Portlander Paul Meyer. Meyer in turn arranged a meeting with several prominent lawyers considered sympathetic to our cause.

Some of these lawyers belonged to the ACLU, perhaps the country's strongest legal advocate for the First Amendment. Having tried a number of free speech cases myself for the Alabama ACLU, I was aware that a case against the Metzgers could raise constitutional questions: Tom and John might very well wrap themselves in the First Amendment. "Any contact we had with the murderers, either direct or through our publications or hotlines, is protected free speech," they might contend.

The free speech question would depend on the specific facts of this case, as yet unknown. Whether the ACLU would choose to assist the Metzgers, as it had assisted the Nazis who wanted to march in Skokie, Illinois, some years earlier, would also depend on the facts. None of the lawyers raised the issue at our meeting.

Two Portland attorneys seemed particularly interested in helping. Steve Walters, a blond forty-four-year-old Stanford Law graduate, was a partner doing corporate work at one of Portland's biggest firms and a volunteer attorney for the ACLU. A former law clerk to Chief Justice Warren Burger, Steve had southern ties, having worked in Georgia for VISTA during the late sixties and early seventies. He was the kind of local counsel we liked to retain—a big-firm lawyer with heart and good contacts in the district attorney's office. This was important. Access to the statements and documents in the state's files after the skinheads' criminal trials would make the investigation for our civil suit much easier.

Elden Rosenthal, a trim, athletic personal-injury lawyer in his early forties, was equally well regarded and well connected. Also a Stanford Law graduate, he seemed particularly knowledgeable on Oregon civil law. He told me that several members of his family had perished in the Holocaust, and he felt strongly about stopping the neo-Nazis.

Walters was at the moment the busier of the two. He was uncertain how much time he could give but said his firm could do the work necessary to establish Engedaw as the personal representative of the estate so a lawsuit could be filed. For now, Rosenthal would handle the matters regularly assumed by local counsel—filing motions, serving papers, interviewing local witnesses and law enforcement officials. I was happy with the duo.

The meeting with the police was equally successful. Larry Siewart was a soft-spoken, mild-mannered, conservatively dressed man of about forty. As Danny had told me, he was a big fan of ours. "Why do we have to rely on two private groups [ADL and the Center] for facts on these skinheads?" he asked as he showed Anita and me into his office in the Portland Justice Center. "The feds couldn't care less about these groups. The courts just turn them loose."

He showed us the original of John Metzger's letter introducing Dave Mazzella to Ken Mieske, then gave us more details. Mazzella had apparently come to Portland shortly after Metzger sent the letter in early October. He had been followed north by fellow Californians Michael Barrett and Mike Gagnon.*

The police search of the apartment Mazzella had been sharing with Steve Strasser had produced Mazzella's personal phone book. Siewart showed us a copy. As I tried to figure out how to coax this critical piece of evidence from the police, I took down the phone numbers of Tom Metzger, John Metzger, and Ken Mieske. Once we filed suit, we would subpoena all relevant phone records in Oregon and California. To determine whether there had been calls from Strasser, Brewster, or Mieske to Metzger and his people, we would need to get all past numbers for the defendants and their key friends in Portland. As my notepad quickly filled up with Things To Do, I suddenly realized the logistical nightmare presented by this case—so far from home.

Siewart said that on the night of the murder, East Side White Pride members had passed out literature in Portland, then gone to the apartment of one of the skinheads. Mazzella had been present throughout the evening.

The skinheads' girlfriends joined the boys later.† Sometime after midnight, Mazzella and others went one way while Mieske, Brewster, and Strasser and their girlfriends went another way—apparently down the street to the fatal confrontation with Mulugeta and his friends. After the murder Siewart told the detectives to pick up Mazzella, who, I now learned for the first time, had provided the information leading to the arrests of his fellow skinheads.

I wanted badly to see Mazzella's statement, but at this stage I didn't have the proper relationship with Siewart to ask for something from an ongoing murder investigation. He did tell me Mazzella had said he was leaving the skinhead life and added that the young leader had been extradited to California in January but had returned earlier this month.

This first news of Mazzella was of mixed value as far as our civil suit was concerned. Because Mazzella was not involved in the murder, we'd be hard pressed to link the Metzgers to the deed. On the other hand, if Mazzella was becoming persona non grata with the local

---

*Gagnon apparently left Portland a few days later, well before the murder. He would never play a major role in our case.
†East Side White Pride did not permit women to become members.

skinheads or Metzger for his loose lips, he might be easier to persuade to talk. "Dave Mazzella could be our Mark Mize, Bob Jones, and Tiger Knowles rolled into one," I scribbled on my pad. In every successful case against the Klan, we had convinced a key Klan insider or sympathizer to turn against the organization, their friends, mentors, and leaders, and to provide critical testimony to sink the ship.

Siewart said Mazzella had served some time on the California assault charge but was now out of jail. Portland authorities did not know where he was—somewhere in California, they believed. No one knew if he would surface for the trial of Mieske, Brewster, or Strasser. As he wasn't an eyewitness to the murder, the state could put on a case without his testimony.

Whether Mazzella appeared or not, I'd be there. I could read a transcript of the trial in Alabama, but nobody has invented a symbol for a court reporter's machine that can convey the body language that's every bit as revealing as the spoken word. Sitting anonymously in the gallery at the murder trial of Henry Hays, the Klansman who had lynched Michael Donald, I'd gauged the personalities of key characters, their knowledge of crucial events, and their abilities on the stand. There would be quite a bit of body language in Portland as these three skinheads tried to save a particular piece of their own anatomies—their asses.

Before leaving town, Anita and I drove to Southeast Thirty-first and Pine. It was a bright, sunny morning. Instead of the rundown rooming-house area I had expected, we found a well-kept neighborhood with small, neat houses on attractively landscaped lots. The murder was so removed in time that I felt little emotion, only sadness that a young man had died here so senselessly. I diagramed the street, knowing I would be back many times before the trial.

Two weeks later the question of whether Mazzella would surface for Mieske's trial became moot. Hopeful that he would receive a more lenient sentence if he made a deal with the state instead of going to trial in a highly charged climate, Mieske pleaded guilty to murder and racial intimidation. As part of the plea agreement he admitted, "I intentionally and unlawfully killed Mulugeta Seraw because of his race."

Danny delivered the news with a big grin. This admission could hurt Metzger if we tied him to the crime. He couldn't argue that this was just a random street fight, not racially motivated and unrelated to the messages he sent urging young warriors to cleanse the nation of blacks.

Or could he?

Shortly after Mieske's plea, we had sent a mailing to Center contributors advising them that we needed their financial support to embark upon "a new case against a group of skinheads who have been charged with brutally murdering a black man." Aware that racist groups received our mailings just as we received theirs, we did not want to tip off the Metzgers by identifying the particular murder or by suggesting that we hoped to sue them and their organizations. If they thought that they were targets of the Center, they might hide evidence or intimidate witnesses.

A week after our mailing, I received a letter from a Portland attorney who described herself as a longtime supporter of the Center, one who was "concerned about the prevalence of racism in this country" and who applauded our victories in certain cases. She expressed concern that the anonymous suit outlined in our solicitation might be connected to the death of Mulugeta Seraw, adding, "I have a client marginally involved in that case and therefore am somewhat familiar with the facts."

A red flag went up as I continued reading:

I appreciate that this case resulted in national and perhaps international publicity, but much of it has been misplaced. Rather than a racist attack by three skinheads against three blacks, what in fact occurred seems to have been simply a street fight between two sets of drunken individuals. The car in which Mr. Seraw was riding blocked the street exit being attempted by the car in which the three skinheads were riding. Epithets were thrown and a fight resulted. Although I regret the brutality of the assault and Mr. Seraw's death, and I recognize that it was out of proportion to the provocation that may have been offered, the fact that he was black and the others were white does not constitute a racist attack. Many of the witnesses involved in the case have said it would have made no difference whether the persons in Mr. Seraw's car were white.

The letter concluded: "While a lawsuit might represent some kind of a symbolic gesture, I question whether the resources of the Southern Poverty Law Center should be directed to such symbolism."

I put down the letter and called Richard Cohen, the Center's skilled legal director and my sounding board since his arrival in 1986. As I waited for Richard to come down the hall, I leafed through the latest edition of Tom Metzger's WAR newspaper. One page featured a derogatory article about Jews titled "North America's No. 1 Enemy." An insulting drawing of a "Yidfly," a Jewish pest, accompanied the piece. The paper featured several other cartoons—did Metzger think that his average subscriber had a hard time reading?—each more inflammatory than the last. Jews, gays, and blacks bore the brunt of the venom in these pictures.

I was reading a poem submitted by a Metzger follower when Richard, a tall, curly-haired Virginian in his mid-thirties, walked in. I showed him the letter from the woman in Portland.

"Disturbing," I said.

"Mieske signed his plea agreement knowing he could be charged with perjury if he wasn't truthful," Richard answered. "It was a racially motivated murder."

"Fine, but if there are witnesses who say Seraw and his friends provoked the attack, or if there's evidence Seraw was drunk . . ."

"You sound like Tom Metzger: 'The skinheads did a civic duty.' "

"Richard, we don't have a chance of connecting Metzger with the murder if what this woman says is true, or if a jury believes it's true. And *she's* a supporter."

"She's a lawyer representing someone involved in the case," said Richard, who has a talent for cutting away the brush.

"We need to find out what really happened that night," I said. "I think Danny and I might pay another visit to the Portland police."

"Make sure you put in for Frequent Flier mileage on this one."

"And another thing . . ."

Richard rolled his eyes. "Yes, Morris."

I held up the WAR newspaper. "We're not into 'symbolic gestures.' I want Tom Metzger's house and bank account for Seraw's family."

DATELINE—OREGON: A new law is being drafted called the Skinhead Law. Anyone killing a black or a Jew gets an automatic death penalty in Oregon. That's okay! Let's get it right out in the open and go for broke. The system plans to destroy all pro-white resistance, if they can. But we have news for these anti-white whites. Hail Robert Mathews and hail the Order and may there be many more.

All twelve [WAR] sectors are cooking. White backlash is spreading fast, like prairie fire. Keep the pressure on. And what have you done for your race against the putrid system today?

—Tom Metzger, White Aryan Resistance telephone hotline, February 17, 1989

CHAPTER FIVE

June 11, 1989

■

Mathews, Alabama

On the day before Danny and I flew to Portland, my wife of five weeks, Elizabeth, and I went for a long horseback ride. We found Chico and Gambler down by our pond, saddled them, and then moved slowly through our pasture and beyond. The morning sun shone bright in the cloudless blue sky, but a gentle breeze rustling across the rolling green hills kept us cool. As we passed each old homestead or farm, I gave Elizabeth an informal history of the land and its owners. "This is where my grandfather's brother John Dees farmed cotton in the thirties. . . . That's where the Barnetts lived. They had twelve hundred and fifty acres, an old plantation house, and black servants dressed up in suits who came running whenever old Miss Barnett rang her bell."

This was familiar territory—my home since birth, my home until I die. I understood the people, their history. My neighbors, *my kin,* still didn't always approve of what I did, just as I didn't always approve of their actions, but we knew we were connected by invisible bonds—historical, cultural, geographical.

This had served me well at the Center. I felt I understood the hopes and fears, the pride and the prejudice, of my adversaries as well as my clients. I could talk to Klansmen more easily than I could talk to many northern civil rights lawyers. I'd grown up with them, gone to school with them. We were more alike than different.

The Klan offered many of these young men something they had not been able to attain in their undistinguished day-to-day lives—social opportunities, the chance to gain leadership roles, a forum to vent their gripes. Klan violence, though horrible, is not the mainstay of Klan activity. Most time is spent cursing the federal government for affirmative action employment policies and welfare programs like food stamps, and reviling Jews for imagined plots to "mongrelize" the "white race."

James Holder, a Klansman who became a key witness in one of our cases, told me he was the black sheep of his family—nothing he did seemed to bring him success until he joined the Klan. There, he quickly used his commando skills learned in Vietnam to gain respect and a leadership role in Glenn Miller's underground paramilitary army.

Lloyd Letson, one of the Invisible Empire Klansmen we sued for assaulting the marchers in Decatur, Alabama, was like any number of my rural neighbors. After we filed the lawsuit, his lawyer contacted me and arranged for a private meeting. Sitting in a Holiday Inn dining room, Lloyd, a short, stocky welder in his mid-twenties, told me he joined the Klan group in 1979 after hearing a fiery speech by the charismatic Imperial Wizard Bill Wilkinson. Lloyd said he had been "sick and tired" of the blacks holding parades on Decatur streets protesting for Tommy Lee Hines, "that nigger" accused of raping several white women.

His infatuation with the Klan quickly died. The leaders were out for power and money, Lloyd said. And he could not understand how they could quote the Bible on the one hand and damn the Jews on the other, "since the Bible says the Jews are God's Chosen People." When the Klan leaders started talking about "the race war to come" and told him to get a camouflage uniform for paramilitary training, he realized this was more than he had bargained for. "God will let lightning strike you dead," he told them when he quit.

After our first meeting, I invited Lloyd and his daddy to come join me in hunting the woods by Catoma Creek swamp, where as a boy I'd hunted with my daddy. I explained that contrary to local opinion, I wasn't out to turn the South into the North, or to destroy the white race. "I'm only seeking justice," I said, telling Lloyd about filing one of the country's first reverse discrimination suits in behalf of white employees of the Macon County, Alabama, School District.

Sitting on the banks of Catoma Creek swamp, Lloyd Letson, Klansman, and I shared a Coca-Cola. Our common roots had overcome our political differences. Lloyd agreed to testify against the Klan.

As my ride with Elizabeth continued, thoughts of Portland crowded out thoughts of Decatur, and I wondered if I could develop that same understanding with the northern, urban skinheads. In my travels to the North, I'd never felt that oneness with the land and its people that I had down home. Could I talk to Dave Mazzella the way I talked to Lloyd Letson? Could I talk to a juror up there as if I were talking to a neighbor across the fence or a juror in Mobile? *You're jumping the gun, Dees,* I thought. *You don't even know where Mazzella is. Don't worry about a jury until you have a case.*

That evening Elizabeth and I took my granddaughter Rebecca to dinner in Montgomery. As the waitress gave us our menus, my mind again began to wander. I was married for the first time in 1955, at the age of eighteen. As a senior in high school, I eloped with Beverly Crum, a sixteen-year-old sophomore. Our two sons—Scooter, now a medical student in Oklahoma after success as a newspaper publisher; and John, in the construction business in Montgomery—had blessed us with three wonderful grandchildren.

I had not been a particularly attentive father to the boys or to my daughter, Ellie, now a college student. My desire to make a name for myself and to earn enough money to buy enough land so that no one could tell me to move (as landlords had told Daddy) had kept me too distant from my kids. The opportunity to close that gap with Ellie and Scooter and John and their children was now at hand. The farm where I'd spent so little time when they were growing up was big enough for them to come stay. Financial independence had long been achieved, and we could now travel together, one big happy family. Elizabeth, too, deserved my attention, an attention I had too often failed to give the women in my life.

Skinheads had murdered others before Mulugeta Seraw, yet I had never brought lawsuits against them. The possibility that we could implicate Tom Metzger was a long shot. Was his downfall so desirable that I was willing to put twenty-five hundred miles between myself and my loved ones for a year?

As I looked across the table at seven-year-old Rebecca, with her red hair and her dancing blue eyes, I thought of the poem I had been reading in Metzger's tabloid when Richard Cohen entered my office. It was titled "Being White Is Not a Crime":

> *White and proud,*
> *That's what I am,*
> *Storming the streets,*
> *Getting rid of the trash.*
> *What's wrong with knowing your race is strong?*
> *Aryan people unite against:*
> *Drugs, Race-mixing, and Crime.*
> *Brothers and Sisters stand by my side*
> *Join the fight for what's right.*

The poem was credited to a twelve-year-old girl.

I took Rebecca's hand. What kind of world would she grow up in? It was indeed important to fight for what's right.

UPDATE—PORTLAND, OREGON: One young fighter, Ken Mieske, received life for winning a fight with an Ethiopian recently. If your rotten government was not letting in all this mud, young white men would not have to be doing this all the time. Never forgive. Don't get mad, just get even. Tell them to get their Ethiopian ass out of the country.

—Tom Metzger, White Aryan Resistance telephone hotline,
June 12, 1989

CHAPTER SIX

June 12, 1989

◼

Portland, Oregon

"This is Detective Nelson with the Portland Police Bureau. Today's date is 11/20/88 . . . and I'm present with Steve Strasser. . . . We're talking about Case 88-16986, which involves the death investigation that occurred on 11/13/88 at Southeast 31st and Pine. Steve, do you understand that we're ready?"

So began the 125-page transcript that rested on a long, document-strewn, wooden table before Danny and me. We were sitting in the Multnomah County (Portland) District Attorney's evidence room for Case 88-16986—the murder of Mulugeta Seraw. We were alone, and we couldn't believe our good fortune. Law enforcement agencies and prosecutors have no obligation to grant a victim's lawyer access to evidence at any time. In rare instances they had allowed us to view evidence, but only *after* trials had taken place or all parties had pleaded guilty. We had considered ourselves lucky on those few occasions; a look at the statements of witnesses and parties, often not presented during the course of a criminal trial, can suggest new leads for our civil suits and greatly reduce our investigative time. Now, remarkably, we had access to the evidence accumulated for a case in progress. "Victim's rights" had real meaning in Oregon.

Case 88-16986 was still very much in progress. Mieske had pled guilty, but Strasser and Kyle Brewster had not. Unless they did, they would stand trial, and the bats, brass knuckles, photographs, autopsy report, and transcripts of taped statements that filled the evidence room would soon fill a courtroom. Where the evidence would go after that was unclear. We had heard rumors that the federal government might bring criminal charges against the three skinheads, which meant that the FBI would take all the evidence. Despite our good relations with the agency, there was no chance we'd be given so much as a glimpse of the evidence. We'd have to begin our investigation into Metzger's connection virtually from scratch—a painful thought in light of our experience on other cases where investigations had dragged on for years, often because witnesses or parties were missing or unwilling to talk.

We already had one of each in Portland. Mazzella was missing, which made the statement he had given the police before disappearing all the more valuable to us. And the one skinhead Danny had located had been less than forthcoming.

During a get-acquainted trip to Portland between my first visit in April and our present joint venture, Danny had paid a call on Steve Nevarou, an ex-skinhead who Siewart thought might prove helpful. In a dimly lit doorway outside a dingy apartment from which heavy-metal music blared, Danny was greeted by Nevarou, a well-built twenty-one-year-old wearing a frown but no shirt. An ink menagerie—tattoos of various shapes and sizes—rose and fell with each breath. Danny, who had identified himself only as "an investigator," began by asking questions about East Side White Pride. Not wanting to alert Nevarou that his main interest was in Mazzella, he danced around for a few minutes before mentioning the Californian. Nevarou responded that Mazzella "was in love with himself," constantly talking about how high he ranked in the hierarchy of White Aryan Resistance, making sure everyone knew how important he was. This would be helpful—Mazzella had apparently played up his affiliation with Tom Metzger—but it wasn't earthshaking. Danny pressed on, but Steve Nevarou was no Lloyd Letson. He abruptly turned chilly and slammed the door in Danny's face.

Thanks to the transcript, we now had access to the statements of Mazzella, the three skinhead girlfriends who had apparently been present during the murder, and one of the perpetrators himself, Steven

R. Strasser, aka Bullwinkle. "Let's start with the night of the murder," I said to Danny, echoing Detective Nelson's conversation with Strasser.

The boys of East Side White Pride and their girlfriends had apparently gathered at the Safeway grocery on Twenty-ninth and Hawthorne about nine on the night of Saturday, November 12. Dave Mazzella brought several of the skinheads in his beat-up military-green van. Ken Mieske, Kyle Brewster, Steve Strasser, and their girls were there. So, too, were Mike Barrett and young men with nicknames like Heckle and Jeckle, Goggles, Pee Wee, and Prick.

East Side White Pride had already decided that this was going to be a "Boys' Night Out." The girls were free to go off and party; the skinheads, dressed in dark leather flight jackets bearing the ESWP patch, wearing their red oxford Doc Martens boots with ten or fourteen eyelets, had work to do.

Beer and wine were purchased and good-byes were said. The girls met back at Patti Copp's to drink Boone's Farm Quencher. Julie Belec finished a bottle on her own, while Heidi Martinson, Strasser's girlfriend, and Copp, who dated Brewster, drank two bottles each and smoked marijuana. Feeling good, they headed downtown to the Pine Street Theatre, a club that featured heavy-metal music and attracted skinheads and punk rockers. The group Nuclear Attack was supposed to be playing.

Pine Street was dead, so the girls headed to a party on Fifty-third and Woodstock. The party was just as dead, so it was back to Pine Street, where at eleven-thirty, things picked up when they spotted a guy wearing a cowboy hat outside the club.

"Hick," the girls called.

Somebody knocked his hat off. He didn't have any hair!

"You a skinhead?" Belec asked.

"No, a Jew."

"Jew, Jew, Jew," a crowd yelled.

Martinson pointed her finger in his face. A young male friend of the girls' known as Buns sneered, "You're a Jew," and the man with the cowboy hat floored Buns with a punch in the nose. While Buns attempted to get up, his friend Craig confronted the puncher. And Craig, too, was hit.

As the "cowboy" walked away, the girls chased after him. "Jew, Jew, Jew."

He hurried into the club to avoid them, then ducked out the back door. The girls saw him getting into his car. Martinson, wearing her own Doc Martens boots, ran up and kicked the door before he finally drove off.

The girls soon grew tired of the club. "We decided, 'Oh well, we didn't have very much fun tonight. There wasn't really nothing to do,'" Belec would explain in her statement to Detective Nelson on November 22. They started for the apartment that one of their group, Desiree Marquis, shared with her skinhead boyfriend, Nick Heise.

While the girls were drinking wine and looking for fun, the boys were conducting business. From the Safeway, the members of East Side White Pride drove to downtown Portland. They parked near the Confetti Club, a nightspot where they were likely to find people willing to listen to their pitch: *The white race is dying. We have to do something about it. Now!*

Mazzella pulled a thick packet of printed fliers from the back of his van. Each of the dozen skins took about twenty-five fliers, and they spread out across the area. This material was provided by John Metzger, Mazzella would later tell Nelson. Under the logo Aryan Youth Movement was an article headlined SCIENTISTS SAY NEGRO STILL IN APE STAGE. The other side of the flier bore the headline NEGRO IS RELATED TO APES—NOT WHITE PEOPLE.

After distributing this "literature" to passersby for about ninety minutes, the skinheads grew restless and thirsty. They took some beer out of the van and drank it while figuring out where to go, what to do.

Over the next hour, they stopped in at two parties. Neither was "racy," skinhead parlance for "alive." Someone suggested going back to Heise's apartment.

On their way, they passed a minimart. Brewster and Strasser decided to make a beer run. Each grabbed a "short case" and hustled out of the store without paying. A clerk caught up with them. They dropped most of the beer, jumped into the van, and took off.

Heise and Marquis lived on Thirty-first and Pine. When the skinheads got to the apartment, the girls had not yet returned from their night at the Pine Street Theatre. The boys drank and played the drinking game "quarters."

At about the time the skinheads settled in at Heise's place, three young Ethiopian men were leaving a gathering in southeast Portland. Mulugeta Seraw, Tilahun Antneh, and Wondwosen Tesfaye had attended a good-bye party for a countryman visiting from Philadelphia. There was food and drink, and the twenty or so guests talked about their lives in America and back in Ethiopia. Around midnight Seraw and Antneh started to say their good-byes. Tesfaye asked if Antneh would drive him home, too. The trio headed back toward Seraw's apartment at Thirty-first and Pine.

Just down the street from Seraw's apartment, the girls arrived with Desiree Marquis at her building. Marquis grew angry when she saw Mazzella's van. Her boyfriend, Nick, had obviously brought home East Side White Pride—this despite the landlord's warning that he would not tolerate one more noisy gathering.

It was noisy. From the street the girls could hear music coming from the apartment. Marquis ran ahead. She entered an apartment full of skinheads. Mieske sat with Heise, a would-be artist planning to paint something on Mieske's Levi's jacket. The room shook to a heavy metal beat. "This is not going to happen at my apartment," Marquis announced.

By the time Martinson reached the stairway to the apartment, some of the skinheads were already on their way down. "Don't even bother. She's kicking everyone out," said one.

Down on the corner of Thirty-first and Pine, the group caught up on what had happened all evening. Then Mazzella, Barrett, and several skinheads piled into the van and headed for home. It was about one in the morning.

Mieske, Strasser, and Brewster and their girlfriends remained on the street talking and drinking. Patti Copp told Brewster and Strasser to finish their beers. She would not drive with any open containers in her car, a law violation her father had railed about.

The story of what happened next differed according to the various statements Danny and I now read. Each participant or witness had a different version, based on individual perspectives, attempts at self-preservation, or legitimate confusion. Some participants—Strasser, for instance—had given more than one statement. Pressed by detectives, these witnesses changed their stories to, at the very least, conform to what the police obviously knew. Although a unanimous account of Mulugeta Seraw's final minutes did not emerge, we could get a strong sense of what happened from the various versions.

As the skinheads finished their beers, Strasser heard Mieske say there were some "monkeys" around the corner. Martinson heard Brewster ask, "Is that a fuckin' nigger?"

"Where?" someone asked.

Brewster pointed down the street, to where a black man stood under a streetlamp, talking and laughing with some people sitting in a car.

The skinheads and their girls climbed into Copp's Nissan Stanza, parked on Pine Street. Copp settled behind the steering wheel, Brewster next to her. Martinson sat on Strasser's lap on the passenger side of the backseat. Belec and Mieske snuggled up behind the driver.

"Let's go fuck 'em up," Brewster said.

Copp now turned her Stanza onto Thirty-first Street. About a hundred yards down the block, an Oldsmobile sat in the middle of the street, with its headlights off. At her boyfriend's direction, Copp drove straight toward this car. Brewster then pulled Copp's emergency brake, bringing the Stanza to an abrupt stop about five feet from the Olds, blocking its path. He told Copp to honk the horn. She did.

"Move the car," Brewster yelled out the window.

When the Ethiopians in the other car did not respond, Brewster became agitated. "Fuck you, niggers," he yelled. "Fuck you, niggers." And he reached for the .25 automatic gun Copp kept in the console between them. Her father had given her the weapon for protection.

"Don't fuckin' touch that gun. That's mine," Copp screamed. She managed to get the gun before Brewster did.

"Go back to your own country," Brewster shouted at the people in the car.

The driver of the other car turned on his headlights. He tried to start the car, but failed. Brewster jumped out of Copp's car. The other car started and pulled out.

Meanwhile, Brewster punched his fingers into the chest of the black man who had been standing by the curb. "Get into your fucking house," Brewster yelled at Mulugeta Seraw.

Then all hell broke loose. Strasser and Mieske, baseball bat in hand, jumped out of Copp's car. Seeing Seraw in trouble, Antneh and Tesfaye had left their car and were on the street too. Tesfaye was quickly knocked to the ground. Mieske broke the rear window of Antneh's car with his bat, while Strasser kicked a window on the car's passenger side so hard that his boot was momentarily stuck in the hole he made. Antneh managed to get back in the car and drive off.

By now Martinson had climbed out. She was looking for her boyfriend, Strasser. Instead, she saw Mieske. He had moved from Antneh's car to join Brewster, who was punching Seraw. Mieske swung the bat. Once, twice, a third time.

Martinson finally spotted Strasser. He was kicking Tesfaye with his boots as Tesfaye crawled on the ground. "Get him," said Martinson.

Tesfaye was crying. He rolled helplessly on the pavement. Martinson told Strasser to stop. Instead, he kicked again . . . and again. Finished at last, he ran to where Brewster and Mieske had been fighting. Seraw was down. Strasser kicked him.

Strasser told the police that he had seen Mieske swing the bat and hit Seraw. While Brewster punched Seraw, Mieske blindsided the Ethiopian, hitting him with the bat across the back of his head. "He like buckled. . . . Then I saw the bat hit again. He was down on his knees and . . . Bam! . . . He fell face first."

"Did you hear him when he hit?" Detective Nelson asked Strasser. "What did it sound like?"

"It sounded really gory, like, I can't even explain, something like maybe taking a bag of chips or something and crunching them up when they're still crisp in the bag."

After Mieske struck Seraw, someone called, "Get back in the car. Let's get out of here." And as Strasser ran to Copp's car, he heard what he would later term the "cry of death," a high-pitched whine from the man on the ground lasting two or three seconds.

Moments after the car pulled off, Tesfaye ran over to Seraw. He desperately shook his unconscious friend, then wailed, "He's dead. He's dead."

In the car, Mieske was laughing.

As Copp sped to her nearby apartment, the passengers wondered if the man on the ground was dead. Brewster and Strasser didn't think so, but Mieske said, "That's the most blood I've seen in my life." Later that night Strasser told Michael Barrett and Dave Mazzella that the blood spurted out of the man's head like water from a sprinkler.

Back at Copp's apartment, Brewster revealed a pair of brass knuckles he'd used in the fight. Martinson told Mieske, "I think you killed that guy."

Now, Mieske wasn't so sure. "It takes a lot more than hitting a guy with a baseball bat," he said.

He was wrong.

When he heard the news the next day, Mieske shook his head. "Oh fuck, he died." He and Belec agreed that if the police came, they would say they were at her house all night. Later Copp and Mieske drove to a deserted beach and burned the bat.

None of the skinheads expressed sorrow. They apparently viewed the killing as a piece of bad luck. "I can't believe that nigger is dead," Mieske told Mazzella.

At times, they all seemed excited by what happened. Goggles had already given "Ken Death" a new nickname—Batman.

I needed some air. I took a deep breath and closed my eyes, and there was Michael Donald hanging from a camphor tree on Herndon Avenue in Mobile.

For so long, the North has hypocritically clung to the notion that such outrages are confined to the South. But hate knows no Mason-Dixon line. I picked up one of the bats the police had seized when searching the skinheads' various residences. It felt heavy, capable of splitting a man's head open in the manner described all too graphically in the medical records and autopsy report before me. The records also revealed that Mulugeta was not legally intoxicated.

Strasser and some of the girls interviewed by the police had suggested that the fight was triggered by the Ethiopians' refusal to move their car, which was blocking the street; race was not a factor. The Portland prosecutors weren't buying that story and neither was I. "I wonder which one of the people that lady who wrote us represents," I said to Danny. "I'd like to see her read through all these statements and then tell me this murder wasn't racially motivated."

But the second part of what she had written still troubled me: "I question whether the resources of the Southern Poverty Law Center should be directed to such symbolism." I had come to Portland with the same uneasy question, and there was nothing in the statements of the participants or eyewitnesses that provided an answer—nothing to link Dave Mazzella to the assault, much less Tom Metzger, who had been fifteen hundred miles away in Fallbrook, California. I put the bat down and picked up Detective Nelson's November 17 interview with Mazzella.

Mazzella had actually given two statements that night. The first focused on what he had heard about the killing from Strasser and others. The second statement interested me more. Here Nelson had asked about Mazzella's activities in Portland.

"The literature you have from California, who do you say puts that out?" Nelson began.

"Aryan Youth Movement," answered Mazzella. He added that he had been to Tom Metzger's house "a thousand times."

"So you . . . are an associate of his? You promote his literature up here?" asked Nelson.

"Oh, anywhere, yeah," Mazzella said, explaining that John Metzger sent literature directly to him.

"So is it like you're working for them?"

"Yeah." Mazzella added that he talked to the Metzgers about twice a week.

"Were you supposed to come and get things organized a little bit more 'cause it was kind of loose up here?"

"Yeah. It's organized now. I'd have to say it's really organized now."

Detective Nelson's skill at asking leading questions rivaled that of any attorney I've seen. "So you got them straight on the skinhead ways, the way you've been taught by the Metzgers?"

"Yeah, we were going around the streets, that's . . . the Metzgers don't teach about 'the skinhead way.' They just teach you the fundamentals of bein' a, you know, a racialist."

I read this last answer to Danny. "Now what do you think being a racialist entails? Murder?"

Danny picked up a bat. "When I played ball we began with 'the fundamentals,' " he said, swinging the bat at an imaginary pitch.

But there was nothing in the remainder of Mazzella's statement that suggested the Metzgers had told him to enlist East Side White Pride to commit any violence, much less the murder of Mulugeta Seraw.

Mazzella stated only that he had worked for Tom Metzger and instructed East Side White Pride in Metzger's ways. What were those ways? Mazzella hadn't said.

We could argue that the violence that was praised, if not also encouraged, in WAR propaganda was the Metzger way, but showing the connection between those words and the death of Mulugeta would be difficult. The Metzgers might also make a strong case that their words—distasteful and disturbing as they might be to many—were protected under the First Amendment. And if Tom and John didn't make this argument, the ACLU, which often intervened in cases where free speech appeared to be an issue, might.

As Danny made copies of the most important documents and took photographs of the key pieces of physical evidence, I found myself doodling on my legal pad. I drew a picture of a gun. I started to draw smoke coming out of the barrel, but caught myself. Instead, I drew a flag like those you see in cartoons. BANG, it read. That summed up our case against Tom Metzger so far. There was no smoking gun, only words.

Danny pulled his rental car into the gas station, took out his overnight bag, and headed for the bathroom. He was only a few miles from the prison in San Bernadino; it was time to look the part. He slipped off his blue jeans and sweatshirt and climbed into a suit. "The sacrifices I make," he cursed.

As he changed his clothes, he decided to change his story, too. He'd play it straight. "Mike, I'm going to level with you," he said to himself as he tried for the third time to get his tie even. "I'm with the Southern Poverty Law Center."

By the time he reached the prison, the sky was darkening and so was his mood. He had called the institution earlier in the day, before flying from Portland to San Francisco. The jail supervisor had told him that because he wasn't an attorney he'd have to go through "normal channels"; there could be no preferential treatment. That meant signing in at the prison and then waiting in line behind about fifty other people who were hoping to see inmates before visiting hours ended.

Michael Barrett had no idea Danny was coming. When prison officials informed him that a Mr. Welch was there to see him, he had no obligation to come to one of the cramped, dirty cubicles in which prisoners and visitors could speak through a screen. Danny's foot tapped wildly as he waited to see if Barrett would come.

Klanwatch intelligence indicated Barrett had been as close to the Metzgers as Mazzella. In 1988, in Riverside, California, he had founded WARskins, a skinhead group affiliated with WAR. He had then recruited across the country. Like Mazzella, he had experienced his share of run-ins with the law for violent acts. He was currently in jail for violating the terms of a parole that had followed incarceration for assault. Danny had located him through a contact with the Bureau of Alcohol, Tobacco, and Firearms. Although John Metzger hadn't mentioned him in his October letter to Mieske, we knew he was a Metzger operative. Since we didn't know where Mazzella was, Barrett was at this point our best hope for understanding the California-Oregon connection . . . if Danny could persuade him to talk.

The Portland police had been frustrated by the young skinhead. When they had picked up Mazzella at Strasser's apartment, Barrett had also been present. Although the detectives did not have a warrant for his arrest, Barrett agreed to come to the station for questioning and allowed the police to conduct forensic tests on four of his baseball bats observed in the apartment. Unfortunately, the cooperation ended soon after this encouraging start. In the evidence room, we had read Barrett's statement. While Mazzella was naming names, Barrett was keeping mum. He acknowledged that he had distributed literature on the night of the murder but refused to identify those who had been with him. And he denied going to Nick Heise's apartment.

According to the police records, Detective Nelson had become so agitated at Barrett's responses that he left the room. Questioned now by Detective Michael Hefley, Barrett did acknowledge he was in the white power movement. He also boasted of appearances on the talk shows hosted by Oprah Winfrey and Morton Downey, noting that the programs had even paid his airfare and lodging. Hefley had then asked the crucial question: Why had he come to Portland? Of course we would have liked to read that Barrett was sent by the Metzgers to stir up trouble. Instead, he explained that he came because he liked the land and there were good jobs available.

Danny would have the opportunity to try and coax more forthcoming answers from him. Barrett now stood on the other side of the cubicle's screen. The leader of WARskins looked more skinny than warlike. He was short and almost frail. There was, however, no doubt of his affiliation. His head was shaved, and he was a walking tattoo parlor. A dark blue scorpion stared out from his right forearm, and a spider and spider web graced his right elbow. Entomology gave way to ideology with two other tattoos. "Sieg Heil" was written across one knuckle, while "War" decorated his right inner elbow.

Danny was just about to begin the introduction he had rehearsed in the gas station when he thought, *Piss on it.* Ever since he'd been a detective, he'd been planning introductions and discarding them at the last minute to play it by ear. "Michael, I'm Danny Welch. I work for a private firm that's hired me to do research on what makes a guy a skinhead. I've been flying all over the country." Danny flashed his private investigator's card and returned it to his pocket before Barrett could read it.

Barrett didn't ask to see the card or question Danny's affiliation. He looked nervous. There weren't too many visitors in suits and ties. Danny didn't want to upset him. The police report indicated Barrett had suffered a head injury in the Navy and had experienced seizures as a result.

The "researcher" began slowly, asking simple questions: What is a skinhead? Why did people join the skinheads? Barrett calmed down as he answered these nonthreatening queries. Then Danny raised the stakes.

"Do you know Dave Mazzella, Mike?"

"Yeah, we're friends."

"Do you know Tom Metzger, too?"

A muscle in Barrett's neck quivered. Danny dropped the subject. Eliciting information from an unknown source is a bit like playing a fish. Once the bait is taken, there is no guarantee of landing him. You have to give him line, let him think he's in control, then bring him in when conditions are just right.

Danny let Barrett run with some easy questions, then came back to Metzger. "I've heard Tom comes to the aid of skinheads when they get in trouble. Have you talked to him since you got here?"

"Nope," Barrett spit out. Danny sensed that Barrett would like to send the scorpion off his arm after Metzger. There was a real possibility that the young man might open up.

"Gee, you're the guy in charge of WARskins, and he's not helping you?"

"Tom's different. I got my feelings about him." Barrett nervously looked around the room. The cubicles on both sides were also occupied.

Time was running out on this visit. Danny had to decide whether he should press Barrett and try to get a signed statement before leaving or wait for a longer, less pressured opportunity. Barrett seemed worried that in those open quarters someone might overhear him.

Any statement's value would be reduced if it weren't notarized; we couldn't file it with the court. On the other hand, Barrett might develop cold feet before Danny saw him again, or he might disappear altogether. He had only a few more months to serve.

This isn't the right time, Danny decided. *I'll take my chances we can reel him in later.* He gave the fish more line. "I heard you had some bats up in Portland."

Silence, then: "Yeah, I brought them up there in a duffel bag when I took the train."

There was only a minute left. Should he at least ask the critical question: *Did the Metzgers send you up there to cause trouble?* Barrett kept glancing around the room. He looked too frightened.

"I decided to wait until he's out of jail, Morris," Danny explained when he returned to the Center.

"I hope you're right, Danny."

But each of us was uneasy. There were two fish swimming out there that we needed to catch if we were to have a chance of getting Tom Metzger. One still hadn't surfaced. One had, and we'd let him off the hook on purpose.

DATELINE—PORTLAND: WAR now has information that shows three skinheads are being railroaded in Portland. Allegedly [Mieske's] defense attorney admitted he hated white separatists and didn't create an active or superior defense. In fact they were advised to plea bargain and plead guilty because the federals would charge them with civil rights [violations]. Such a deal. The Ethiopian primates blocked the skins' automobile with theirs, came out of the car screaming racial slurs, confronted the skins and so the skins had to fight them. Now the courts have lied about this case, the press have lied, the politicians lied, and a defense attorney threw the fight. Now, boys and girls, who's your real enemy here? Most of the people involved are white. White mutants as I would call them, or Jew mutants. The rest were white zombies that put these guys down the tube. Remember that!

This is WAR. At the tone, leave your message, a progress report. Special ops, run silent, run deep, and then sometimes periscope depth. And use courier. Do not target yourself.

> —Tom Metzger, White Aryan Resistance telephone hotline,
> June 19, 1989

CHAPTER SEVEN

July 6, 1989
∎
Montgomery, Alabama

The photographs of "Aryan Woodstock 2" in the WAR newspaper angered me. Six weeks earlier, over the Memorial Day holiday, Tom Metzger and friends had gathered in Catoosa, Oklahoma, for a weekend of what he called Reich 'N Roll. There, tattooed skinhead musicians had entertained a crowd of several hundred.

Everyone in the pictures was young. A mother in her early twenties posed with her infant daughter in front of a Confederate flag. Three smiling teenage girls "sieg-heiled" for the camera. Two boys, no more than eight or nine years old, stood near the stage in front of a banner bearing a skull and crossbones. A young man and woman strolled arm in arm down an outdoor aisle formed by skinheads and others giving the Nazi salute. Was this some twisted wedding ceremony?

Accompanying these photos was a reprint of a speech Tom Metzger had delivered to the assembly. He began by hailing Robert Mathews's violent group and proclaiming that the Order's "declaration of war [against the federal government] is just as valid today as it was in 1984. . . . The right wing is dead. The Marxists are dead. It's a white revolution."

Metzger then made the inevitable allusion to Nazi Germany. Asserting that young people in the United States have been divided by traditional politics, he stressed the benefits of Aryan unity: "If you remember what happened in Germany, they ceased to be divided and they began to kick ass." With WAR uniting the once-divided young, the "New Order" could begin, Metzger told his audience. And who would lead the movement? "Skinheads are in the forefront," he said.

The skinheads at Woodstock 2 and across the United States were the American version of a British movement that had begun in the early seventies when young men and women with shaved heads had first appeared, as a reaction to the popular "mods." The "skins" did not simply look different. Whereas the longhairs were, in the skinheads' eyes, middle class, liberal, and effete, the skins saw themselves as working class, patriotic, anti-immigrant, and tough.

Not all of these early skinheads were violent or racist. Still, there was a large enough radical contingent to spark the interest of British neo-Nazi groups like the National Front, which actively recruited skinheads. Soon the streets of London and other English cities became the site of periodic clashes between skinheads and minorities, often Asian. "Paki-bashing"—attacking Pakistani immigrants—became particularly popular.

Music was (and is) an integral part of the skinhead culture. "Oi" music, a kind of Cockney rock, arose as a means to express disgust with the establishment. Leading the booted, lockstep march down this avenue was the band Skrewdriver. Ian Stuart, the group's leader, was a National Front organizer with a history of racial violence. One Skrewdriver song, "Prisoner of Peace," paid homage to Adolf Hitler's deputy Rudolf Hess. Another effort, "White Power," bemoaned the takeover of England by immigrants. "Once we had an Empire, and now we've got a slum," went the lyrics. Skrewdriver's "Nigger, Nigger" was even more explicit: "Nigger, nigger, go, go, go."

Many early U.S. skinheads shared the look but not the ideology of their overseas counterparts. As one skinhead said, the style "stood for unity. . . . Everybody who had a shaved head, you considered them a brother."

But by the mid-eighties, brotherhood was not a principal concern of skinhead groups like Chicago's Romantic Violence. Leader Clark Martell, whose call for action appeared in Metzger's newspaper, had a long history of neo-Nazi activities. He was arrested for painting swastikas on village property in suburban Oak Park, Illinois, and for hitting a counterdemonstrator during a white power rally in Ann Arbor, Michigan.

"I am a violent person. I love the white race, and if you love something, you're the most vicious person on earth," Martell told a gathering of white supremacists. Other skinheads in other cities professed similar views and committed similar acts—disrupting rock concerts, defacing synagogues, assaulting and sometimes murdering blacks, Asians, Jews, and gays. By the end of the decade, Klanwatch would have files on some seventy different skins groups from coast to coast. A sampling: Blitzkrieg of Harrisburg, Pennsylvania; Buffalo-Rochester Aryan Skinheads (BRASH) of Rochester, New York; Christian Identity Skins of Las Vegas; Confederate Hammer Skins of Dallas and Memphis; Nordic F.I.S.T. of Minneapolis–St. Paul; Suicidals of Orange County, California; Tulsa Boot Boys of Tulsa, Oklahoma.

Skinheads had first appeared in Portland in the early 1980s. At the time their violence was limited for the most part to nightclubs where punk rock groups competed with heavy-metal, racist bands in the Skrewdriver tradition. Punk rockers were often the target of such violence, as skins would attempt to control the "pit," or dance floor.

In 1986, about fifty bat- and knife-wielding skinheads disrupted a punk rock concert at the Pine Street Theatre, where the girlfriends of East Side White Pride would later attack the Jewish "cowboy." That same year skinheads from Portland attended a meeting of Aryan leaders in Idaho, and Rick Cooper, a neo-Nazi from California, established himself in the Portland area. Cooper published a virulent racist tract called the *National Socialist Vanguard Report* and befriended local skins.

By the end of 1987, the skinheads had taken their act from the Pine Street Theatre to Pine Street itself. Larry Siewart and the Portland police began seeing what we now call hate crimes. A black man was physically and verbally assaulted. A Jewish business was vandalized. An Asian man and his Caucasian wife and their daughter were confronted on the street by skinheads disgusted by their "mixed marriage."

In May a local newspaper, *Willamette Week,* ran an article about a Portland skinhead gang, POWAR (Preservation of the White American Race). Portland's ABC television affiliate then followed with a town hall forum featuring POWAR members and an audience of concerned citizens. The media coverage bestowed a certain notoriety, if not legitimacy, on the movement, and skinhead groups began to attract new members. Police estimated that two hundred skinheads now made Portland their home. Among this number were Ken Mieske, Kyle Brewster, Steve Strasser, and George "Goggles" Flynt of East Side White Pride.

The growth of the skinhead movement had not escaped Tom Metzger's attention. He claimed to have been drawn to the skinheads by their music. "I grew up with early rock and roll—Elvis Presley, Jerry Lee Lewis, Fats Domino," he told *Rolling Stone* magazine. "I don't always catch all the words [in skinhead music], but I'm impressed with the power of it. I feel this anger coming from these white street kids—I get taken up in it."

Music, of course, was the major lure for attracting "white street kids" to the Aryan Woodstock, where John Metzger, like his father, sang the praises of racialism and revolution. After dedicating his speech to the late Robert Mathews, John said: "You know, we have a lot of other things besides concerts. We network all the hundreds of small little groups that all add up to one kickin'-ass revolutionary machine. We all work together now."

John was long on rhetoric and short on specifics. But one line from his speech struck me: "We are a normal people in an abnormal time."

Normal people. Who were these young kids in the Tulsa Boot Boys and the Suicidals, in Nordic F.I.S.T. and East Side White Pride?

The mother of a former skinhead from Florida gave the best answer. Skinheads were "tofu kids," she said, "because tofu takes on the flavor of whatever it's cooked with."

Ken Mieske certainly fit this description. "If a rugby team had come along and asked Ken to join, he probably would have. Instead, it was the racists," one of his friends told us. This reminded me of so many of the young Klansmen I had met. While they no doubt had racist propensities, they would have been just as happy and proud to wear the bowling shirt of the local tavern rather than the sheets of the local klavern. Unfortunately, for many the Klan was the only group to express interest in them.

We had never spoken to Mieske, who had been in jail since killing Mulugeta and was by all accounts extremely hostile toward the police, the criminal-justice system, and anyone associated with the Seraw family. But we had learned a good deal about him from newspaper articles and conversations with the police.

Mieske was born in 1964 near Seattle. Abandoned early by his mother, he was adopted by a family friend. He left home young, and by the age of sixteen was a long-haired Seattle street kid.

In 1982, Mieske met Cody Wallis in Seattle. Wallis, a thirty-two-year-old Portland restaurant owner and rock promoter, invited Mieske to Portland. Mieske appeared several months later, and Wallis gave him a job and a place to sleep. Although Wallis, who is gay, hinted in interviews after the murder that a sexual relationship may have existed briefly, the overall relationship was more like that of foster parent and son.

Wallis booked some acts into the Pine Street Theatre and found Mieske work there. Soon Mieske developed a fascination with a variation of heavy-metal music called death metal, a genre distinguished by high-tech guitar and outrageous, death-related lyrics. Mieske began calling himself Ken Death and persuaded his mentor to book death-metal groups like Slayer.

He moved out of Wallis's house and lived with friends. In 1984, at the age of nineteen, he met twelve-year-old Julie Belec. They spent most of their time listening to music and going to parties.

About this time Mieske began to get into trouble. He was convicted in February 1984 for attempted possession of cocaine. While still on probation eighteen months later, he was arrested for stealing meat and money from a submarine sandwich shop. After serving a short jail term, he returned to the Portland music scene.

In 1986, a local producer gave Mieske a minor part in a music video for "Boy in a Bubble," a cut from Paul Simon's *Graceland* album. But Mieske's musical tastes continued to be extreme. When skinhead groups began playing Pine Street Theatre, he was there.

Wallis said that Mieske had not demonstrated any racist tendencies when he first arrived in Portland. Indeed, Ken had counted many blacks, Hispanics, and gays among his friends. Although he had associated with the skinheads frequenting Portland's clubs, it was only after a return to prison in late 1986 that his racist attitudes emerged. Belec, Wallis, and other friends believed Mieske was recruited into the white supremacist movement while doing time for burglary at Pendleton Correctional Institute. This did not surprise me. The prisons were fertile territory for several white supremacists, who created "prison ministries." By couching their ideology in the language of the Identity religion, these racists were often able to bypass restrictions on prisoner mail. And by claiming to be a "church group," white supremacist prison gangs could hold meetings and recruit members from among fellow inmates. The largest of these gangs was called Aryan Brotherhood.

After prison Mieske moved into a room with the now sixteen-year-old Belec in her parents' home. An attractive blue-eyed blonde, she apparently shared his newfound racism. When the police searched her quarters after the Seraw killing, they found a great deal of racist literature. She was fascinated with Rudolf Hess.

As 1988 began, Ken Death concentrated his efforts on two groups—East Side White Pride and Machine, a death-metal band that invited him to become lead vocalist. On September 10, Machine performed at a local club. Later that evening Mieske, who still wore his hair at shoulder length despite his ESWP ties, was arrested in connection with an assault on a Safeway store security guard by skinheads. He was released when the guard could not identify him as one of the attackers.

On November 5, Mieske and Machine performed at Pine Street Theatre. By this time he wore his hair short, like most of the others in East Side White Pride. During the performance he encouraged the audience to vote in the upcoming election for a measure that would overturn Governor Neil Goldschmidt's executive order banning discrimination based on sexual orientation.

Mieske seemed to fit what many believe is the classic skinhead pattern. He had been abandoned as a child and had lived on the streets; he was mixed up sexually and into drugs; he became a petty criminal toughened by doing time with hardcore prisoners. But what were we to make of fellow ESWP members Kyle Brewster and "Goggles" Flynt? Brewster had apparently been involved with drugs as an adolescent and then turned himself around. He had been homecoming king at his high school. In a commencement speech Governor Goldschmidt had singled him out for praise.

Flynt was the son of a prominent Portland attorney. His mother was an executive. No broken home, no life on the streets, no mixed sexual signals. He had apparently always felt like an outsider. A punk rocker by the time he entered high school, he had been fascinated by the skinheads, who always seemed to get the better of the punks on the dance floor and in the streets. When he was tapped by East Side White Pride, he enjoyed the best of both worlds: he had become an insider in an outsider group.

But what exactly did that group do? In Heidi Martinson's interview with the Portland police, she said that East Side White Pride read racist literature, listened to music from Skrewdriver, and partied. There was virtually no organized activity, she explained, *until Dave Mazzella came up from California.* Mazzella confirmed this information—so important to building our case—in his statement to the Portland police. East Side White Pride had been "very loose" prior to his arrival, he told detectives Nelson and Hefley. Many in the group used drugs, something the Metzgers condemned in their speeches and writing. "They [ESWP] were very sloppily organized. I mean they were depressing. They were not what I'm used to—a tight-knit group . . . sit down, everyone knows what to do. I come up here and no one's active, everyone's kinda, 'we gotta do this, we gotta do that,' you know, just a lot of talk."

Within six weeks of his arrival, East Side White Pride had done a lot more than talk. Mazzella mentioned participating with the group in several racial assaults. He described leading the "boys' night out" to distribute the Metzgers' literature and recruit new members. He boasted to the detectives of his close ties with both Tom and John Metzger. But he never specifically pinpointed his instructions from the Metzgers or acknowledged any connection with the death of Mulugeta Seraw.

Reading about the history of the skinheads and trying to understand why someone would join their ranks made me anxious. I wanted to put aside the statements, newspaper articles, special reports. I wanted to sit in a room with Dave Mazzella and talk, ask questions, get answers.

On a steamy July afternoon in Santa Ana, California, this happened.

DATELINE—FONTANA, CALIFORNIA: On Sunday the seventeenth, a march with guest Martin Luther King III was held [to commemorate the Martin Luther King holiday]. Several white separatists attempted to demonstrate at that occasion. . . . David Mazzella, vice president of Aryan Youth, was stopped at the express command of federal agents and arrested by local Fontana police. . . . The charge was possession of a perfectly legal gun for personal protection, along with a baseball bat. Federal swine did not see the obvious baseball and the glove that sat beside the bat. . . . Mazzella's bail was twenty-five hundred dollars. His charge was a felony. Can you believe that? I want to thank these Big Brother goons for giving young white Americans a lesson in total government oppression.

> —Tom Metzger, White Aryan Resistance telephone hotline,
> January 22, 1988

CHAPTER EIGHT

July 12, 1989

■

Santa Ana, California

Dave Mazzella took a final drag on his cigarette, killed it in an ashtray, and immediately lit another. For better or worse, this nervous kid sitting across from me in the Ramada Inn held the key to our lawsuit.

Just a day earlier, Irwin Suall, the Anti-Defamation League's long-time fact-finding director in New York, had phoned me at the Center with the surprising news that Mazzella had called. Mazzella apparently wanted to make a fresh start, following in the footsteps of a handful of other skinhead turncoats who, aware of ADL's interest, had allowed the organization to debrief them.

I had told Irwin I'd be on the next plane to Los Angeles. "Please don't do anything until I get there," I said. Our case would most likely live or die on the basis of what Mazzella would say.

In the pictures I'd seen Ken Mieske was so menacing that he looked as if he belonged behind bars. Mazzella, on the other hand, looked at first glance as if he belonged behind a computer. The vice president of Aryan Youth Movement, who had been arrested several times for assault, was a pale, skinny twenty-year-old. He wore glasses, and his dishwater blond hair was short and uneven—apparently he was growing it out. The tattoo on his arm of an eagle holding a swastika seemed curiously out of place.

Betsy Rosenthal, the ADL staff attorney assigned to interview Mazzella, had not told him that I would be present, but he seemed pleased when she introduced me. "I know all about you," he said. "You've won some big cases in Texas, North Carolina, and Alabama. Metzger thinks you're a race traitor."

I seized on this odd kind of familiarity and complimented him on his role in WAR. "You must be quite a leader, Dave. I know you were on with Morton Downey and Oprah and that Sally Jessy Raphael," I said. "That takes a lot of self-confidence."

He shrugged. "I guess."

"And it takes a lot of courage to decide to change your life and come forward the way you have. You can do a world of good for other young folks, Dave."

I wanted him to see how his leadership skills could be used for good ends. I did not criticize him but said that Metzger had hurt a lot of people with his message of hate. I reminded him about Mulugeta.

Dave had come to talk, not to confess. He had thought Betsy would ask him for general information about WAR and the skinhead movement. I wanted specific facts about Portland and the Metzgers' involvement. I didn't tell him that I'd read his statement to the Portland police after the murder or that I had seen other police files. I wanted to see if what he told us now would be consistent with his past accounts, truthful, beneficial to our cause. I wanted to see what kind of witness he would make: would he be articulate, bright, comfortable, and, most important, believable?

A baby comes into the world free of prejudice and malice. What turns the innocent child into a violent, hateful human being? Dave Mazzella's parents did not teach him to despise blacks, Jews, and other minorities. They did not counsel that brass knuckles and baseball bats were acceptable ways to "communicate" or resolve disputes.

Dave's father was a "socialist at heart," Dave told me—a Vietnam veteran who never glorified war, the proprietor of a small appliance-repair business in northern California who lived to take his big motorcycle into the hills. His mother, Linda Mazzella, Dave added, was a good, gentle, open-minded woman struggling to provide stability to the household, in contrast to her free-spirited mate. Apparently it was a losing battle. In 1980 the business went under, and Dave Mazzella, Sr., left Linda, Dave, and Dave's older sister. He moved from their home in Mariposa, a small town south of Sacramento, to southern California.

At the time when twenty-year-old Mulugeta Seraw was adjusting to his new life in America, eleven-year-old Dave Mazzella was also adjusting. His father neither wrote nor sent child support. Linda, earning the minimum wage as a secretary, did her best to support the family. Soon she met and married, in Dave's words, "Ron, a Jewish man from Redwood City."

Dave was unhappy in his new home . . . and unmanageable. He became involved in the punk rock scene, spending most of his nights at the local mall. He was picked up for shoplifting and suspended from school for smoking pot.

Linda sent him to live with his father, and later with his grandparents, but such changes in scenery did not change his behavior. While staying with his mother's parents, he was expelled from eighth grade for distributing Valium to his classmates. He also "got into self-mutilation."

"What kind of self-mutilation, Dave?" I asked, half afraid to hear the answer.

"You know, where you carve things in your arms and things. I had swastikas carved and all."

I shivered.

Shortly after starting high school in 1984, with his hair spiked, his ear pierced, Dave began listening to a radio talk show that often featured discussions about neo-Nazis and white supremacists. As a child, Dave had loved World War II movies and, for reasons he could not explain, "had always been fascinated by the German part of it, the Nazis and all." He was part German, but that heritage had never been stressed, and he did not think that accounted for the attraction. The fact that he did not get along with his Jewish stepfather, stepsister, and stepbrother did eventually make the Nazis' ideas as appealing as their paraphernalia. "I saw a lot of things happen to my mom that kind of started building that anger that I used as an excuse later on in life," he explained.

Dave contacted the radio show and asked for the printed material discussed on the air. One of the pieces listed a post office box for Rick

Cooper's *National Socialist Vanguard Report.* Dave wrote Cooper, asking for all past issues. The packet from Cooper listed names and addresses of additional neo-Nazi organizations. Dave wrote to all of them, and soon each day brought something new in the mail. Home from school before his mother, Dave hid all the material under his bed.

When my boys were growing up, we worried about their hiding *Playboy* magazines. How frightening that things had come to this.

Dave devoured this literature. Soon, one organization in particular interested him. The White Student Union (WSU), founded and led by Greg Withrow in Sacramento, directed its white power message to those in high school and college. Withrow sent Dave literature to distribute at the high school, then phoned. "I felt important," Dave said. "I didn't want to be the same as everyone."

Blending the "whites have rights, too" message with standard neo-Nazi fare, WSU was gaining notoriety on campuses and in the media. Withrow encouraged Dave to start his own chapter of the organization. "I was excited," said Dave. "By this time I was developing hatred for all the races—Jews, blacks, Hispanics."

"Did the literature make sense to you?" I asked.

"Yes." He paused, then said, "My mom was on her third marriage, and I just felt like I wasn't wanted. I mean my grandparents, my dad . . . I just had nothing going for me. It was an escape route. It helped me through hard times. It inspired me."

Dave had said he wanted to be different, but I heard a young man who wanted to belong. His family hadn't offered that opportunity, and hate filled the vacuum created by the absence of love.

The literature, Dave told me, did what all good propaganda did. It painted a compelling one-sided picture. "I was going to school with blacks, and the majority of them were pretty good. But you never looked at the good side. You looked at the bad side, like: blacks are harassing whites, and that's wrong. I started getting so fed up with seeing whites not doing anything, not fighting back."

Withrow put Dave in touch with two white supremacists from the San Jose area, Ted Lewis and Paul Hoffman, who took him to his first Klan rally. At fifteen, Dave went to Modesto, where he heard Imperial Wizard Bill Albers. Lewis and Hoffman even provided a spare Klan robe, complete with the insignia of the night rider on horseback, torch in hand—a skewed version of the fashionable Ralph Lauren polo pony logo. The evening climaxed in a cross burning.

Dave came away excited. He had felt isolated passing out newspapers on his own. Now he saw there were kindred spirits. "I felt connected."

Initially Dave distributed his materials without attracting much attention. When no one was looking, he'd stick WSU literature bearing his own post office box number into lockers or telephone booths or leave papers around libraries where they were sure to be seen. After several months, he began riding buses across the county, getting off at high schools. "I'd run across the campus, take a handful of papers, throw them in the air, and let the wind spread them all over the place."

Developing more confidence as he continued communicating with Withrow, Dave gradually became less clandestine. He started trying to recruit classmates to his WSU chapter. Word spread around the school, and the student newspaper ran an article. The administration reprimanded him but took no other action. Dave's mother, who had been unaware of his activities for the first six months, was equally critical . . . and ineffectual.

Some people, however, were receptive. Dave saw himself as a salesman. "I had all these pitches—the Holocaust was a hoax. I had it all memorized from the literature. I had statistics the Aryan Nation [a major white supremacist organization based in Idaho] put out. I'd say: 'Do you know less than fifteen percent of the world's population is white, and in sixty years it will be less than five percent?' "

The dire statement that the white race was dying caught people's attention. Those responding came from all social and economic strata. There were preppies and punks, rich kids and poor kids. They shared white skin and troubles. "I think I was offering them a way out, because at that age, most people are really impressionable."

Most of these California kids, Dave explained, were turned off by the old-fashioned Ku Klux Klan. "But I was flying something totally different from the KKK banner. It was neo-Nazi. Like, rockers already wore the Iron Cross." Now Dave gave his friends SS armbands to wear.

Dave carried his own armband in his pocket. When he went skateboarding along the expressway, he put it on, "trying to shock people."

Dave had been involved with WSU for about one year when

Withrow drove down from Sacramento to meet him at the pizza parlor where he worked after school. With the president of WSU was his wholesome-looking blond teenage vice president, John Metzger.

John was no stranger to Dave. They had spoken on the telephone several times. In trying to reach John, Dave had even talked on the phone with Tom Metzger a few times. With this mention of Tom Metzger, I looked at Betsy. Now we were getting close to the subject of my inquiry.

Although he was excited to meet the twenty-four-year-old Withrow, Dave really wanted to meet Tom Metzger. Dave read the WAR newspaper religiously, and director Metzger was his hero. "Just like you might want to meet a rock star or baseball player, it was my goal," he told me.

Soon Dave began attending WAR meetings. Over pizza in a San Francisco apartment, members would detail their activities. Dave would report that he was distributing more and more literature and that he was putting up swastikas and writing WHITE POWER on walls in Mountain View, Cupertino, and Sunnyvale.

This paper-and-graffiti blitzkrieg eventually earned him the attention of more than student newspapers. The *San Jose Mercury* and other publications requested interviews. Dave obliged, taking one reporter to a Klan rally.

Radio and television were not far behind. By the time Dave accepted an invitation to appear on *A.M. San Francisco,* he had become a skinhead. A friend named Matt had encouraged the switch from punk to skin. Dave had not yet shaved his head, but he considered himself "part of the culture," hanging out with the twenty or thirty skins in the Bay Area and wearing the appropriate jacket and boots. "They were racially prejudiced," Dave said, but they were not connected to any white supremacist movement. Having read so much literature, he felt more sophisticated politically than the skinheads, he told me, but "I really liked the uniform."

Tom Metzger also appeared on *A.M. San Francisco.* Dave was not disappointed by this first meeting with his hero. Metzger, more comfortable in front of a camera, rescued Dave several times when he stumbled over his own words. After the show, the WAR leader invited Dave back to his hotel room, where he "seduced" him politically. Metzger had a VCR in his room loaded with a videotape of his latest cable offering. For good measure, he also gave Dave some literature.

When Dave returned home, he found his belongings in the front yard. By chance, his mother had seen the show and no longer wanted him in the house.

After a few days, Linda allowed her son to return. But he started spending less time at home and more time with Matt, who shaved Dave's scalp. "It took a while to get used to it," Dave said.

"What did your parents say?" I asked.

"They were shocked, but I said, 'You're always telling me to cut my hair because it's sticking up.' " He smiled.

During the months after the appearance on *A.M. San Francisco,* Dave's relationship with Tom Metzger grew stronger. They talked on the telephone frequently, and Dave felt comfortable discussing not only the problems of America but his own problems. Metzger became something of a father figure, Dave said. "I had total respect for him at this point. I would do anything for him." When Dave was suspended from school for several violations, including distributing literature, Metzger suggested suing, but Dave's mother would not sign the necessary papers for her son, a minor.

After his first national TV appearance, Dave's stock shot up with Bay Area skinheads. The movement was becoming more organized. Dave's group wore blue sweatshirts with American flags and Olde English lettering in white heralding the name they had selected: American Firm. A group of young skinhead men and women gathered almost every night, usually on the street. "We'd pick a place and go preachin' and drinkin'," Dave said.

One night they met in the parking lot of San Jose's Coyote Creek Park with members of the San Jose Skins. Suddenly an elderly black woman came by yelling, "They're going to lynch me, they're going to lynch me." A skinhead had stopped her at a bridge in the park and told her that because she was black, she would have to pay a toll. Then he started chasing her.

The skinhead was later arrested and charged with racial intimidation. The incident captured the attention of the media, and Dave, the best known of the local skins, received several calls from reporters. "I coined the term that skinheads were 'front-line warriors,' " he told me. The pride or nostalgia in his voice troubled me. I began to wonder if he had truly made the break from the past, when he had been, in his mind, such a celebrity. It is difficult to go cold turkey—to give up the only thing that has ever given one a feeling of self-importance.

Dave said that he had eventually moved from the Bay Area to Costa Mesa, just half an hour from the Metzgers'. He began visiting their home and meeting others in the WAR hierarchy, including skinhead Marty Cox; Dave Wiley, a computer wizard who helped run the cable TV show and telephone hotlines; and Brad Robarge, an Orange County skin who would eventually marry one of Metzger's daughters. WAR was apparently a family business. Dave said Metzger's wife, Kathleen, was deeply involved "behind the scenes."

"How often were you at the house?" I asked

"Every other week. I spent all my time either going over there or talking with them or hanging out with John [Metzger] and helping the Orange County skinhead chapter." Dave also hooked up with Michael Barrett, who had recruited about 75 percent of the skinheads in Southern California to affiliate with WARskins.

Skinhead gang fighting was intensifying and becoming increasingly racial. The skins would cruise the streets looking for trouble, "hoping we'd run into a mixed-race couple or someone we could start taunting."

Could we tie the Metzgers to such violence? I thought to myself.

Yes. Dave said that Tom Metzger had clearly encouraged this activity and carefully instructed his recruits. Metzger constantly talked about violent racial incidents and counseled that the skinheads should try to provoke others to take the first swing. That way the skinheads could retaliate violently but claim self-defense. If the police stopped or arrested the skinheads, they should remain silent, said Tom. Dave told us that Metzger passed out pamphlets reminding the warriors of their constitutional right to remain silent if arrested. Eager to please his "second father," Dave took part in a series of violent racial confrontations. When he reported his successes, Metzger congratulated him, adding, "Be careful. Don't get caught. You can't do anyone any good in jail."

"The violence was a form of frustration because the white revolution wasn't happening quickly enough," Dave explained. "Tom preached it wasn't going to happen overnight, and he knew we needed outlets to vent our frustration."

It was frightening how effective the ideology was. I could see the susceptibility of these unsophisticated youths under Metzger's spell. Hungry for acceptance and self-importance, they were little different from the starving street urchins manipulated by Fagin in *Oliver Twist*.

Metzger rewarded his urchins for their violent acts. He invited Dave to join him on the nationally syndicated *Sally Jessy Raphael* television show, where Dave received star treatment. The show paid his airfare and had a limousine waiting at the airport to whisk him to a good hotel in New Haven, Connecticut, for the taping.

By this time Tom had merged Withrow's WSU into WAR and given it a new name, Aryan Youth Movement. He had replaced Withrow and installed his son, John, his ideological clone, as president. In New Haven Tom asked Dave to serve as vice president of AYM. Dave told us that the promotion was made not in spite of his violent ways but because of them.

The Raphael show also featured Klansmen. These good ol' Southern boys quickly made it clear they wanted nothing to do with the skinhead from the West Coast. "They didn't trust me or like me," Dave said. "They wouldn't even shake my hand."

The Klansmen, in Metzger's view, were missing the boat. "Tom's attitude was: White supremacist organizations were getting older, and they needed some kind of link to youth. He knew skinheads were dedicated; they got things done," Dave told us.

If the skinheads got into trouble, the Metzgers would help them. In January 1988, Dave crammed several skinheads into his van and headed for Fontana, California, where Martin Luther King III was to address a rally in memory of his father. Armed with shields, stun guns, baseball bats, chains, and knives, the skinheads planned to "go in there and get King, make some news." The police pulled them over before they got a chance, arresting Dave. Dave called WAR headquarters, and John, along with Dave Mazzella, Sr., came and bailed him out of jail.

Dave was, he admitted to Betsy and me, under Metzger's spell. A few months after the Fontana incident, he asked Metzger to officiate at his marriage. Former Identity church minister Metzger was willing to perform the ceremony until he heard a rumor that Sylvia, the bride-to-be, might be a Native American. The director would not participate in the muddying of the pure white race with Native American blood. It would look bad for WAR, he said. He told Dave to prove Sylvia was white by producing her birth certificate and photographs of her parents.

Eighteen-year-old Dave didn't question the directive. When the proper documentation was in hand, Metzger not only married the two, he provided the "entertainment" at the outdoor ceremony— videos promoting racism. He even brought a portable generator to supply the electricity so the films could be shown.

I wanted to say: *How can someone be so sick that he spreads hatred at a wedding.* But now was not the time to get emotional. I held my tongue.

Sylvia soon became pregnant, and the marriage quickly fell apart. By the fall of 1988, the Metzgers had a new assignment for Dave, whose status within the organization had grown with each violent incident. At the Oklahoma Aryan Fest, Tom and John had learned that East Side White Pride and POWAR, rival skinhead factions in Portland, were feuding. They sensed an opportunity to win new WAR recruits.

Tom had previously received correspondence from Mieske and Brewster. He gave their names to Mazzella, who wrote back. By the time he was ready to leave for Portland, John had already written the letter to Ken Death so important to our case: "You'll get a feel of how we work when you meet Dave Mazzella. . . ."

When he arrived in the city in early October with Mike Gagnon, another skinhead associated with WAR, and a van full of WAR literature, Dave's first stop was the Mieske-Belec place. There he called Tom and put him on the phone with Mieske, who was thrilled to talk to his hero.

Over the next hour, Dave told Betsy and me how, *in his capacity as WAR vice president,* he had organized East Side White Pride and taught them the fundamentals of being a racialist that he had learned from Tom, including violence. These lessons had involved brutal confrontations with minorities in Portland. He had kept the Metzgers apprised of his activities by means of phone calls and letters.

GREAT STUFF, I scribbled on my notepad. This information strongly suggested that Mulugeta's death was a result of the Metzger-to-Mazzella-to–East Side White Pride connection.

When Dave finished, I felt for the first time that we actually had a good chance of bringing down Tom Metzger's growing empire. Still, there were too many ifs for me to feel comfortable.

We had a chance only *if* Dave testified in court as he had talked to me; *if* we could find other evidence to corroborate his story; *if* he and his story would hold up under cross-examination; *if* a judge would at trial's end instruct the jury that the connection Dave described made the Metzgers liable; *if* the jury could understand how a man sitting in his living room fifteen hundred miles away from Portland was culpable for the death of a man he had never heard of and had never specifically instructed anyone to kill.

This last part was tricky enough. And I honestly didn't know if we'd even get that far. I believed what Dave Mazzella had told me, but I wasn't certain how he would come across as a witness. Dave was intelligent but very nervous. Metzger had been like a father to him. How would Dave hold up in court in the presence of that father figure? Could he say what he said to me with Metzger staring at him? Could he say what he said with other skinheads staring at him?

After Dave had returned to California from Portland, Metzger's friend Marty Cox had beaten him up—apparently in retaliation for Dave's rumored snitching. This raised another worry: if Metzger's warriors learned that Dave was going to testify against their hero, they might see to it that Dave never made it to the courthouse.

Nervously lighting another cigarette, Dave had no idea of the worries that I knew would cause me many sleepless nights between now and a trial. He had no idea I was thinking about using him as our star witness.

Now was not the right time to tell him. I wanted to get a statement from him, a notarized statement—something he might feel would bind him legally, if not morally. Then I would work on developing the bond, the trust, the relationship, necessary to make this young man a powerful witness.

I asked if he would sign a statement summarizing what he had told Betsy and me.

"It's the truth," he said. "I don't see why not."

We arranged to meet the next day. I spent the first sleepless night writing and rewriting the statement from the notes I'd taken, wondering if he would even show up to sign it.

This is not the Klan, and this is not Alabama. Morris Dees may be a big boy in Montgomery, but out here he ain't jack. And when I knock this guy off his saddle, it'll make me the biggest thing in the country. I'm going to cost this guy so much money, he's going to wish he never came out here. He's going to get bogged down like the Germans did in Russia. You've got another Stalingrad here.

—Tom Metzger, *Los Angeles Times* interview, February 18, 1990

CHAPTER NINE

January 24, 1990
■
San Diego, California

San Diego was not Stalingrad, but after my first confrontation with Tom and John Metzger, I was indeed sorry I'd made the long trip west. After spending several days and nights in Montgomery preparing for the pair's depositions, a team from the Center and I had arrived in California to find father and son not only intent on bogging us down but capable of doing so.

Based in large part on the affidavit that Dave Mazzella had signed as promised, we had sued Tom, John, WAR, Ken Mieske, and Kyle Brewster in October, after Brewster and Steve Strasser had also pled guilty to the murder of Mulugeta Seraw.*

We had initially filed the lawsuit in federal court in Portland on behalf of Mulugeta's uncle Engedaw Berhanu, the representative of the estate. The Donald case, like all our other major Klan cases, had been tried in the federal system; under the Ku Klux Klan Act passed

---

*Brewster and Strasser pled guilty to first-degree manslaughter as well as assault and intimidation charges. Brewster received a sentence of twenty years with a ten-year minimum. Strasser received twenty years with a nine-year minimum. We did not sue Strasser because he had played a lesser role in the murder and because, based on his willingness to cooperate with the Portland police, we believed he might be willing to cooperate with us.

by Congress in 1871, this was the venue to seek the civil remedies for victims of Klan violence. Federal courts had also been a friendlier forum for blacks than state courts, where popularly elected judges were often biased. But soon after filing *Berhanu* v. *Metzger, et al.*, we had determined that we would be better off in state court for two reasons. First, Elden Rosenthal, our local counsel, tried most of his cases there. He was well respected and more comfortable on that turf. Even more important, the rules of discovery in Oregon state court did not require parties to disclose as much information to their opponents as the federal rules did. This was a welcome oddity; usually state rules require broad disclosure of potential witnesses and evidence before a trial.

Obviously, a good trial lawyer wants to reveal as little as possible about his case to the other side. This was particularly true in this instance. We did not want the defendants to know we had such physical evidence as John Metzger's letter to Ken Death. And we certainly didn't want them to know we had located Dave Mazzella, had secured his potentially devastating affidavit, and were planning to use him as our star witness. The less Tom knew about our case in advance of trial, the less time he would have to fabricate lies in response to our witnesses.

There was another reason for keeping Mazzella's role a secret. When Mieske had been arrested, he had snarled to a policeman, "Whoever snitched us off is dead." We didn't want the defendants or their friends to feel it was important to get to Dave—either to make good on Mieske's threat or to "persuade" him to reconsider his testimony.

Our suit, voluntarily dismissed from federal court and immediately filed in state court in late November, was officially captioned as an "action for wrongful death and racial intimidation." We alleged that through "intentional acts" or in the alternative "reckless acts" or "negligent acts," including the selection of Mazzella as their agent, the Metzgers had "incited or encouraged the members of East Side White Pride to commit violent acts against blacks in order to promote white supremacy." As a result, Mulugeta Seraw had lost his life.*

---

*There is a difference between acting intentionally, recklessly, or merely negligently. Complaints almost always employ this form of alternative pleading because final proof may support one theory but not another.

Reading the complaint, I couldn't help remembering the first time I had conceived of a civil suit seeking to hold an organization and its top officials liable for the criminal deeds of underlings they had encouraged or incited. Eighteen years earlier these underlings had been not skinheads but "plumbers."

In June 1972, five men were arrested for breaking into the Watergate headquarters of the Democratic National Committee (DNC). Among them was James McCord, security director of CREEP—the Committee to Re-elect the President (Nixon)—and of the Republican National Committee (RNC). I figured that someone at CREEP or the RNC was behind the Watergate break-in. At the time I was chief fund-raiser for the Democratic presidential candidate, George McGovern. I called McGovern's campaign manager, Gary Hart, and asked him what he thought of the idea of having the DNC file suit against the burglars, RNC, CREEP, and organization officials for, among other things, violating the First Amendment rights of the party and voters. Hart was skeptical but accepted my offer to come up to Washington, D.C., from Montgomery with my law clerk, Charles Abernathy.

Abernathy, now a professor at Georgetown Law Center, and I presented our theories to an old friend, Joe Califano, who along with the famed Edward Bennett Williams served as DNC general counsel. Within a few days—less than two weeks after the break-in and some time before Deep Throat's revelations began appearing in *The Washington Post*—the DNC had filed suit against RNC and CREEP and organization officials for the acts of their agents and employees. My involvement in the Watergate affair stopped at this point. The case was ultimately settled for $750,000 after President Nixon resigned.

All the president's men had been represented by the best counsel available. The Metzgers, on the other hand, claimed to be representing themselves. When Danny Welch, Center investigator Joe Roy, Klanwatch research director Sara Bullard, ADL attorney Richard Shevitz, and I arrived for the depositions, Tom and John were officially without lawyers.

For the next nine months, they would cry that they were unable to find more than a handful of attorneys willing to represent their "unpopular" views and that they could not afford these lawyers' fees. But it was apparent that someone with a law degree was working behind the scenes on their behalf. Just the day before the depositions, they had filed a well-conceived motion to dismiss our complaint. Some of the ancillary language in the motion was unmistakably Tom's: "Is the Pope to become liable for assaults on homosexuals for declaring homosexuality a sin? Is *Playboy* magazine to be liable for inciting lust in a rapist's heart?" But the legal theories advanced, including lack of jurisdiction in Oregon over the California-based Metzgers and our failure to join, or sue, indispensable parties (the unnamed agents of WAR whom we alleged encouraged the violence), evidenced a lawyer's handiwork.

Such handiwork was also apparent in the cases cited and in two other pleadings. The first, filed in Oregon, was a cross-complaint in which the Metzgers sued the Seraw estate and Mulugeta's companions, Tilahun Antneh and Wondwosen Tesfaye. Here the Metzgers countercharged that the Ethiopians had been responsible for the death of Seraw because they, not the skinheads, had started the fight, motivated by their own "malice and racial hatred" against whites.

I was ceremoniously served with papers announcing the second action when I entered the room for the deposition. Filed in state court in San Diego, this complaint charged Engedaw and me with malicious prosecution because we had dismissed our federal lawsuit. Ignoring the fact that we had refiled the case in state court, Tom Metzger claimed he had lost several thousand dollars worth of TV repair work as the result of our supposedly frivolous federal court suit and had spent hundreds more defending himself. The Metzgers sought $10 million in damages. As outlandish as these two actions appeared, they would require serious responses and therefore succeeded in slowing our momentum.

Nowhere, however, was the unseen hand of a lawyer more apparent than in the ploy John Metzger pulled on the very morning we were to depose him. On that day John, who had never been to college, much less law school—his most recent job had been as a clerk at a nuclear power plant (a frightening thought!)—filed for bankruptcy. He claimed he was $2,000 in arrears and faced potential liability of $10 million more if he lost our case. Bankruptcy is a federal action, and such a filing has the effect of automatically staying other actions against the individual (our lawsuit, for example) pending a court's determination of the bankruptcy's legitimacy; John, obviously counseled to follow this course by a lawyer, could not be deposed in our case.

I was furious. We play hardball in trying these cases, and we expect the other side to do so. Still, there are certain courtesies to be observed. You don't wait until counsel spends more than $2,500 to travel across the country for a deposition before revealing there was no need for the trip.

John would eventually plead naïveté and respond that we had to be in San Diego for Tom Metzger's deposition anyway. Tom, reluctant to ruin his apparently quite profitable WAR business, fearful of the embarrassing publicity, and confident that he could handle us, had not declared bankruptcy. Still, his deposition was marked by obstructionist, dilatory tactics as well.

The Metzgers arrived for the depositions wearing different suits— Tom in brown, John in baby blue—but identical expressions: sneers that left no doubt that they felt philosophically and morally superior to me and my team and also believed they were winning the first round of the legal battle. The two men moved—actually *strutted*—the same way and sat similarly in their chairs. Each leaned back as if he were in a La-Z-Boy recliner and looked upward as if there were handwriting to read on the ceiling if not the wall.

They were compact men, Tom stouter than John, and jowlier, too. He wore a toupee that was the same color if not the same material as his suit. John had blond hair, blue eyes, and a face so pink I doubted he had begun shaving. If not for the scowl and the slit-eyed gaze, he would have made a fine poster boy for the Aryan cause.

Ordinarily I try to remain on amicable terms with opponents like the Metzgers despite the evil they may have done. Maybe this is due to my genial Southern upbringing. It doesn't hurt to be pleasant to your enemy, and sometimes you can gain an advantage in this way.

This pragmatism has served me well in several cases. When I met Benny Hayes, the UKA Grand Titan who had influenced his son Henry and Tiger Knowles to lynch Michael Donald, I had extended my hand in peace and indicated a willingness to help his son avoid the death penalty, which I have long opposed. On a subsequent visit, he showed me secret Klan documents that proved essential to winning our civil case against, among others, him.

Despite this experience and similar ones, I could not bring myself to be friendly to the Metzgers. Unlike many of the good ol' boy Klansmen, Metzger was deeply evil. Like Robert Mathews and the Order members, he would gladly have exterminated all Jews. His hate for me was also evident. With nothing to gain from small talk, I did my best to be civil.

As Tom and I sat across from each other in a large room in a San Diego office building, my anger at John's eleventh-hour bankruptcy move was, uncharacteristically, visible. The deposition did nothing to soothe me. Tom answered my first three questions, stating his full name and address and acknowledging that he lived in a single-family dwelling. Then:

Q: And who else lives at this address with you?

A: At this point I must say that since this case involves a death, a murder, allegedly, that at this point on I will take the Fifth.

Q: You mean you are going to take the Fifth Amendment with respect to the entire deposition?

A: That's right.

I was disturbed but not completely surprised. Preparing for the deposition—reading WAR literature and newspapers, listening to telephone hotlines, poring over other material collected over the years by Klanwatch and brilliantly digested for me by Sara Bullard—had taken an immense amount of time. However, we had figured Metzger would play rougher than some of the naïve defendants who in past cases had let us take damaging depositions.

I explained that it was his privilege to take the Fifth Amendment, but that if he did so "in a frivolous way or for the purpose of delay," the court could make him pay for our considerable expenses in coming to and preparing for the deposition. I added that he could not take the Fifth at his deposition and then decide to testify at the civil trial; this was against the Oregon state rules, as well as the rules of every other jurisdiction. As I couldn't imagine the egocentric Metzger forgoing the opportunity to climb on the soapbox at a trial that could potentially receive national publicity, I thought he might agree to answer my questions now and save a return trip. But he refused to answer virtually everything I asked for the next forty-five minutes.

"I need this aggravation like a hole in the head," I said to Danny as we gathered up the papers we had spent such a long time preparing in anticipation of the two depositions. "We come halfway across the world, don't get a damn thing from Tom, and John files for Chapter Thirteen, which means we have to find a lawyer out here to fight that, not to mention that I've just been sued for ten million dollars." I might have added that we could expect the Metzgers to resist our subpoenas for phone records and bank records, creating more delays and further legal wrangling. These skirmishes are to be expected in almost any proceeding, and I knew our Richard Cohen, a scholar, writer, and tactician without peer, would help coordinate these various actions and plot our legal strategy. Still, the prospect of directing so many different court battles in Oregon and California from a command post in Alabama did not appeal to me.

Danny wisely kept loading a briefcase without responding to my frustration. Then, without looking up, he handed me an envelope. Inside was a check made out to the Center from James McElroy, Attorney at Law. Danny explained that McElroy, who had an office in the building, was a fan of ours. When he'd heard we were here, he had approached Danny during a break, made the contribution, and asked if he might meet me.

An hour later, after a delightful conversation in Jim "Mac" McElroy's office, the Center had entered into what would prove to be one of its most rewarding alliances. McElroy, a successful plaintiff's personal-injury lawyer in his early forties, was honest, without pretense, and in step with us philosophically. He wasted no time in accepting my offer to become our local counsel in San Diego. His first task would be to defend us in the Metzgers' suit charging malicious prosecution.*

The meeting with McElroy was not the only positive result of the journey. A few days before the depositions, Danny and Joe Roy had flown to Los Angeles, then driven to San Bernadino to meet Michael Barrett. Barrett, who had been paroled several weeks earlier, had no reason to leave us his forwarding address. Fortunately, Danny utilized a law enforcement connection to get Barrett's address from his parole officer.

---

*We hired another San Diego law firm, Gray, Cary, Ames & Grye, to respond to John Metzger's bankruptcy action. Lawyers Barbara Orr, David Mandel, and David Osias did the work guided by the Center's Richard Cohen.

Apparently long estranged from his own family, Barrett had been given shelter by an older woman whose daughter he had known. Danny had called to reintroduce himself, still using the story that he was doing research on the skinheads. Barrett had agreed to meet him at the TCBY yogurt shop, where he was now working.

Barrett appeared the same thin, unimposing young man he had been the previous summer, with a couple of noticeable exceptions—he had let his hair grow out, and the tattoos that he had seemed to flaunt were now covered. Danny and Joe engaged in an hour's conversation with him, discussing everything from his work to the pros and cons of living in California, Alabama, and a variety of other locales.

Gradually Danny became serious. He explained that he and Joe worked at the Center, and he told Barrett about the lawsuit against the Metzgers, Mieske, and Brewster. Still uncertain of Barrett's feelings about Metzger, Danny carefully avoided suggesting that Tom was our major target. He did not, however, mince words about the director of WAR. "You know, Michael, Tom Metzger has harmed a lot of young people in his time." When Barrett nodded, Danny added, "He exploited you, ruined your life, didn't he?" And tears came to the eyes of Michael Barrett, former skinhead leader.

"Michael, I don't know if you ever saw the picture of Mulugeta Seraw after East Side White Pride got done with him. It's gruesome. Here was an innocent man trying to go to school, better his life here in this country. I mean this guy could barely understand English, much less know who the skinheads were."

Barrett nodded again.

"Did Tom ever help you in jail?" Danny asked.

Barrett looked down at the floor. "No," he said quietly. He had been abandoned by his onetime hero as well as by his family.

Danny knew it was time to move forward. "Michael, I'd like to ask you a lot of questions, and I'd like to take some pretty detailed notes."

When the questioning was over, Danny looked at Barrett warmly. "This has been real helpful. What I'd like to do is go back to the hotel so I can type up my notes, so we can put it into some kind of affidavit form that the attorneys can read, and then get it notarized. All this is the truth, isn't it?"

"Yes."

Danny and Joe drove Barrett home and arranged to pick him up the next day. After he had disappeared into the house, the two veteran investigators looked at each other, then started shouting with glee. "You'd have thought we'd just won the lottery," Danny later told me.

They picked Barrett up the next morning. "Read this and see if it's correct," said Danny, who had borrowed a typewriter at his hotel to prepare the affidavit. While Barrett went over the document, Joe searched a phone book for the closest notary public. None were listed in the San Bernadino yellow pages.

"Damn," said Danny. There was no telling how long Barrett would remain agreeable if they had to drive through the valley looking for a notary.

So far, however, Barrett was being most cooperative. "This is fine," he said, handing Danny the affidavit. He added, "I think there's a notary at a liquor store near here where you can cash checks." There was, but Danny's relief was short-lived. California law required presentation of identification. As Barrett had none, the notary refused to stamp the affidavit.

"Wait just a second," Danny said. Searching through his briefcase, he found a not-so-recent newspaper article about Barrett accompanied by a picture of the young man in full skinhead splendor. Although Barrett now had hair on his head, it was obvious that he was the person identified in the photograph. After several minutes, Danny finally persuaded the notary to accept the clipping as a valid form of identification.

Barrett had not asked about the consequences of providing an affidavit that hurt Tom Metzger, and neither Danny nor Joe had offered an unsolicited opinion. Now, as they left the liquor store for the TCBY shop, Barrett wondered what would happen. "Will Tom find out about this?" he asked. "Am I going to have to testify?"

"I don't know if Tom has to know. It depends on the rules of the court, I think," Danny said truthfully. "As for testifying, your affidavit may be enough so that you don't have to come to court."

Barrett betrayed no fear but said quietly, "I'd rather Tom doesn't know about this."

Danny showed me the affidavit that night in San Diego. He was excited . . . for good reason. This was potent material. But I sensed an underlying sadness. "I feel sorry for Michael," he explained. "He's a nice guy, Morris, a genuinely nice guy. He's just a kid from the streets who got caught up in Tom's smooth talk. He's scared of Metzger, and he's all alone. He's alive, but he's a victim just as sure as Mulugeta was."

Danny stayed behind after the Metzger "depositions" to explore one more Southern California lead. A law enforcement officer in the San Diego area with whom Danny had recently become friendly had placed a man undercover with the Metzgers and WAR for about a year. This informant, one Pete Gibbons, had apparently worked his way into WAR's inner circle, successfully persuading the Metzgers he shared their racist beliefs. Gibbons was not a police officer but what some might call a wanna-be, enamored of the police. At any rate he had been good at what he'd done. Although he had left Metzger before the Seraw killing, we were most interested in talking with him. Danny's contact set up a secret meeting, and Danny rendezvoused with Gibbons at the ADL office in San Diego after dark. Gibbons, a well-tanned, laid-back man in his late twenties, impressed Danny with his excellent information if not with his self-congratulatory tone. This skilled mole corroborated much of what Mazzella had told us.

Barrett's statement was important for what it revealed about the Metzgers—that they had operated in Oregon and encouraged violence. But it was equally important for what it allowed us *not* to reveal—Dave Mazzella and the key letter from John Metzger to Ken Death.

The Metzgers' motion to dismiss our complaint alleged, among other things, that the Oregon court had no jurisdiction over the Metzgers because they were not residents of Oregon, did not conduct any business in the state, and had no contact with the plaintiff there. If this were true, the Metzgers deserved to win their motion. Well-established case law prevents suing an out-of-state resident who has no contacts or dealings in the state.

There was no doubt that Tom Metzger was working in Oregon *after* the Seraw murder. In February 1990, he broadcast a message on his telephone hotline while he was in Portland:

WAR has come to the decision that Portland needs even more cultural enrichment. We're going to try to lease some big buses and give free transportation to our Southern California darling non-white dopeheads, street people, and bring 'em all to beautiful downtown Portland. . . .

And now that WAR plans to colorize Portland, like Ted Turner, even more we want all you brain dead whites to come down, take a ticket and adopt a niglet or a gooklet for your very own. Move 'em right in. Show 'em how much you like to integrate.

Recordings like this might pack an emotional wallop if played for a jury, but we needed to demonstrate to a judge that the Metzgers had been active in Oregon *before* Mulugeta's death as well. Dave Mazzella's affidavit, in which he clearly explained that the Metzgers had sent him to Oregon in his role as an officer of WAR, would be sufficient for us to prevail at this point in the proceedings. However, if we revealed that affidavit, we would be alerting the Metzgers to Mazzella's defection and putting our key witness in harm's way. Barrett's cooperation meant we could, for the time being anyway, continue to keep Mazzella a secret.

In the affidavit Barrett, too, acknowledged that the Metzgers had sent him to Oregon. He added that he had told the members of East Side White Pride to create physical trouble for blacks and Jews, whom the Metzgers portrayed as enemies. "We told them to be sure to use violence if they got the opportunity and to be sure and beat the hell out of the enemy. . . . We were telling them what Tom and John Metzger told us to say to skinheads we were organizing. We got ESWP all fired up to carry out Tom and John Metzger's goals of harming blacks and Jews."

Barrett also said that while in Oregon he had "kept in almost daily contact by telephone with WAR and the Metzgers. I was acting on behalf of WAR," he stated. He then added this revealing information: "Mazzella informed them [the Metzgers] of the murder before the police had learned who committed the crime and before Mieske, Brewster, and Strasser were arrested. Tom told us to keep our mouths shut and not to talk to the police."

Mazzella had told us this, too. Given the choice, we preferred that he, rather than Barrett, tell it to a jury. Having talked with Tom under these circumstances, he was in the best position to reveal the specifics of the startling conversation. Indeed, Barrett might be prohibited from testifying to this because of the hearsay rules that forbid relating a conversation that one was not a party to. Here, then, was another reason Mazzella was so critical to our case and why getting Tom's phone records that might substantiate communication with his Oregon emissaries was also important.

Barrett's affidavit, attached to our opposition to the Metzgers' motion to dismiss the case, created waves from San Diego to Portland. FORMER SKINHEAD LINKS METZGERS TO RACIST SLAYING headlined the *San Diego Union*. In the accompanying article, Metzger denied that he had incited the skinheads to violence, characterizing Seraw's death as the result of "a spontaneous street fight that could not have been predicted by anyone." He also called Barrett a liar who had been run out of Riverside, California, "by other skinheads because he got into drugs" before going to Portland.

We knew that Metzger would have difficulty finding Barrett, who had no ties to his family and no permanent address. Still, we regretted that by filing the affidavit we might expose him to the wrath of the Metzgers and their loyalists. It was a very difficult decision, but one that we felt was necessary in the long run. I must confess that we were pleased that WAR's energies were apparently going to be directed at this ex-soldier rather than Mazzella, who by virtue of his family connections would be easier to locate.

As often as possible over the next several months, I furthered the notion that Barrett was our key witness. The first time a reporter asked me about the importance of Dave Mazzella to our case, I played dumb. "Who?" I asked. Sometimes when we attended hearings or depositions with the Metzgers, I would write Barrett's name in bold letters on my legal pad accompanied by a big star. Later, I'd make the notation FIND DAVE MAZZELLA. It's common for opponents to take a look at unattended papers during breaks in the action, and the Metzgers were no less curious than others we've faced. I'd find an excuse to leave the room, making sure my pad was in a place where the Metzgers would see the misleading message.

Of course we knew Mazzella's whereabouts. He was in Medford,

Oregon, with his mother. In the days after our first meeting in July, he had lived with his father and his father's new wife and two young stepsons in Garden Grove, California. As usual, tension eventually developed with the stepparent. When Dave played a tape of the raunchy comedian Andrew Dice Clay within earshot of the boys, his stepmother prevailed upon David senior to banish him.

Dave was getting ready to move to Medford in October 1989 when we flew him to Montgomery just before filing the lawsuit. In addition to desiring a second debriefing, I wanted to establish a bond with him. We needed each other at this point. He could help us win our case, and we could help him turn his life around. As corny as this may seem, I truly believed it (in fact, I believe it with respect to most of our witnesses who see the error of their ways and help us fight their former colleagues). Dave was basically a good kid in need of two things— someone who cared about him and some means of achieving self-esteem. Tom Metzger had cared for him; now I wanted to. Perversely, he had achieved self-esteem by becoming the nation's most visible skinhead and working his way up to WAR vice president; now, he could achieve it by being the repentant racist who balanced the scales of justice by making Metzger pay for his sins.

Dave's visit came at a hectic time. After we had won the Donald case in 1987, Mrs. Donald and I had been honored by the Alabama NAACP. My speech to the organization's convention recalled the contributions of the slain heroes of the civil rights era. Later that evening, several young people in attendance, black and white, told me they knew little about Medgar Evers, Emmett Till, Viola Liuzzo, and others less famous than Dr. King who had died in the battle for civil rights. On the drive home, I had conceived of a memorial for those who gave their lives for the movement.

With the blessing of the Center's directors, we had commissioned Maya Lin, the talented young architect who had designed the Vietnam Memorial, to create a fitting remembrance that would grace the plaza in front of the Center. We hoped this civil rights memorial would draw and inspire visitors from across the country. We were to dedicate the memorial on November 5, 1989, in a ceremony bringing together national leaders, surviving civil rights heroes like Rosa Parks, and the families of those who had died for the cause. We expected thousands of caring citizens as well.

On the day Dave came to Montgomery—about four weeks before the dedication—the large black granite table bearing the names of the dead also arrived, ready for installation. Dave seemed genuinely impressed and moved by the histories of the forty men and women whose names had been etched into the stone.

I took a picture of Dave and my daughter, Ellie, by the memorial as the workmen installed it—one of the first photographs taken of the monument. The irony was not lost on either of us. Less than two years earlier Dave Mazzella, by his own admission, had been indirectly responsible for a murder not unlike many commemorated here in granite. Now he had the rare opportunity to redeem himself. I hoped he wouldn't blow it.

I gave Dave the grand tour of Montgomery. We went down to the Tallapoosa River looking for alligators. We went to the fields where I'd worked as a boy, and I taught Dave the fine art of picking cotton. I was confident that if we remained in close contact, we could keep him on the straight and narrow.

Four months after this visit to Montgomery, I learned that I was wrong.

Dave Mazzella went off the screen. As they say in radar, he went off the screen.

—Tom Metzger, *Los Angeles Times* interview, February 18, 1990

CHAPTER TEN

February 20, 1990
■
Medford, Oregon

Danny Welch would later tell me that even after he and Joe Roy had taken the long flight from Atlanta to Portland, then driven the six hours south to Medford, they didn't look as tired as Dave Mazzella's mother. Linda Mazzella Ford had called me the previous day immediately after learning that Dave was once again in trouble. The local sheriff had arrested him for assault, robbery, and unlawful possession of a weapon.

When Dave had visited the Center in October, he had spent a good deal of time with Danny. Afterward, Danny had told me he thought Dave was still in danger of slipping back into his past violent, racist ways—not because he relished hurting people or deeply believed the white supremacist credo, but because the skinhead world was the only place in which he had ever been somebody. Over the next four months, both Danny and I had talked regularly with Dave, reinforcing the notion that he was a hero to courageously come forward to help stop the Metzgers. Danny had also spoken with Linda Ford several times, finding her the good mother worried about her son's well-being.

Here "well-being" had two meanings. Linda hoped Dave had finally abandoned his skinhead ways. She also worried that Tom Metzger, whom she believed had brainwashed Dave and other young, impressionable recruits, might hurt her son if he found out about his defection and could locate him. We had counseled her and Dave that the best way to avoid WAR was to keep a low profile—steer clear of the small band of skinheads in the Medford area, avoid contact with former skinhead friends and Metzger supporters, and by all means stay out of trouble with the police. An arrest could lead to unwanted publicity.

Dave seemed to have followed our advice with positive results until February 18. He was working in a lumber mill, living with his mother and stepfather, and had a new girlfriend. There had been no problems. Metzger, as he told the *Los Angeles Times,* had no idea of his former vice president's whereabouts.

Now, however, Dave was coming dangerously close to reappearing on the radar screen. Blond, in her forties, Linda showed the strain of watching Dave get into so much trouble in his twenty-one years. Danny sensed there was guilt, too, mixed in with the worry. Linda did not share any of Dave's past hatred for blacks, Jews, and others, but she seemed to feel partially responsible for his embracing the philosophy. She and Dave senior had not provided a stable home life for their son. She knew that shuttling him back and forth between households where new and unfriendly stepfathers and stepmothers appeared had contributed to his delinquency.

Since Dave's move to Medford there had been a degree of stability. Linda now wondered whether trouble would always follow Dave like a shadow. Dave insisted he was innocent this time and she believed him.

After a lengthy conversation with Dave and his new girlfriend, Danny and Joe also believed him. Dave was embarrassed about what had happened—there had been a confrontation he should have avoided—but he claimed that the sheriff's office was "making a mountain out of a molehill."

Apparently, Dave's former girlfriend had come to Medford after running away from her California home. Accompanied by three friends, she asked if they might stay with Dave for a few days. He said yes. One of the houseguests had then stolen a hunting knife from Dave's mom's house. Dave and a group of friends had confronted the fellow, and in the scuffle that ensued the offender ended up in a lake—whether he was thrown in or jumped to escape attack was unclear. Dave and others had then thrown rocks at him, and Dave had walked off with the young man's jacket. Thus, the robbery charges. When the police questioned Dave, they searched his truck and found an unregistered gun, a .380 semiautomatic.

Dave told Danny and Joe that his accuser had already left town and that he had admitted he had stolen the knife and was in the wrong. Dave's new girlfriend, like his mother, backed up his story. As Dave couldn't afford an attorney, the court assigned him one, a skilled public defender named David Orf. Since the accuser had recanted his own story and left the state, the assault and robbery charges were quickly dropped.

Dave (and our trial team) had dodged a bullet. The press had not picked up on the incident, and the affair would blow over. But there was a lesson for Dave. In speaking to a deputy in the sheriff's office, Danny and Joe had sensed that the local authorities were watching the former skinhead closely. "They think you're going to start some big-time stuff here," Danny explained to Dave. "You might even say they're out for you."

"It was no big deal," Dave insisted.

"I know, man, but just keep your nose clean. Try not to get into fights."

This was good advice. Unfortunately in the months ahead, Dave was not always able to follow it, causing his mother and our trial team no end of frustration and worry.

We were thankful that the February 18 editions of Portland's *Oregonian* and Medford's *Mail Tribune* made no mention of Dave's arrest. That same day, however, a lengthy feature article in the San Diego County edition of the *Los Angeles Times* caused us great concern. Richard Serrano, an enterprising *Times* reporter, had somehow persuaded authorities in Portland not only to talk about Metzger but to show him statements and exhibits from the murder investigation that we had hoped and expected would remain secret.

Key among these exhibits was the letter from John Metzger to Ken Death. Serrano immediately recognized its explosive impact. Our plan had been to ask John Metzger at trial if he had written any letters to any members of East Side White Pride before Seraw's murder. We fully expected him to say he had not. We would then show him the letter to Ken Death in his own handwriting, severely damaging his credibility before the jury and demonstrating the Metzger/Mazzella/Mieske link. We had a handwriting expert ready to impeach him at this point if he still denied writing the letter.

Presumably the Metzgers knew of the letter before the article was published; John had written it. But they may have forgotten about it. As it was handwritten, odds were they didn't have a copy to remind them of its existence. They certainly hadn't known that we had it. With its publication in the *Times,* they now knew we did.

Serrano also quoted extensively from the statement Mazzella had given to the police after being picked up on the outstanding warrant a few days after the Seraw murder. The article included Dave's description of himself as WAR's man in Portland and his mission to teach East Side White Pride "the skinhead ways."

We were not happy to see the media reveal the cards we had so jealously guarded. When Serrano had called me for an interview, I had been disappointed that someone had given the reporter access to the files (although the Portland authorities had the right to do so; we had, after all, first secured this material through their good graces). I had asked Serrano not to publish some of the material as it might be damaging to our case. He refused, citing his obligation as a journalist to report such information.

There was some news in the article that we were happy to see. "Tom Metzger acknowledged that [Mazzella and Barrett] were once key members of his network and that he officiated at Mazzella's wedding," Serrano reported. Such public statements would make it difficult for Metzger to distance himself from our key witness come trial time.

Metzger had granted Serrano an extensive interview in his Fallbrook home, where they sat, according to the reporter, by a wall featuring a White Aryan Resistance flag and a skull and crossbones on a field of black. During their conversation, "Metzger pulled several knives out of his pocket and placed them on a shelf."

Metzger had also placed on the table several legal theories that interested us. First there was the First Amendment defense. He noted that the Manson family had murdered after hearing the Beatles' "White Album," yet no one had tried to hold John Lennon and Paul McCartney liable for the deaths. He added that his literature had "nothing to do with going out and physically killing individual black people on the street corner."

Insisting again that the murder was merely a result of a street fight among drunks, he said of Mieske, Brewster, and Strasser: "We didn't even know those guys." The Metzgers had also forwarded this argument in their motion to dismiss: "Plaintiff does not claim that Tom Metzger had any knowledge of the alleged plan to assault Seraw, let alone agreed to join in the plan. Therefore, it is impossible to have been part of any conspiracy. . . ."

On its face this seemed logical, and we worried that jurors might be reluctant to find that Tom and John, based in Fallbrook, were liable for what appeared to be a spontaneous confrontation in Portland involving individuals with whom they had had no direct contact other than a brief phone conversation between Tom Metzger and Mieske when Mazzella arrived in town.

There was, however, a two-word answer to this argument: vicarious liability. As Richard Cohen noted in his well-crafted opposition to the motion to dismiss: case law holds that if a party provides "substantial assistance or encouragement" to the perpetrator, he can be held liable for the perpetrator's acts. Richard also argued that our complaint forwarded a second theory of vicarious liability, namely, civil conspiracy. Under Oregon law, if two or more persons (in this case, the Metzgers' agents and the skinheads) agree on a common objective (here, the pursuit of white supremacist goals through violent means) and overt acts occur (the attack on Seraw), then a civil conspiracy exists and all are accountable.

Barrett's affidavit, we knew, would be sufficient to overcome Metzger's argument that the court lacked jurisdiction. But what of the argument that we had failed to sue "indispensable parties"—the WAR agents who, we alleged, encouraged the Portland violence. If a judge ruled in the Metzgers' favor and required us to amend our complaint by also suing Barrett and Mazzella, our case could suffer greatly. Making these two allies defendants could easily change our current positive relationship with them. We might have been able to explain to them that suing them was just a formality. Nevertheless, they could be forgiven for beginning to wonder who was friend and who was foe. They would also have something in common with the

Metzgers again: defending themselves against the Southern Poverty Law Center. Fortunately, Richard was able to find Oregon case law that supported our position. In early March, the court ruled in our favor. The Metzgers' motion to dismiss was denied in its entirety, and we did not have to expose Dave Mazzella.

This ruling ensured that there would be a trial . . . sooner or later. We hoped it would be sooner. The less time the Metzgers had to find Dave and the less time Dave had to self-destruct, the better.

Dave had come close to the radar screen once again. Less than three weeks after his first brush with the Jackson County authorities, he had been arrested a second time. This time the charges were more serious. Dave stood accused of assault for breaking another man's jaw.

Dave's public defender, David Orf, gave us the unpleasant details. Shortly before midnight on March 4, Dave had witnessed a fight between two of his acquaintances in the alley across from his apartment. As the fight ended, Dave apparently stepped in and grabbed one of the combatants. They began fighting, and Dave landed a strong blow to the jaw.

Dave told the police he was sorry, explaining that he had been intoxicated and that he became aggressive when he drank too much. He had tried to apologize to the victim and had agreed to pay medical expenses. He was charged with second-degree assault.

I talked to him on the phone shortly after his release on a $500 security bond. I let him tell me what happened. Trying to hide my disappointment in him, I played the role of friend. "I can see how you might have lost your temper," I said. We discussed how alcohol almost always seemed to play a role in his troubles, and I urged him to get professional help.

"I'm sorry. I'm really sorry," he kept repeating. "I'm letting you down. I'm sorry."

"I'm more concerned about you right now," I said. "Don't worry about letting me down. You just take care of yourself." But before I hung up, I did remind him how important he was to victory over the Metzgers.

With Dave becoming more and more of a problem, I wished we could go to trial immediately. We were, however, far from ready to try the case. There were depositions to take, phone and bank records to secure, and various motions to file or answer. Over the course of the next six months, we would prevail on virtually all of these motions, eventually gaining the phone records that indicated contact between the Metzgers in California and Mazzella and the members of East Side White Pride in Oregon and the bank records that demonstrated how the Metzgers conducted the business of White Aryan Resistance and Aryan Youth Movement. In California, the lawyers we retained were also able to stymie the Metzgers' effort to delay. The court there dismissed John Metzger's bankruptcy action because his claim failed to comply with bankruptcy rules.

With this dismissal, the stay on taking John's deposition was automatically lifted. This was critical to us. Depositions serve two important purposes during the pretrial "discovery" period. They provide information necessary to build a case, and, equally important, they pin down the testimony of parties or witnesses. As depositions are taken under oath and recorded by a court reporter, a deponent cannot change his story at trial without risking having his credibility challenged because of the change. Although John might invoke the Fifth Amendment as his father had, we were anxious to depose him and lay the groundwork for impeaching him at trial. We were also anxious to depose Mieske and Brewster, as well as the girlfriends who had witnessed the murder.*

Because you can talk to your own client or a sympathetic codefendant at will before trial, there is rarely anything to be gained by taking his or her deposition. We were at first astonished when we received notice that John Metzger intended to take his father's deposition. What purpose would it serve? Tom had stonewalled us by taking the Fifth. John could talk to Tom privately whenever he wanted. Why give us the opportunity to question him under oath at this time?

Then we realized that Tom had finally decided that he could not pass up the opportunity to take center stage and testify at the trial. To do so, he would have to drop his Fifth Amendment defense and answer questions at a deposition. Apparently he didn't have the courage to let us know directly that he had changed his mind. John's notice served that purpose. Whatever Tom's motivation, we were delighted

---

*If John did invoke the Fifth Amendment at his deposition, he would not be permitted to testify in court. Therefore, he would look guilty, and Mazzella's account would go unchallenged. Thus, it was important that we persist in trying to take his deposition and get him on the record with his decision, whatever that might be.

to have the opportunity to question him. We immediately gave notice that we, too, would take Tom's deposition. We scheduled John's for the same day in late March.

Tom Metzger's eyes narrowed. The veins in his neck bulged. "It's not simply the facts of this case that the Southern Poverty Law Center is interested in," he growled at me. "The interest . . . is to find any and all friends and associates of Tom Metzger . . . for the express purpose of trying to destroy them. . . . You're as crooked as a dog's hind leg."

Crooked as a dog's hind leg. I liked the image. Indeed it was an apt description of *Tom's* actions. My question that had triggered his outrage concerned one of those actions. Shortly after we had filed our lawsuit, Tom had transferred the deed to the family home to his wife, Kathleen. I wanted to know about the circumstances. The information I elicited here might prove helpful if we sued to prevent this transparent (and illegal) attempt to avoid losing this asset if he lost the case.

The rancorous response to my question about the transfer typified the climate of the all-day deposition. The Metzgers had arrived accompanied by Carl Straight, a tall, muscular redheaded man in his early forties with the mug of a boxer. Straight, a longtime bodyguard and confidant of the Metzgers, was there, Tom explained, "for security reasons." Tom alleged that his enemies had recently fired a crossbow into his home, barely missing Kathleen. Later in the deposition Tom would suggest, without any substantiation, that our supporters might have been responsible for this alleged attack.

Straight's behavior suggested he was interested less in protecting Tom than in intimidating me. He spent most of the day trying to stare me down. At times the task was too much for him, and the menacing mien would disappear, replaced by a vapid look that was truly frightening.

John Metzger had started the day by announcing that he would not be deposed despite the lifting of the bankruptcy court's stay. His reason? He had not had time to prepare himself.

My temperature rose. "You can play your games if you like. We will take your deposition at some point," I said impatiently.

John had already indicated that he could afford to pay for only one hour of the court reporter's time in taking his father's deposition.

Ordinarily, the party who schedules a deposition foots the entire bill, but, anxious to move ahead, we had agreed to pick up the cost for the time when we were asking questions. Now, fearing we'd have to make yet another trip back, I offered to assume *all* costs if John would consent to being deposed the following day. He still refused. I angrily warned that if we had to return again, the court might require him to pay our considerable expenses. He was undeterred.

John spent his hour throwing softballs to his father. He began by trying to establish that Tom had no agents, business dealings, or personal contacts in Oregon; he had visited the state only once, some seventeen years earlier. Tom then explained that prior to Seraw's death, he had only heard rumors of the existence of East Side White Pride and did not recall receiving any phone calls from Oregon before the murder. He disavowed the fliers that East Side White Pride had passed out in the hours preceding what he characterized as a street fight initiated by the Ethiopians.

The Oregon phone records we had secured by this time reflected that Ken Mieske had called Metzger collect from jail at least twice and that Mazzella had called Tom from Mieske's house six weeks prior to the murder. John's next line of questions tried to deflect this potent proof of contact. Did Tom know who Mieske was when the telephone rang November 20, one week after the murder?

"No, in fact I asked the operator, because we get calls from people all over. . . . Mieske yelled in the background, 'I'm the one who had the fight with the Ethiopian.' "

And what had Tom told Mieske?

Merely this, Tom insisted: "I hope you have a good lawyer and know what your constitutional rights are. Beyond that I have nothing to say to you."

Mieske had called Tom again around Christmastime. Why?

The imprisoned skinhead just wanted to say hello, Tom maintained.

John then moved to the decoy that appeared to be our smoking gun, Michael Barrett's affidavit. Tom stated that he had met Barrett on "very few occasions" and that the young man's notion of a WAR-skins/WAR alliance was fantasy. He discounted Barrett's statement that Tom had taught him that blacks and Jews were enemies, explaining that Barrett had already defaced a synagogue by the time they crossed paths. He then asserted that he hadn't sent Barrett to Portland, and he certainly hadn't given him any baseball bats to bring to Oregon, as Barrett alleged. "Mr. Barrett is perjuring himself," Tom said flatly.

Tom concluded with a bit of self-serving revisionist philosophy that he would repeat in the months to come:

> I will not deny that . . . there are elements of the black race and the Jewish people that are enemies of racial separatists in their ideology, but that does not mean that I have instructed . . . anyone to commit violence against these people.
>
> I simply tell people: If you are attacked physically, you must fight and do whatever the law . . . permits you to do to protect yourself.

When the hourglass ran down and John's money ran out, we began our cross-examination. Pete Gibbons, the undercover informant, had told us that Metzger was motivated as much by greed as by ideology. In addition to selling subscriptions to the WAR newspaper and soliciting contributions to the organization, Metzger marketed hate paraphernalia. At the back of his tabloid, illustrated advertisements offered "Aryan entertainment" from the "nation's largest white separatist library." Videocassettes of Aryan Woodstock were priced at $20.00. Record albums appealing to skinheads were also hawked, at what seemed a considerable markup. Most subscribers, contributors, and purchasers sent cash, Gibbons said. We therefore suspected that some of the hate money was unaccounted for in the records we had subpoenaed from Metzger's bank.

We wanted to get some sense of how much money Metzger was making, how many contributors he had, how the money was spent. Such information would enable us at trial to present a picture of how WAR operated, its scope. Metzger would appear even more despicable if he seemed to be making a good deal of money from what he portrayed as a righteous ideological crusade. Big money figures would also help build the case for high punitive damages, and a pecuniary motive would undercut Metzger's First Amendment defense.

From day one Metzger had protested he was just a poor TV repairmen. He said he operated the repair business separately from WAR, but he acknowledged that each was a sole proprietorship and that the money from one sometimes went to pay bills for the other.

Metzger's dual bookkeeping system may have worked to his advantage in his cash-oriented business, but it made our task more difficult. Still, we managed to reveal the questionable ethics of this man who had no problem in passing judgment on the character of entire peoples. We'd read his newspapers, publications, fliers, interviews, speeches, and transcripts of his telephone hotline messages, and we'd watched his cable show exhaustively. In all this material, he gave the clear impression that WAR was a not-for-profit organization. We suspected that many unwitting contributors believed this was the case.

Now, Metzger acknowledged that WAR was not formally a nonprofit organization but added that it never earned a profit. I wasn't satisfied with this answer.

"The question is: Have you led your WAR associates or members . . . to believe that they're making contributions or donations to a nonprofit organization?"

"No," he answered. "They're simply giving their donations to White Aryan Resistance, and they trust me that it will be handled in their behalf or benefit."

I asked if he had ever described himself as a "trustee" of WAR, a characterization suggesting a charitable organization.

No, he said. He did not recall using the term "trustee."

I then showed him an issue of the WAR newspaper that included a form for people to will property or money to WAR. "I bequeath to Tom Metzger, as trustee for White Aryan Resistance . . . the sum of . . ."

Metzger tried to straighten that crooked hind leg of his. He had simply taken the form from another periodical, he insisted, then finally admitted, "Perhaps there was an error there. Should have been just Tom Metzger."

Having seen how WAR operated and generated money for its director/trustee, I asked Metzger to explain the structure of the organization. The WAR he described at this deposition was certainly more amorphous, more invisible, than the WAR he wrote about in his newspaper or talked about on his hotline. "WAR is an idea that was created by myself to work with the broadest number of Caucasian people possible in a loose association of people who tend to agree, at least in part, to share ideas," he explained. There was no formal membership, no dues, no officers or board, no organized activity. "It's strictly an organization using ideas, First Amendment activity."

"Is that right?" I smiled. It sounded like one big encounter group, whose encounters were purely philosophical—not the "kick ass," "gas the niggers" organization I'd read about in his material. "Is there a goal of WAR?" I asked.

"Yeah. The overall goal . . . is the fight against what we regard as a repressive regime, corporate control in America and Washington, and to help work for the best . . . long-range interests of Caucasian people and their liberties."

Was a white revolution the goal?

"Yes," Metzger said, but added, "You jump to the conclusion that by revolution I mean violent revolution. There are many revolutions that are not violent."

I showed him a copy of an interview published in the *Indianapolis Record* in April 1989. There, he was quoted as calling for a revolution and the partitioning of urban areas into ethnically segregated territories. "After this, Metzger says, individuals who have the heritage of many nations flowing in their veins 'will not be accepted into the white state.' "

Metzger responded that he thought the statement might have been taken out of context, but he acknowledged that WAR already adopted the "one-sixteenth rule [of association] . . . taken from the Southern race laws of long ago." This forbade association with folks who were more than one-sixteenth nonwhite.

Envisioning our Portland jury, I got specific. "Would a Greek person fall within the one-sixteenth rule?"

"Many Greeks would. . . . Some wouldn't."

The same was true of Spanish people and even Swedes. "They've had quite a bunch of the mixing during World War Two," Metzger explained with a straight face.

"What about Jews?"

"Jews are not acceptable."

"Why?"

"That's just what we decided." He would later explain that the United States was "disproportionately influenced by Jews."

I showed Metzger a number of articles from his newspapers that seemed to encourage direct action against minorities and call for the revolution that would create an all-white state. He adamantly denied that he had at any time encouraged violence. This, of course, was a key to our case. But hadn't he written the following in 1986: "If white racists can't recognize an effective street-fighting revolutionary white army when they see one, then that's their tough luck. They'll pay for their blindness in the future if they don't support militant white fighters now."

"Yes," Metzger said. But he insisted he was only suggesting that racial separatists be able to defend themselves from attack.

This was the Metzger line. He did not encourage violence unless it was in self-defense, in response to someone else's first move. So the effective street-fighting revolutionary white army was for what purpose? I asked.

"For self-defense."

And what of his statement at Aryan Fest II that Jews were panic-stricken because "skinheads kick ass." This, too, was a reference to the skinheads' ability to act in self-defense, Metzger said.

I was anxious to see if a jury would believe this incredible explanation. Even if they were as skeptical as I was, however, the jury would still have to find that the Metzgers, through their agents, encouraged East Side White Pride to commit the violence that led to Mulugeta's death.

My next line of questions focused on Metzger's ties to skinheads in general. He acknowledged supporting skinheads—although not financially—and he admitted telling a *San Francisco Independence* reporter: "They are becoming part of our overall movement. They've gone beyond the bullshit stage."

Now, without betraying that we had spoken to Dave Mazzella or suggesting that he was helping us, I moved from the general to the specific. "You answered some questions from your son on Mr. Gagnon, and Mr. Mazzella, and Strasser and Barrett," I began, burying Mazzella in the middle of the catalog. "I'm going to follow up. . . . What role did Dave Mazzella play in WAR?"

"Well, he sort of assumed an honorary title in our youth group. He appeared on a couple of television shows, but he didn't do much else."

"Now, didn't you consider him a key member of your organization until you expelled him?"

"Not after the television shows, no."

The expulsion I was referring to had come long after the Seraw murder. The television shows Metzger spoke of predated Dave's trip to Portland. Metzger said that he had lost faith in Mazzella after Dave had failed to take responsibility for his pregnant wife. Under any circumstances, Tom said, his contact with Mazzella had been limited. Mazzella had been at his house, WAR headquarters, "maybe half a dozen times max."

What had Mazzella done when he was there?

"Talked about girls and had a beer," Metzger answered. That was all he could recall.

Throughout the deposition Metzger dismissed much in his more incendiary speeches and writings as hyperbole, clowning around, and what he called "disinformation" to confuse enemies like the Southern Poverty Law Center. His cryptic hotline messages to "special operatives" working in various sectors of the country were an example of this, he said. So, too, he now said, was his hotline message that the skinheads in Portland had done "a civic duty" in killing Mulugeta Seraw. "They [Mieske, Brewster, and Strasser] were legally lynched and everyone knows it," Metzger added. "Some disinformation. Saying it sounds like the skinheads did a civic duty, that's my satire."

"Would you tell me if you would—" I began.

"I hate crack dealers," Metzger interrupted.

"You have information that Mr. Seraw was a crack dealer or that Mr. Antneh or Mr. Tesfaye were crack dealers?"

"We'll find out when we go to trial." Metzger leered.

That day couldn't come fast enough for me. Metzger had left the deposition with a smug look on his face. No doubt he thought he'd outfoxed us by playing the innocent or by being evasive. What he did not realize was that by admitting to the validity of the telephone hotline tapes and taking responsibility for their content, he had saved me from what could have been a time-consuming, contentious battle at trial to lay a foundation to introduce this pertinent material. At dinner that night in one of McElroy's favorite pubs, our trial team celebrated a successful day. I drank a bottle of wine myself as we laughed about Tom's naïveté in thinking he had snookered us. Joe

Roy went to the jukebox and put in quarters to play every country-western song listed. Soon Kenny Rogers was singing about "The Gambler," who knew when to hold his cards and when to fold them. Tom Metzger had played his hand wrong this day.

Tom's failure to hold his cards had allowed his true colors to come through—fifteen-sixteenths white—but we hadn't stripped him totally naked of his First Amendment cloak. We hadn't wanted to—better to show the emperor with no clothes before the jury and the world rather than one court reporter. We had a great deal of information—not disinformation—that we had not revealed, including telling photographs and videotapes. To paraphrase Mr. Metzger, he'd find out about it when we went to trial.

Here is our answer to race mixing:

Awake and arise, O warriors, to fight.
Awake to the call of thunder at night.
The time is now, you must answer a call
and stand and fight 'til death makes you fall.
You have slept too long, you must join the chase
and slaughter the beast that would darken your race.
Don helmet and sword and pick up your shield.
Let your eyes glow with hate, swear never to yield.

—Tom Metzger, White Aryan Resistance telephone hotline,
April 16, 1990

CHAPTER ELEVEN

June 17, 1990

Los Angeles, California

I looked across my hotel room at Dave Mazzella and was suddenly haunted by a frightening image. On a warm summer night in 1987, the Sacramento police had found a young white man lying on the sidewalk in front of a bar. He was tied to an eight-foot board. His neck had been slashed. His arms were stretched out to his sides. Both hands had been nailed palm up to the board with No. 8 sinker-type nails. Greg Withrow, the founder of the White Student Union, the former head of Aryan Youth Movement, had been crucified.

Still alive, despite the razor that had been dragged across his throat, Withrow refused to identify his attackers. Later he would acknowledge that they had been skinheads and explain that he did not want to cooperate with the police because he was afraid of further attacks.

No one familiar with Withrow's activities had to search very hard for a motive. Earlier that day, the blond, mustached, twenty-six-year-old Aryan leader had appeared on a local television show, *Good Morning, Bay Area,* and announced that he was quitting his racist ways for love. A waitress named Sylvia with whom he worked at a Sacramento club had shown him the errors of his past. Now he proudly wore her name tattooed only a few inches away from a variety of ink swastikas.

The "conversion" had stunned the white supremacist community. Withrow had been a leader, an innovator, ever since he founded the White Student Union in 1979 as an eighteen-year-old student at Sacramento's American River College. At various times, he had belonged to the Ku Klux Klan, the American Nazi Party, the Sacramento Area Skinheads, and White Aryan Resistance. Tom Metzger had long been his adviser, and he worked closely with John Metzger. Withrow's organization shared Metzger's Fallbrook post office box.

Like John, Withrow had been trained for this life by his father, who at various times had been an auto mechanic, a bartender, and a professional gambler. "Some fathers raise their kids to be doctors, lawyers, or ballerinas. I was raised to be sort of a Führer," he told a *Los Angeles Times* reporter in 1989. As soon as the boy could read, Albert Withrow had fed his son a steady diet of racist literature.

Withrow had done his best to please his father. At the National Aryan Congress's July 1986 meeting in Idaho, he had exhorted a gathering of four hundred racists to strive for "total genocide" of non-Aryans in North America. The audience responded with a standing ovation and shouts of "Sieg Heil."

As a skinhead, he said, he had taken part in numerous attacks on non-Aryans, including frequent armed assaults against Japanese tourists in San Francisco. The police in various northern California cities knew him well and had arrested him many times for everything from assault and battery to possession of drugs.

When he met Sylvia, who disdained his white supremacist beliefs, Withrow was torn between hate and love. Then his father died. "I had this thought that, 'Gee, maybe I don't have to carry this on anymore,' " Withrow told the *Los Angeles Times*. "Then I thought, 'No, no, no, it's my duty. Honor my family, my ancestors, my race, my nation.' I just kept forgetting to honor myself."

Love finally won out. Withrow went to Fallbrook to let his mentor, Tom Metzger, know he was leaving the movement. According to Withrow, Metzger was furious. The crucifixion followed his televised announcement. One month later, his hands damaged forever, Withrow appeared on the *Donahue* show with, among others, his new enemy John Metzger. While they were in New York, Withrow said, John told him that he deserved to die for abandoning the movement.*

No doubt the Metzgers would feel the same way about Dave Mazzella in seventy-two hours when they learned that he had not only forsaken their cause but was working with the enemy. After much debate, we had "noticed" the depositions of Mazzella and Michael Barrett for June 20.† Now, preparing Dave for the upcoming questioning, I couldn't help thinking that our decision to take his deposition might expose him to the same fate as Withrow's, or worse.

We had by this time lost track of Michael Barrett; we did not know if we could locate him in time to attend. But we hoped the Metzgers would concentrate their preparation on him since his affidavit was our most publicized weapon.

Unfortunately, after Mazzella's deposition we would no longer be able to hide the fact that he, not Barrett, was our real key witness. This raised the most difficult and hotly debated question our trial team would face during the discovery period. Was it worth taking Dave's deposition to get his sworn testimony on the record? The downside was obvious: we would be revealing our number one witness and the thrust of our case, thus leaving the Metzgers plenty of time to create a defense and try to discredit, intimidate, or harm Dave. The crucifixion of Greg Withrow loomed over all of us.

The upside of taking the deposition was equally compelling. Since his move to Oregon, Dave had proved himself unable to keep out of trouble or stay in one place. The obvious and prudent move was to preserve his testimony by an evidence deposition that could be presented in court if Dave was not able to attend. Elden Rosenthal, our local counsel, had been adamant about this before he left for England for most of the summer. He saw this case as a typical tort action‡—if a witness had something to say, it didn't matter when or how he said

---

*We had no proof that John or Tom Metzger had anything to do with the assault on Withrow.

†"Noticing" a deposition means sending notice to the other parties in a lawsuit that you intend to take a certain person's deposition on a particular date. Whether or not the person to be deposed shows up and the deposition goes ahead as scheduled is something the attorneys cannot necessarily control.

‡A tort is a wrongful act, not including a breach of contract or trust, that results in injury to another's person, property, reputation, or the like, and for which the injured party is entitled to compensation.

it. "It's crazy to take the risk that we might not have his testimony at trial," he said.

Richard Cohen, the Center's legal director, agreed with Elden. Surprising Metzger with Dave at the trial would indeed be devastating, he said. But many things could happen to Dave between June and October. Those who didn't want the Metzgers to lose might locate him and have him killed, or persuade him to change the story he had told us, or not to testify at all. On his own he might return to the skinhead way of life and refuse to cooperate; the ADL as well as the Jackson County, Oregon, authorities were already suggesting Dave was flirting with SOS, the Southern Oregon Skinheads.

Richard and Elden presented other troubling scenarios. Dave might simply disappear, or he might get himself into trouble with the law and be unable to come to the trial.

Everything my fellow lawyers suggested was true. Still, I resisted. I had spent considerably more time with Dave than they had. I sensed that despite his instability, he would stick with us. He had done nothing to indicate he was going to change his story before trial. We could continue to keep an eye on him through phone calls, visits, and conversations with his mother, who appeared anxious to see Metzger defeated. And the likelihood of the Metzgers' trying to harm Dave was greater if we flushed him out of the bush. If we didn't take his deposition, the Metzgers would have no reason to believe that we knew Dave's whereabouts or that he would testify for us. Therefore there would be no reason for them to risk further trouble by harming him.

Yes, a deposition read at trial would be better than nothing if Dave was unavailable. But how much better? In taking the deposition, we could only anticipate issues that might arise at the trial and need to be addressed; such a deposition would be incomplete. Moreover, depositions read into the record rarely move a jury. Jurors want to see the star witness, observe his or her behavior, enjoy the drama; reading depositions at trial may be necessary at times, but it is boring. And Metzger would know Dave's testimony and make up lies to rebut it.

We had faced a similar question in the Donald case. There, one of the keys to beating the United Klans of America had been establishing that the organization had engaged in a pattern of violence to further its goal—the supremacy of the white race. We had been able to docu-

ment the UKA's involvement in the 1961 attacks on the Freedom
Riders, its participation in the 1963 Birmingham church bombing,
and its role in the 1965 murder of Viola Liuzzo. After that, however,
the trail was cold until the Donald lynching in 1981. Sixteen years, we
feared, was too big a gap to prove the continuing pattern.

We did know of a 1979 attack on the home of the NAACP president
in Childersburg, Alabama, by UKA members. But we had no one to
testify to the organization's involvement. Klanwatch research revealed that at the trial of the Childersburg defendants, a local UKA
officer had turned state's evidence. After testifying for the government, Exalted Cyclops Randy Ward had entered a federal witness-
protection program. Remarkably, our investigator Joe Roy tracked
him down, and we eventually persuaded Ward to meet with us. He
had much to tell us but was reluctant to testify at trial. He was trying
to put the Klan days behind him and was also fearful of revealing his
new identity.

Our immediate inclination was to take Ward's deposition; this
could easily have been arranged so that he wouldn't have to testify in
person. He was a bigger question mark than Mazzella. There was a
greater chance he would not show up for the trial. But I sensed he was
with us and decided to take the risk of not deposing him. In the end,
he came to the trial and was an important witness.

Initially I was willing to take the same chance with Mazzella. As
Dave's personal troubles increased, however, I decided I had an obli-
gation to my client to preserve at least the basics of a case against
Metzger. Deposing Dave would accomplish that.

Richard and Elden noted that we could assure Dave some measure
of protection by suggesting that he refuse to reveal his address because
he feared for his safety. To further confuse Metzger about where Dave
lived, we scheduled the deposition in Los Angeles.*

I had spent much time in Montgomery preparing for the deposition
and had arrived in Los Angeles three days early with a briefcase full
of files and a thirty-page outline for a "cram session" with Dave. I had

---

*Metzger and his supporters apparently knew where Dave's mother lived. She had
been receiving suspicious phone calls from unidentified persons asking for Dave, and
she had observed a strange car in front of the house one night. Metzger would have
to go to court to get an order compelling Dave to reveal his address. This move was
highly unlikely.

last seen him in April. After making bail in his March assault case, he had enrolled in a truck-driving school in Ashland. He and a girlfriend were living in a small room in a place called Mom's Motel.

School and the girlfriend had not worked out. When Dave met me in Los Angeles, he was out of work. He had just pled guilty to the February unregistered weapons charge, agreeing to forfeit the gun, pay a $120 fine, and perform twenty hours of community service. The assault trial was still pending.

I had rented a suite for our meeting. We ordered some food from room service and then spent ten hours going over events as if for the first time. I found myself adding more and more information in red ink in the margins of my outline. Dave was obviously being truthful, and his memory was astounding. He recalled, for example, the name of the café near San Francisco where Metzger had met him to deliver a load of WAR newspapers. Then he remembered that Metzger had published a photo of this meeting in the WAR tabloid.

As the hours wore on, I realized I would need two or three more days of debriefing and then another week to reorganize my deposition outline. Although Dave was certain about many details, it was important for us to verify them. We did not want to provide Metzger the opportunity to destroy his credibility. Unfortunately, such verification would also take time.

I knew I would not be ready to depose Dave on June 20. And I was back to that original question: Did I really want to depose him at all? While Dave sat in the living room of my suite during a midmorning break on our second day, I excused myself and went out on the balcony.

Dave will be with us come trial time, I thought. *This story is just too good to expose before then.*

I went into my bedroom and called Richard. "I'm going to cancel Dave's deposition," I told him.

"Until when?"

"Forever."

"Dees," he said, his voice rising disapprovingly.

After several minutes, we reached a compromise. I agreed that if Dave appeared to be straying off our radar screen between now and the trial, I'd strongly consider rescheduling his deposition.

Before I put Dave on the airplane back to Oregon, I told him how important it was that he stay out of trouble with the law and refrain from communicating with anyone who might tip off the Metzgers to his whereabouts. He had already written his former wife, Sylvia, in Tennessee. We feared she might tell Metzger where he could find him. Dave promised he would try his best, and I honestly believed he could keep these two commandments until October 8, the date Judge Ancer Haggerty had set for trial.

Judge Haggerty's designation as trial judge in March had been, in our eyes, poetic justice. In Oregon's court system, the judge who presides at trial does not hear all pretrial motions unless the case is officially deemed "complex." Different judges may handle the various initial motions. We had sought to have the case designated complex in the hope that a single judge would grow impatient with the Metzgers' dilatory tactics.

Our motion for such a designation was heard by Donald Londer, chief judge of Multnomah County. Elden Rosenthal was present to argue our position. When Tom Metzger heard the name Londer, he remarked that it sounded Jewish. He then insisted he didn't want a Jewish judge.

Judge Londer advised Metzger that Judge Haggerty, who was relatively new to the bench and did not have a particularly busy docket, was the next judge in line to hear a complex case. He then asked if Metzger had any objection to Judge Haggerty. Metzger said Judge Haggerty would be fine.

Perhaps Metzger thought he now would be judged by an Irishman, maybe even someone who met the one-sixteenth rule of association. He couldn't have been more mistaken. Judge Haggerty was black.

The assignment of Judge Haggerty and the setting of a trial date were among several notable events occurring between Tom's deposition in March and my mid-June trip to Los Angeles for Dave's deposition. The cat-and-mouse game with John Metzger had continued. We had filed a motion asking the court to compel him to submit to his deposition, but he had obtained another delay by refiling for bankruptcy. Stymied in this skirmish, we had won a major battle in April when Judge Haggerty had thrown out the defendants' cross-complaint that alleged that the three Ethiopians—Antneh, Tesfaye, and Seraw—were responsible for the fight and therefore should be liable for any judgment the jury in our case might assess against the Metzgers. At the hearing on this motion, Metzger told Judge Haggerty that the Southern Poverty Law Center and Klanwatch "are two major organizations committed in print to the destruction of Tom Metzger." He also criticized a "nationwide media blitz" aimed at raising "massive amounts of money with wild attacks on Tom Metzger." This was a reference to a Center fund-raising appeal that included a photo of Mulugeta's injuries and a letter asking for money to support the case and bring down the Metzgers. We enclosed the photo in a sealed envelope, warning the squeamish not to look.

Mailings like this have often angered not only targets like the Metzgers but also people who profess to share the Center's goals. Many of those who applaud our ideology bemoan our tactics as shameless, undignified, excessive, inflammatory. My response is blunt: It takes hundreds of thousands of dollars to try a case like this. I will not hesitate to go for the gut to raise money so I can put on the best case possible for my clients. More important, such mailings break the shield of disbelief that things like this still happen. Our contributors at that time might have been familiar with what Klan victims looked like. This was our first effort against skinheads and neo-Nazis who bludgeoned their victims with bats instead of lynching them. The photo was a wake-up call to our supporters, particularly those in the North, who believed "It can't happen here." Portland now knew better.

After Judge Haggerty ruled that the cross-complaint did not have to be joined with our case, Metzger left the courtroom. Several people followed him through the courthouse to his car, chanting, "Ban the Nazis, ban the Klan/No more Metzgers in our land." Metzger, like most demagogues, thrives on such confrontations. He smiled, then tried to do a jig to the beat of their protests. But such lightheartedness toward his detractors belied Metzger's ever-escalating message of hate to his supporters. At the very time Metzger was dancing in Portland, he was offering "Hateful Stickers," one hundred for six dollars, in his WAR newspaper. The fifteen different designs included an Aryan giving a Nazi salute, with the captions "Let's kick some ass" and "Skinheads"; a commando with a rifle under a banner reading "Take aim for your future"; "Get out gook scum," decorated with a skull and bones and a swastika; and a drawing of a black man, captioned

"A brain is a terrible thing to waste, that's why niggers don't have any." Presumably these adhesive peel-off stickers could be placed on everything from automobile bumpers to student notebooks.

On the same day that Judge Haggerty ruled, we traveled about fifty miles south to the Oregon Correctional Institution in Salem to depose Kyle Brewster and Ken Mieske. From a tactical standpoint, one might have thought the Metzgers would distance themselves from these confessed killers; the closer the ties, the more plausible a jury might find the connection. Having pleaded guilty to the murder, admitting it was racially motivated and forgoing the right to argue self-defense, the two skinheads, it seemed, had violated the Metzgers' professed credo that violence was justified only when defending oneself.

But Tom and John embraced Mieske and Brewster. In the next issue of *WAR,* Tom proudly ran a photograph, taken after the deposition, showing him shaking hands with Brewster, and another of John shaking hands with Mieske.

In addition to professing (in public anyway) that force was justified only in self-defense, the Metzgers had continually reminded followers of their Fifth Amendment rights. Brewster, who looked like a young Dennis Hopper—desperate and evil—took the Fifth. His meaningless deposition was over quickly. Mieske, alias Ken Death, on the other hand, decided to answer my questions. Or more properly, he danced around my questions but did not invoke the Fifth Amendment.

Ken Death had apparently bulked up considerably in the prison weight room since his incarceration; he looked far stronger than in the photos I had seen. His light brown hair was long and shaggy. Mieske showed little remorse for his behavior. Here was twenty-five years of volcanic anger that had erupted once and, given the opportunity, would erupt again. He made it clear that he didn't like me, and I did not waste time pretending I liked him.

Mieske did his best to protect himself and the Metzgers. He claimed that far from representing the Metzgers' interests in Oregon, Mazzella had told him he was dropping out of WAR and AYM. And he insisted Mazzella had not tried to organize East Side White Pride. "How can he organize something when he can't even go out and find himself a job and take care of himself?" he growled. "It wasn't like [Mazzella and Barrett] were coming up here and they are the gods of California. . . . They came up here and they were bums and we put them up."

And what of the crucial letter John Metzger had addressed to Ken Death one month before the murder? Mieske insisted: "I have never seen the letter before. I had a bunch of mail Julie [Belec] never let me know was there. See, I was in the concert business. I would go away for three, four days and come back, and she would say, 'Here is some mail here and there is a pile lying over there in the corner of the room.'"

After this unbelievable response, we moved to the period after Seraw's death. Well before Richard Serrano's *Los Angeles Times* article, Mieske had come to believe Mazzella was an informer. Despite Mieske's claim that he had never had contact with the Metzgers and his statement that Mazzella had distanced himself from WAR and AYM, Mieske had communicated his suspicions about Dave in a letter to the Metzgers.

"Why did you feel you needed to tell them Dave Mazzella was an informer?" I asked.

"I told everybody, because he is a rat and a piece of shit, as far as I'm concerned. He is a liar. He is a chronic liar. He used to make up stories. . . . He lied through the whole case. He is a liar just like Steve Strasser. Steve Strasser is a psychotic liar too." Mieske paused and glared at me before snarling, "Pretty good witnesses you got there. As far as I'm concerned, if they knew how to tell the truth, half of this shit wouldn't have happened."

"Are you through?" I asked quietly.

Mieske had referred to Mazzella and Strasser as witnesses. For a moment I wondered if he had somehow learned that we planned to use Dave. I dismissed the notion, fairly certain that he was identifying the pair as the witnesses who had led to his downfall in the criminal proceeding. Through his defense attorney in the murder case, he had received copies of police statements identifying Mazzella as "the snitch." Strasser had also cooperated with the police.

Whether Strasser would cooperate with us, too, was, at present, up in the air. I had met with him in the Portland jailhouse before he was sent to prison and had asked for his help. Strasser, a slow-speaking, dark-haired six-footer, had been noncommittal. Once he was settled in prison in mid-March, I had written him a letter asking for his help. I had also suggested he might have his racist tattoos removed.

Strasser's response dated March 29, 1990, only stoked my anger at

Tom Metzger for preying on impressionable and pathetic lost young-sters. He expressed remorse for his role in the confrontation with the Ethiopians and said he was sorry for the suffering of friends and relatives "on both sides." He was trying to improve himself by taking classes in anger management and substance abuse, he wrote, and he hoped to return to "socioty [*sic*] as a responsible citizen," But although he was interested in tattoo removal and was anxious to know the names of antiracist groups in Oregon, he did not respond to my request for help.

Before heading to Oregon for the depositions, I had written back with information about antiracist groups, taking the opportunity to enclose an affidavit that I hoped he would sign in advance of testifying at trial. He again refused to commit himself to helping us. Sometimes it's easier to erase tattoos than to erase the past. Strasser also had to live with the fear of reprisal in a prison community that included Mieske, Brewster, and a substantial number of Aryan Brotherhood members.

Because there was still a good deal of time before the trial, we were in no rush to take Strasser's deposition. If he did eventually ally himself with us, we could prepare him for trial without deposing him—unless we felt he would change his mind at the trial or be unavailable to testify in person.

Strasser's testimony was not essential. We could build our case without him. We were, quite honestly, as interested in giving the appearance that he would be our key witness as we were in using him. By not suing him, we led the Metzgers to believe that he was already in our camp. Tactics. The defendants could concentrate their efforts on rebutting him rather than our secret weapon, Dave Mazzella.

Mieske's deposition had gone well for us, despite his evasive responses and outright lies apparently designed to protect the Metzgers. We had the murderer's account of events on the record now. He had denied seeing the letter from John Metzger and denied talking to Tom Metzger when Mazzella arrived in Portland. If at the trial he changed his story about the letter, phone call, or anything else, we could show he lied at his deposition. If he clung to what he had said at the deposition, it would be up to the jury to decide whether he was telling the truth . . . in light of some of the surprises we had in store.

One of those surprises was Julie Belec, Mieske's partner in love and in hate. I had not had the opportunity to speak with her prior to the day of her deposition and was uncertain what she might say—whether she'd be helpful or harmful.

We had heard that Julie still loved Mieske. How would that color her testimony? If I could find out before the deposition, I'd know how to proceed once she was sworn in and was speaking on the record. Concerned that Julie might skip town before the trial, we had decided to treat her deposition as one that would be read before the jury at trial because the witness was not available to testify in person. With this, quite possibly, my only opportunity to examine her, there was little room for error. I didn't want to ask her any questions that might backfire.

We had scheduled the deposition for 1:00 P.M. at a law office we were using, but we had subpoenaed Julie to arrive at noon. She did. As we anticipated, the Metzgers were not yet present. I didn't know if Julie comprehended the case's cast of characters, or if she had a clear understanding of who I was and whom I represented. I didn't offer that information immediately. "Miss Belec, I'd like to talk to you about your testimony and deposition," I said softly.

I was surprised by how pretty she was. Many of the skinhead women had a hard, angry look, but this petite blond seventeen-year-old had a soft expression. Hate had not yet aged her. She was dressed neatly in designer jeans and a white silk blouse.

I knew the police had found a great deal of hate literature that she claimed was hers. I knew that just hours before Seraw was beaten, Julie had attacked the man who had said he was Jewish at the Pine Street Theatre. I knew she had provided a phony alibi for Mieske. Still, I was surprised when she proclaimed that she remained in love with the demon whom I had seen in prison only a few days earlier. We learned from prison officials that Mieske was actually receiving love letters in prison from Julie and several other young women. Some of these letters were sexually explicit; Mieske's correspondents fantasized about him in graphic detail.

Prison rules forbade minors from visiting inmates, so Julie could only write Mieske. This worked in our favor. Had she been able to see him or phone him before her deposition, she might have learned what he told us at his deposition and then tailored her testimony to support his lies. Instead, she was on her own.*

I had already told Elden that I wanted to speak with Julie alone. We did not want this teenage girl to feel at the mercy of a bunch of grown men/interrogators. I took Julie to a conference room. Formality might also be intimidating. I had my coat and tie off and sleeves rolled up before she arrived.

We hoped Julie would verify that Mieske had read the "Ken Death" letter from John Metzger. She did. We also hoped she would stand by her statement to the police after the murder, a statement that looked good for our case. She did not. She contradicted her earlier version, insisting now that the Ethiopians had started the street fight.

"Is everything you told the police true, Julie?" I asked, figuring she had forgotten what she had told detectives eighteen months earlier.

"I'm not sure."

I looked at my watch. The Metzgers would be here soon. The short session had proved helpful; I now knew how to phrase my questions.

When the Metzgers arrived, they were unaware that Julie and I had spoken. Although they had every right to excuse themselves and talk with Julie privately as we waited for the court reporter, they never asked to do so. I did my best to distract them, swallowing my dislike for them and engaging in meaningless banter on everything from politics to the weather until the reporter arrived.

When the deposition began, I followed a narrow line of questioning. Had Mieske received and read the "Ken Death" letter? Yes. When Mazzella arrived in Portland had he called Tom Metzger and put Mieske on the line? Yes. Had some of the fliers found in the room she shared with Mieske belonged to him? Yes. (At his deposition Mieske had indicated all the literature was hers.)

With these specifics quickly out of the way, I moved to a final area of inquiry. Julie had been a witness to the confrontation with the Ethiopians. Sitting in Patti Copp's car, she had seen the clubbing and kicking. After reminding her that she had given the police a video-taped statement only a week after the incident, I asked if she had told

*Since Mieske's deposition was just forty-eight hours before Belec's, he apparently was unable to write her about what he had said.

the detectives the truth, as best she remembered it. Yes, she now said.

"Has your memory improved over time? Do you remember more now?"

"No, I pretty much forgot about the incident."

It was difficult to believe she could forget something so deadly, but her answer certainly helped us. If she did appear at the trial, she would be hard-pressed to change her testimony and repudiate her police statement, which was so beneficial to our case.

Tom Metzger did not ask her anything about the incident itself. He did ask if Mazzella had ever indicated that he had been sent by the Metzgers to "inflict violence on people of other races." Julie said no. She later added that she had never seen anything to lead her to believe that WAR "advocated killing people of other races."

This testimony would have minimal impact on our case; the fact that Julie herself had not heard Mazzella advocate violence did not prove he had not done so. Still, on redirect examination after Metzger finished, I searched for the young woman's motives.

"Do you believe like Mr. Mieske that blacks are subhumans?" I asked.

Reaching down to retie the laces on one of her shoes, Julie answered matter-of-factly: "I wouldn't really say subhuman. I guess I'm more of a supremacist. I think I'm better than them."

"And at this time do you look favorably on Mr. Metzger and his WAR and WAR youth organizations?"

Julie looked at Metzger and nodded. "Yes."

Her deposition had been short but sweet. She had made a liar out of her boyfriend, who had insisted he had never seen John Metzger's key letter or talked by phone to Tom. Jurors are seeking the truth and deeply resent lying witnesses. Julie would impeach Mieske on these two key points.

When the deposition was over, she went off with the Metzgers. I'm sure that when they talked Tom brought her up to date on what her boyfriend had said two days earlier at his own deposition. If Tom had talked to her in advance of the deposition, as we did, she might have testified differently. Instead, she told the truth.

Another skinhead girlfriend at the murder scene, Heidi Martinson, had given Elden an affidavit that also helped our case. Heidi, who had been dating Steve Strasser at the time of the murder, was now involved with Goggles Flynt. Flynt had also provided a beneficial affidavit months earlier when I had met with him at his father's law office.

Heidi and Goggles had renounced their pasts. "I guess I was just power tripping," Goggles explained. "I wanted people to be afraid of me." Heidi, a large, amiable bleached blonde, was now working as a secretary. Goggles worked at a factory.

Elden had also spoken with Patti Copp, Brewster's girlfriend. Her lawyer had allowed the interview but had refused to permit his client to sign a statement or affidavit. In his post-interview notes, Elden described Copp as "a very hard-looking twenty-year-old woman. . . . She would be attractive except for the fact that her face looks like it's 30 years old."

Copp's version of the beating not only contradicted Martinson's, it contradicted the statement she had given the Portland police—a statement that supported our case. In November 1988, presumably when her memory was fresher, Copp had told the police some very damaging things, among them that Brewster had told her to pull up close and block the Ethiopians' car, that Brewster had put the bat and gun in her car, and that Brewster hit and kicked Seraw. She also stated that East Side White Pride was into "nigger bashing," a description that tied in nicely to terminology used in the WAR literature Mazzella had brought to Portland.

Now, eighteen months later, she told Elden a different story. She did not remember Brewster's telling her to pull closer to the other car. She did not believe either Brewster or Strasser had hit or kicked Seraw. Although she had broken up with Brewster and was now in therapy dealing with their "destructive relationship," she insisted Brewster got a "bum rap." She claimed that at first she didn't even know the skin color of the occupants of the car that stopped in front of Seraw's building. "She does not believe there was any racial motivation in the assault, that if it had been white guys the situation would have come down the same," Elden noted.

How could her version have changed so much? Copp explained to Elden that the Portland police had taken advantage of her, interrogating her for long periods and making her say things that were untrue.

Elden summarized his memorandum with the following evaluation: "This woman is not going to be a good witness for us. If we put her on the witness stand to say the things we like, stuff would come out that we don't like on cross-examination. It is unlikely we will be able to bend her testimony."

Elden was one of the best tort lawyers in Oregon. He was, as I wrote to him, "batting a thousand with the court on motions." But I disagreed with his assessment of Copp. "These cases just are not like traditional lawsuits," I explained in a letter to him. "What you think would make a bad witness in a typical tort case usually works just the opposite in a Klan case."

It might not be necessary to call Copp as a witness, I continued. If, however, Heidi Martinson was unavailable, Copp would do just fine. As with Julie Belec, anything Copp said that was negative to our case could be contradicted by her police statement. We could examine her as we would a defendant or hostile witness: "You're saying that your memory is better now and that you lied to the police then?" we could ask. We could then put on the policeman who took her statement. I felt confident that the jury would believe him instead of Copp, who insisted that Brewster had been railroaded. Besides, she had been accompanied by lawyers during the police interrogation. Would a jury believe that those lawyers allowed the police to make their client say things that weren't true?

I wrote Elden that he should not worry about Metzger's ability to cross-examine Copp. "There is good, quick, and pointed comeback to anything Tom might get from her. The best of all is that she feels the cops screwed her. The jury will think the cops were trying to maintain peace in Portland and stop these monsters."

With the statements and depositions of Copp, Mieske, Belec, Martinson, Flynt, Mazzella, Barrett, and even Tom Metzger, our case was coming into focus. The blur of events of November 12 and 13 was becoming a series of snapshots. The invisible hand of the Metzgers was slowly being revealed. As these pictures emerged, we grew more convinced that this was not a case in which the Metzgers could legitimately create the defense that they were merely exercising their First Amendment rights.

We hoped the ACLU would agree with this assessment and refrain from giving Metzger the assistance he had requested. The organization's involvement would give the defendants an air of legitimacy we felt they did not deserve. Accordingly, I had written to the Oregon chapter's executive director, Stevie Remington. In my letter I spoke about my own background with the organization. In the 1960s, I had been a volunteer attorney for the Alabama ACLU, participating in several free speech cases. And when the ACLU faced a revolt from members in 1977 for its controversial intervention on behalf of Nazis seeking to march in Skokie, I had helped draft the organization's successful explanation and highly profitable fund-raising appeal to supporters. More important, I gave Ms. Remington the facts of the Metzger case, explaining why it did not involve the First Amendment.

The ACLU could have made a major commitment and provided representation to the Metzgers. It did not. The organization could also have chosen not to get involved at all, as we hoped. It didn't choose this alternative either. Instead, in May 1990 the Oregon chapter filed a motion for leave to appear as amicus curiae, or friend of the court. This is a common stance for the ACLU and other legal-oriented organizations representing all sorts of viewpoints. In this instance, the ACLU sought the court's leave to present arguments and information concerning civil liberties issues. Because the Metzgers had asserted that the activities upon which we had based our claim constituted in part what the ACLU termed "expression and political activity that is protected by the First Amendment," the Oregon chapter sought "leave to submit legal memoranda . . . to assist the Court's analysis." Practically speaking, "friend of the court" meant friend of the Metzgers. If the ACLU did involve itself on issues of constitutionally protected free speech, it would be on behalf of the defendants.

We opposed the motion, arguing that freedom of expression simply was not the issue here. We realized, however, that we had little chance of persuading Judge Haggerty to bar the ACLU—or other organizations—from becoming amicus curiae.* At this stage of the proceedings there was, arguably, a question as to whether the First Amendment might come into play. Only after we presented our case and the Metzgers offered their defense would the constitutional issue (or lack of one) come into focus. In late May, Judge Haggerty granted the ACLU's motion.

If Tom Metzger could persuade a jury that he did nothing more than *talk about* violence in the abstract, he would prevail at the trial. Dave Mazzella was the key to proving Tom did much more. As the

*The National Lawyers Guild later filed a brief supporting our position.

summer wore on and the trial grew closer, I kept my fingers crossed that Dave could stay out of trouble.

He couldn't.

According to the Jackson County sheriff's office, a group of about ten skinheads, male and female members of SOS, had gathered at a cemetery near Emigrant Lake outside Ashland on the evening of August 4. They were drinking. Dave was among them.

Shortly before midnight, the authorities alleged, Dave had participated in what appeared to be a jump-in—a fight in which several skinheads attack one individual. Dave was said to have watched the jump-in, involving himself only after the victim, nineteen-year-old Anthony Bounds, was on the ground. After telling the attackers to back away, Dave had for ten minutes kicked the fallen young man with his heavy, military-type boots. Instructing those present to say that Bounds had been injured when he fell off a motorcycle, Dave then loaded his victim into his truck and drove him to a hospital emergency room. Bounds suffered a broken jaw and other less serious injuries.

Apparently Bounds was able to talk despite the broken jaw. He identified Dave as his assailant. The police arrested Dave on August 8. Danny and I were in Ashland within twenty-four hours.

David Orf, Mazzella's public defender, met us at the Jackson County jail. A fair-haired man in his late thirties, he told us he was a longtime Center supporter. He arranged for us to see our wayward witness in an attorney's visiting room.

Mazzella entered wearing jail clothes and a sheepish grin. "I'm sorry about this," he said. "But it really wasn't my fault."

I had called him before leaving Montgomery and he had told me "what really happened." He had indeed been at the cemetery with his new girlfriend, Ruth, and there had been a few skinheads present. He knew some of these people, but he had not returned to their fold. He was not a member of SOS.

"I was drinking," Dave had admitted, "but then Ruth and I went to sleep in my van." Some time later, he was awakened by someone who told him that a skinhead named Henry Sullivan had hurt Bounds. Dave put Bounds in the van and rushed him to the hospital.

Dave had given me the name of a friend who could exonerate him. Before boarding the plane, I had called this young man. He had corroborated Dave's story to some extent. I had taped our conversation and upon arriving at the jail had turned the tape over to Orf.

I didn't tell Dave about the tape. I was very stern with him, suggesting I wasn't sure I believed him. He was deflated but still wanted to please, still wanted to be the hero.

I was worried that Tom Metzger might set Dave up for a fall—locate Dave and get someone Dave trusted to visit him. I pointed out to Dave all the bad things this could lead to and again warned him not to communicate with anyone about this case or the Metzger case.

Despite Dave's protest that he was innocent, a local judge found the sheriff's version compelling enough to revoke Dave's bail on his March assault charge and set bond at $25,000. This meant Dave needed $2,500 to make bail. He didn't have it, and his exasperated mother was not about to give it to him. Linda Ford had decided her son needed some "tough love" and that a stay in jail might shake him into reforming.

After I got over the shock of this latest arrest, I realized Dave's new troubles presented us with as much of an opportunity to make a good point as it did the Metzgers. If the assault charge held up, the Metzgers could raise questions about Dave's credibility. How could he insist that he had encouraged violence at the Metzgers' behest when it was clear he was capable of using force without any direction at all? But this argument would play into our hands. Dave Mazzella, we could tell the jury, was, *is,* a loose cannon. And that is precisely why the Metzgers recruited him, made him an officer, and sent him to Portland. Tom and John knew what to expect from their violence-prone agent when they sent him on missions. And even if the Metzgers could persuade the jury that they hadn't intended for Mazzella to carry out racial violence, we could counter that they knew, or should have known, that he would, based on prior experience. They were therefore liable for the reckless selection of an agent. Under either scenario, Dave didn't have to be a choirboy for us to present him to the jury.

I saw one other benefit from the incident. We knew exactly where Dave would be for the foreseeable future. Our team could stop losing sleep over the fear that he might disappear, be done in, or do himself in.

The Holy Church of the White Fighting Machine of the Cross

San Diego, California
September 17, 1990

Dear Morris:

Are you trying to steal Tom Metzger's house? Shame, shame. There could be very bad things happen to you if you carry out this exercise in futility. You are taking on too much, Morris baby, you are messing (or trying to mess) with white power. Nobody messes with white power. You go against nature. . . . We want you to drop all of the charges in the lawsuit in Portland and stop messing with Tommy. We don't want to have to do anything bad to you even if you are the lowest form of scum whitey goyim alive. It would hurt us badly to take you out. . . . You can't stop white men from trying to save the race in Amerika [*sic*]. You would do better to stop guys like Sharpton from going into the white man's neighborhood, in Jew York [*sic*].

. . . The time has come for you to back right off from Tommy. . . . Morris, you haven't dealt with us. We're real bad, honey. We hurt.

. . . You are causing us to spend all of the funds it has taken us a long time to get for the movement, so your sin is real bad. It's not fair to us or the race. . . . We know of many white men in the movement that want you real bad, baby.

. . . Tom didn't write this, but he is not your concern any longer.

CHAPTER TWELVE

September 20, 1990
■
Montgomery, Alabama

The letter from the Holy Church of the White Fighting Machine of the Cross arrived within minutes of the fax from Jim McElroy. GROUP PROBED IN COURTHOUSE BOMBING read the headline of the *San Diego Tribune* article that Mac had sent. The newspaper reported that the FBI was investigating the "Holy Church" in connection with the September 15 midnight bombing of the federal courthouse in San Diego. The group had become suspect after writing a letter to San Diego television station KNSD explaining "the reasons for the detonation of the device," which had damaged the courthouse entrance. The letter also warned "all concerned to drop the lawsuit in Portland, Oregon, against WHITE POWER."

I do not take any threats lightly. In 1983, the Center was badly damaged by a fire orchestrated by the Klan. In 1984, security guards spotted two heavily armed intruders on my property. At the time of Robert Mathews's death, an Order operative was in Alabama tracking my movements so the group could kill me. As a result, elaborate round-the-clock measures are always in place at the Center and my private residence.

Klanwatch has information concerning well over three hundred white supremacist groups in the United States. None of our staff had ever heard of the Holy Church of the White Fighting Machine of the Cross. If the warning letter to me had been the group's only communication, I might have been able to pass it off as the work of a crank. But the courthouse bombing made that impossible. Tom Metzger's friends and followers had already shown their proclivity for violence. I was concerned.

The Center has an excellent working relationship with the FBI. The role that agents have played and continue to play in providing me protection cannot be discussed without compromising security. After receiving McElroy's fax, Danny immediately called the bureau. Agents investigating the bombing told him to take the threat seriously.

It is impossible to dismiss a death threat totally, but it's not that difficult to put it at the back of your mind when you're racing down the homestretch, preparing for one of the most important trials of your life. *Berhanu* v. *Metzger, et al.* was less than three weeks away. There was an incredible amount of work to do—structuring the case, preparing for witnesses, contemplating jury selection, worrying about getting Mazzella from jail in Medford to the courthouse in Portland, selecting and creating exhibits, preparing and responding to last-minute motions.

We had wanted a speedy trial and we were getting it, thanks largely to Richard Cohen and Elden Rosenthal. Since we had filed suit, Metzger and his offstage lawyers had at every turn tried to stall us with bankruptcy actions, countersuits, and attempts to add other parties. This effort had culminated on August 30, when Tom filed a "motion to continue" in which he asked Judge Haggerty to delay the start of the trial beyond October 8 because the defense needed more time to complete discovery. "Plaintiff now admits he is able to contact three 'alleged' agents of defendant whereas plaintiff said he could not locate same one month ago," the motion stated.*

The motion worried us. A major trial is like a championship prizefight. Like a boxer, a lawyer prepares himself to be ready mentally—and physically, too—on a certain date. As a trial approaches, I direct all my energy to the upcoming battle, thinking of little else, even increasing the level of my daily workout. It's difficult for me to with-

---

*Apparently, Metzger assumed that because we had canceled the depositions, we did not know the whereabouts of any of these alleged agents.

stand the rigors of a lengthy trial if I'm not in peak physical condition. A postponement, particularly a long one, is difficult for the body and psyche not only of the lead trial lawyer but of the entire team that has been gearing up for battle.

Lawyers do learn to live with continuances. I could adjust to the disappointment of a last-minute delay. More troubling was the prospect that witnesses like Heidi Martinson, whose whereabouts we now knew, might depart town without leaving forwarding addresses. Skinheads and their friends are a nomadic lot, and this young woman owed us nothing. Indeed, testifying would serve only to bring up bad memories, place her in an unwanted spotlight, and alienate her from past and present friends.

Dave Mazzella's availability might also be affected. Dave had pleaded guilty to a lesser charge of assault in connection with the March 5 fight in the alley across from his apartment. Sentencing was set for November 1, and a prison term of some months was quite likely.

A party wishing to bring an incarcerated person to court as a witness must file a motion seeking the prisoner's presence. The presiding judge then has broad discretion in determining whether to grant the motion. Some judges almost categorically deny such motions, citing security considerations, expense, or the nonessential nature of the witness's testimony. In this event, a party must rely on having the inmate's testimony read to the jury or presented in a videotaped deposition.

We did not know how Judge Haggerty would rule. If the Metzger trial, which we expected to last two to three weeks, took place before the November sentencing, we might not have to find out. Dave was not currently serving a sentence in jail; he was there because he could not make bail. If he could come up with the bail money, then we need not file a motion. We felt confident that we could work with public defender Orf to ensure that bail was raised.

Within a week of receiving Metzger's motion to delay, Richard and Elden had filed a compelling response stating our grounds for strenuously objecting to any postponement. They first noted that just three weeks earlier Judge Haggerty had asked all parties if there was a problem with the October 8 trial date. Neither Metzger nor any of the defendants had indicated any difficulty with proceeding.

They further noted that Metzger had long known the identities of the persons that we alleged had acted as his agents; in our February opposition to Metzger's motion to dismiss, we had alluded to the roles of Mazzella, Barrett, and Mike Gagnon. "Even assuming that Mr. Metzger understood during the past month that plaintiff's counsel did not know where these persons could be found, he has had more than six months to use his own resources and network of associates to find them. It is not incumbent on plaintiff's counsel to do Metzger's work for him," we wrote, citing case law on the point. We added that under Oregon law a party is not mandated to disclose the location of a witness if doing so is likely to expose the witness to grave danger. Richard and Elden made the case for such danger by quoting from Metzger's newspapers and telephone hotlines about the need to bring traitors to justice. They also noted what had happened to Greg Withrow after he left the Metzger flock, and they cited Mieske's threat to kill whoever snitched.

Despite the power of our response, we feared Judge Haggerty might nevertheless give Metzger more time for discovery and grant the continuance. Many judges are disposed to grant a continuance to a party showing a good-faith attempt to complete discovery. Persuaded of extenuating circumstances, such as the previous unavailability of witnesses, a judge may push the trial date back. Judges also frequently accommodate nonlawyers representing themselves in complex litigation, reasoning that they are unschooled in civil procedures. While it was clear that outside attorneys were advising the Metzgers, the pair was, officially at least, without counsel.

Tom Metzger had filed several motions during July and August. We had been able to avoid constant commutes to Portland by relying on our local counsel and, when necessary, utilizing telephone conference calls that included the judge, the Metzgers, and someone from our Center trial team. The September 13 hearing on the motion to continue was, however, so important that I wanted Richard in the courtroom. As Richard prepared to head west armed with a briefcase full of cases to support our opposition to the continuance, Metzger himself unwittingly provided us with our strongest argument.

Tom's letter to Dave Mazzella was postmarked September 8.

Dear Dave,

It's been a long time and I would like to touch base with you on the Portland case. I have no idea which side of the fence you are on, or if you are riding the fence. . . .

As you know the allegations against myself and John are absurd. People in Portland have already told me you didn't encourage them to kill anyone. The whole thing was a stupid street fight that got out of hand. . . .

We have files of statements about how Morris Dees takes advantage of these type of cases to raise tens of millions of dollars for himself. . . .

All I ask of you is: what, in your own words, is going on and what is your status in our case? Will you willingly make a statement if I visit you at the jail?

Mazzella had immediately shown David Orf the letter. Orf had counseled him not to respond. The local authorities had already suggested that Mazzella had reunited with the skinheads. Orf told Dave that communication with one of the nation's top white supremacists would hurt his own chances of getting a reduced sentence on the assault charges. With Dave's permission, Orf then rushed a copy of the letter to us.

Mazzella professed not to know how Tom had tracked him to the Jackson County jail.* For our purposes it didn't matter *how* Tom had found Dave; it mattered *that* he *had* found Dave. The defendants' plaintive cry that they were being hampered in discovery by our refusal to reveal the whereabouts of their "alleged" agents now seemed ridiculous.

We felt confident that if Richard and Elden revealed the letter at the upcoming hearing, Judge Haggerty would refuse to postpone the trial and perhaps even chastise Metzger for making false representations to the court. But should we play that card? By letting Metzger know that we were aware he had written to Mazzella, we would also be letting

---

*We later came to suspect that Medford skinheads had sent Metzger ally Rick Cooper a short article about Mazzella that appeared in a local paper. Cooper then probably forwarded it to Tom.

him know that Mazzella was on our side of the fence. Otherwise, how would we have the letter?

Once Tom knew where Dave stood, he would in all likelihood take his deposition, thus removing the element of surprise we desired and affording the defense time to fabricate a response to Dave's story. And if the deposition was taken, Judge Haggerty might deny a motion to bring Dave to court, reasoning that because the deposition could be read into evidence at trial, Dave's presence was unnecessary. In light of this scenario, was it worth revealing our star witness in order to guarantee that the trial proceed on October 8?

"If it looks as if the judge is going to rule in our favor, then don't show the letter," I said to Richard as he left for the airport. "But if it looks as if he's going to grant the continuance based on the inability to find Mazzella, then bring it out. I don't want this trial postponed."

Richard nodded. "You know, Tom might tell Judge Haggerty that he just found Mazzella and needs time to take his deposition and then prepare his defense in response to what Dave says."

"I'll bet you that won't happen, Richard. Tom doesn't know whose side Dave is on right now, but he probably thinks Dave will write him back and invite him to the jail in Medford, and then he'll win Dave over and surprise us come trial. He's such a smug bastard, I'll bet he doesn't even tell the judge he found Dave."

That is exactly what happened. At the hearing Metzger made no mention that he had located Mazzella. Elden and Richard stressed that Metzger had not conducted his discovery diligently. In the months since we had filed suit, he had taken only one deposition, that of our client, Engedaw Berhanu. We weren't responsible for the fact that he had waited to begin his inquiry at the eleventh hour.

After listening to Judge Haggerty's comments during the hearing, Richard and Elden gambled on not revealing the letter. Judge Haggerty then announced his decision: the trial would proceed as scheduled. I was ecstatic. We could move full speed ahead.

Metzger should have responded by immediately scheduling Dave's deposition. Instead he wrote Chief Judge Londer, seeking removal of Judge Haggerty from the case.

Dear Judge Londer:
. . . Judge Haggerty has consistently bent over backwards to

accommodate the plaintiff's attorneys. The last straw was to deny a reasonable set over for trial. . . .

It is my sincere belief that Judge Haggerty is incompetent to render proper decisions on such a complex case. Very important constitutional issues are being trashed in the process.

I realize that the plaintiffs want a show trial and media blitz to fit the fund raising efforts of the ADL and Southern Poverty Law Center. If the court also cynically allows this travesty to continue on its present course, then there is obviously no chance at complete discovery and/or justice.

Don't expect me to sit there like Judge Wapner's court* while I and my son are legally lynched. We will simply join the circus.

Judge Londer did not respond, and hours later the threat implicit in Metzger's letter became explicit when the Holy Church of the White Fighting Machine of the Cross preyed on the San Diego courthouse.†

Even before the bombing, Danny Welch had shifted gears. He continued to help prepare for the courtroom battle in Portland, but his primary focus was on ensuring that no battles took place outside the courtroom.

It is considerably easier to provide security on your own turf—at the Center, at my home, around Montgomery in general—than in a city twenty-five hundred miles away. We expected to be in Portland for the better part of a month. We would need to move safely in this city, where we didn't know the police, the danger spots, and the safest routes nearly as well as we knew them back home. We would need to move freely in our hotel, between hotel and courthouse, between courthouse and Elden Rosenthal's law offices, within the courthouse, and, if possible, about town. We'd all function a lot better if we could go to restaurants, movie theaters, and pool halls and use the city's many running paths.

A secure home base/hotel was a top priority. On our earlier trips to Portland, we had stayed in the downtown area within walking distance of the courthouse, police headquarters, and Elden's firm. But

*Judge Joseph Wapner presides over the popular syndicated television program *The People's Court.*
†We have no evidence linking the Metzgers to the bombing.

Danny's thorough check of all the downtown hotels revealed that not one was sufficiently safe for our purposes. Stairwells, hallways, parking lots, and common areas could not be satisfactorily secured for our trial team, which would number about one dozen. Danny finally found a hotel across the Willamette River that met our requirements. We would register under assumed names. Otherwise, those who wished us harm could track us down by calling hotel switchboards.

The question of who would provide security in the hotel and elsewhere was paramount. As the trial approached, Danny, a former policeman, lobbied our friends in the Portland Police Bureau to detail several people to protect the Center team as well as local counsel. Such an effort is enormously costly and necessitates shifting personnel from one area to another. Unconvinced of a serious security threat at first, the bureau was initially unwilling to make such a sweeping commitment. As a result Danny hired two local private investigators, one of them an ex-cop with strong contacts on the force. The ADL, officially listed as co-counsel and intent on monitoring the trial, also made arrangements for private security—a former Israeli soldier who had protected some of the wealthiest Jewish families in South America and elsewhere.

If the San Diego bombing and the letter threatening me were not enough to convince Portland officials to pull out all the stops on security, Tom Metzger's behavior in the days before the trial was. He used his telephone hotline to encourage skinheads and other supporters to converge on Portland.

Shortly before the trial, the police agreed to provide round-the-clock protection, including hotel hall patrols and escorts, for both our party and the Metzgers. Judge Haggerty and Elden, too, were assigned protection. Police guarded Elden's home and his office and accompanied him wherever he went, even to his weekly basketball game at the local Jewish community center.*

A trial is a collaborative effort, and in the weeks leading up to the Portland showdown, I had numerous collaborators. Many Center

---

*In some ways Elden and his family suffered the most from this tight security. Not only were they less accustomed to it than Center members, they were at home—with officers on the premises—not in a hotel.

lawyers and staff persons worked on various aspects of the case. None was more effective than Sara Bullard, who, like Danny, had from the beginning seen the Seraw murder as the best opportunity to bring down the Metzgers. Sara, a diminutive thirty-three-year-old, had come to the Center from the North Carolina Human Relations Council after watching us try our case against white supremacist Glenn Miller.

By spring, Sara, an excellent writer and researcher, had culled from newspapers, telephone hotline transcripts, and transcripts of television appearances an indispensable annotated hundred-page collection of quotations from Tom and John Metzger. In August, she found what may have been the most important quotation of all.

For some weeks Sara had been trying to track down a *Seattle Times* article in which John Metzger had been quoted. I had been alerted to this article after reading another piece, "Violence by Skinheads Spreads Across Nation," in the *Los Angeles Times.* That article, written just one month after the Seraw murder, noted: "John Metzger was quoted by the *Seattle Times* as saying '. . . skinheads today are deadlier than the skinheads of just two years ago. They're more disciplined.' "

I thought that quotation might be effective in court and wanted the original *Seattle Times* piece. Initially, the people at that paper whom Sara contacted were unable to find the article. Sara eventually searched our files and found it in the stacks of material sent to us by a clipping service that we pay to provide newspaper and magazine articles on subjects of interest to the Center.

"Dear God," I exclaimed after reading it. Exactly three weeks after Seraw's murder, loose-lipped John Metzger had done more than profess awareness of the skinheads' deadliness. After saying he was surprised that skinhead recruiting efforts in Portland had been so successful, he had admitted a link to Mazzella, whose role in informing on Mieske, Brewster, and Strasser had not yet been made public. In the article reporter Walter Hatch, presumably on the basis of his interview with John, identified Dave Mazzella as "vice president of Metzger's group, who had moved to Portland in October to organize racist skinheads." Hatch went on to write: "If local skinheads request his help, Metzger said, he would send Mazzella or another organizer to Seattle to try to repeat the success in Portland."

"This is as important as the letter to Ken Death," I told Sara. Unfortunately, unless John Metzger admitted that Hatch had accurately represented his words, we could not, under the rules of evidence, introduce the article in court without reporter Hatch's testimony. The Metzgers had made several foolish mistakes during discovery, but we were certain that John, if he testified, would deny making such a statement. "It's critical that we take Hatch's deposition, Sara," I said.

When I called Hatch in Seattle, he quickly referred me to his editor, who told me the newspaper had a policy of refusing to allow reporters to give statements about the sources and material used to prepare articles. Otherwise, he explained, individuals might be reluctant to talk to reporters. The editor referred me to the newspaper's attorney, a partner at one of Seattle's biggest law firms. The lawyer echoed the editor, citing precedents in which the First Amendment had successfully been invoked to protect a reporter from revealing information. I explained our particular case, clearly one of good versus evil, and the need for Hatch's testimony. I said we didn't want to know Hatch's sources; we only wanted him to verify what was printed.

After several calls the lawyer agreed that I could take Hatch's deposition if I limited questions to the article itself. I could not ask him about the notes of his interview with John or other material that did not appear in the paper. Hatch would not come to Portland to testify, but the deposition could be introduced into evidence if the court deemed it admissible. The lawyer told me that this was the first time he had ever allowed a reporter to be deposed, and I should consider myself lucky. I did. The newspaper could have stalled us forever if we had been forced to go to court to compel Hatch's testimony.

Knowing that the deposition might be introduced into evidence, we decided to record Walter Hatch on videotape. The jury would certainly pay more attention to his testimony if they could see him, rather than hear a stand-in read from his deposition transcript. Before the deposition began, I foolishly told the Metzgers of the limitations imposed by the *Seattle Times*'s attorney. I adhered to those limitations and was done deposing Hatch, an articulate, straightforward young man, in about ten minutes. He gave us all we wanted.

Tom Metzger immediately disregarded the established rules—probably just to be contrary, because I had outlined restrictions. He began by noting that Hatch had identified John as a neo-Nazi. What, Tom inquired, was Hatch's definition of a neo-Nazi?

The newspaper's attorney with whom I had dealt had sent an associate to monitor the deposition. The young man objected to this question, and to most of Tom's other queries over the next several minutes. As he instructed Hatch not to answer many of these questions, my heart sank. This deposition would be admissible in court only if all parties received a full and fair chance to examine the witness.

In inquiring about Hatch's views about the Anti-Defamation League, South Africa, the Japanese alliance with Germany during World War II, and the reporter's membership in various organizations, Metzger was asking questions that were irrelevant if not offensive. Finally, the attorney reached his boiling point and threatened to terminate the deposition if such questioning continued. I quickly asked for a break in the proceedings.

"If this thing is terminated, we won't be able to use Hatch's testimony and get the article into evidence," I told him in private.

The attorney was more interested in his client than in our case.

"Please talk to your boss," I asked.

After a lengthy conference, the attorney reported that Metzger would be allowed to pursue his ridiculous lines of questioning. And Tom did . . . for almost three hours.

Putting up with such inanity seemed a relatively small price to pay if the Hatch videotape could be shown at trial. However, when Richard Cohen read the deposition transcript in Montgomery, he feared that Metzger might not have received the requisite fair chance to cross-examine. "If Tom objects to this at trial, Judge Haggerty would not be out of line in excluding it" was our legal director's unfortunate assessment.

We'd have to wait at least three weeks to find out.

With the trial rapidly approaching, Elden flew to Montgomery for a weekend of brainstorming with Richard and me. We discussed potential witnesses. We reviewed key documents, including Metzger's telephone records, bank records, and newspapers. We discussed the major themes of the case. And, perhaps most important, we debated how to structure our presentation.

Determining what witnesses to call, the order in which to call them, and what points to make with each witness was critical. We would, in effect, be telling a story at the trial. While it was clear from the attention the case had already gained that the media and much of the nation would be watching, my basic concern was that the story made sense and kept the interest of twelve people—the jury.

Where should we begin this story? We could start by focusing on Tom Metzger, the prince of darkness—describe his roots, his organization, his change from radical political candidate to revolutionary, his recruiting techniques, his philosophy, his incitement of violence. After introducing the Pied Piper of Hate, we could then move to Dave Mazzella, chronicling his evolution from punk to skinhead to Metzger fan to Metzger operative. Once Dave described his mission to Portland and his activities there, we would examine those present at the murder: Julie Belec, Heidi Martinson, hostile witness Ken Mieske, and perhaps Steve Strasser. With the murder finally described, we would then focus on damages. A doctor would describe Mulugeta's injuries. A financial expert would describe his earning potential had he lived. Uncle Engedaw, other friends, and fellow workers would present a picture of the young man who died so senselessly. We planned to bring Mulugeta's father from Ethiopia to testify as well.

This approach seemed completely logical . . . and totally unsatisfying. "Something's missing," I said.

"There's no drama," said Richard. "You'll put the jury to sleep if you start with Tom. I'd start with the murder itself. Who did it? Why did they do it? What happened? And who are we going to hold responsible? We should treat this like a criminal case, only this time we're the prosecutors."

In my thirty years of practice, I have represented clients in hundreds of criminal proceedings, over thirty of them death-penalty cases. My role in these trials has always been defense attorney, never prosecutor, with one exception. After Glenn Miller violated the terms of a court order in which he promised to refrain from operating a paramilitary organization, we brought criminal contempt charges against him. When the U.S. District Court in North Carolina ruled that the local U.S. attorney was the proper party to bring the action, Richard and

I were appointed special prosecutors. I had enjoyed wearing a different hat, particularly one that allowed me to take advantage of the vast
resources that the government has in trying a case.

Although we might adopt the mind-set of prosecutors and structure
our case as if it were a criminal prosecution, we were not bringing
criminal charges against the Metzgers. They would pay damages, not
go to jail, if found guilty by the jury, and we did not have to persuade
a jury that they were culpable of a crime. In a criminal prosecution,
the state must prove its case beyond a reasonable doubt, a more
demanding task than that facing us in our civil suit; Judge Haggerty
would instruct the jury to decide based on a "preponderance of the
evidence."*

With the structure of our presentation falling into place, we could
now determine who would present what. We decided that Elden and
I would share the major courtroom responsibilities—interviewing
prospective jurors, delivering the opening statement and closing argument, and examining and cross-examining witnesses. We did not want
to be viewed as outsiders, legal guns-for-hire with no interest in the
affairs of the city. Elden would be the upstanding Portlander outraged
that the Metzgers had sent their agents up from California to foment
violence, kill an innocent resident, and give the city a bad name.

Jim McElroy and Richard Cohen were more than qualified to examine witnesses, but too many lawyers could spoil this case. We
wanted to avoid giving the jury the impression that a large team of
attorneys was taking on the undermanned Metzgers. There would be
plenty for Mac and Richard to do, anyway. Mac would help prepare
star witness Mazzella for his testimony and work with undercover
agent Pete Gibbons, whom we might or might not call.

Elden and Richard, as they had throughout the case, would handle
all legal arguments. Their most important job would be to maneuver
us around First Amendment obstacles, but they had several other
concerns before the trial. We wanted to prohibit testimony from John

*While we would not officially be prosecutors, we would be in one sense representing
the state's interest. Oregon, like many states, allows juries to award punitive damages
in cases such as ours. Such damages, intended to punish the defendant for particularly
offensive behavior, can be awarded to plaintiff above and beyond damages that will
compensate him for his real or actual loss. In most states, the plaintiff is entitled to
all the punitive damages awarded, but in Oregon, the state shares punitive damages
with the plaintiff.

Metzger and Kyle Brewster because they had evaded discovery by invoking the Fifth Amendment at their depositions. We also wanted to prohibit references to the Center or the ADL. As Richard would eventually note in a motion, "To deflect attention away from his own conduct, Tom Metzger has repeatedly attacked the activities of the Southern Poverty Law Center (SPLC), the ADL, and SPLC attorney Morris Dees during the course of this litigation. Metzger has sought to portray himself as the victim of a conspiracy between two leftist organizations bent on raising money for themselves by persecuting them." To make his point, Metzger had filed with the court Center fund-raising letters, a magazine article critical of the Center and me, and material accusing the Center of using false testimony in one of our Klan cases. This information was not only irrelevant but patently false. Even if it had some marginal relevance, however, its probative value was far outweighed by the confusion and prejudice it would create. In one letter to the court, Metzger had accused us of wanting to put on a "show trial," but it was clear from his behavior that he was the one who wanted a circus. Introducing sensational, false material about us would help create the desired atmosphere.

This was an important point for us to win. We did not want *Berhanu* v. *Metzger* to turn into Metzger versus Dees or David versus Goliath. I don't know whether Metzger's attempts to make this happen resulted from intelligent calculation or paranoia. Whatever the origin, if he could portray himself as the small businessman/private citizen/victim of the intrusive U.S. government and its lackeys like me, he might score points with the jury.

As the days passed, we kept waiting for the bad news that Metzger was going to depose Mazzella. He never did. But we were not yet home free with our key witness. Dave's mother told us that although she remained sympathetic to our cause, she would not bail him out of jail.

Would Judge Haggerty grant a motion to allow jail officials to bring him to Portland if some other source of bail money was not found? We could file the motion and find out. But there was a downside here. We would be alerting Metzger that we planned to call Dave as a witness.

There was, however, another way of divining how the judge would rule. We filed a motion to bring Strasser to the trial from prison. When

MICHAEL LLOYD

Left: Mulugeta Seraw, the Ethiopian college student beaten to death by Portland skinheads in 1988: **Above:** Tekuneh, Seraw's father, and Henok, Seraw's son, listening to testimony through an interpreter. **Below:** The Ethiopian community in Portland attends Seraw's funeral.

MICHAEL LLOYD

Top left: The skinheads smashed the windows and taillight of the car carrying Seraw. **Above:** East Side White Pride (ESWP) bat seized by police who searched skinhead Steve Strasser's apartment. **Left:** Morris Dees questions skinhead Kenneth Mieske about the beating death of Seraw. **Below, left to right:** Portland skinheads Kyle Brewster, Kenneth ("Ken Death") Mieske, and Steve Strasser pleaded guilty to killing Seraw.

Left: Tom Metzger, White Aryan Resistance (WAR) leader. **Below left:** Dave Mazzella, vice president of WAR Youth, testifies against WAR and the Metzgers. **Below:** John Metzger. **Below right:** Mazzella (*center*) poses with skinheads Michael Barrett and Mike Gagnon in 1987.

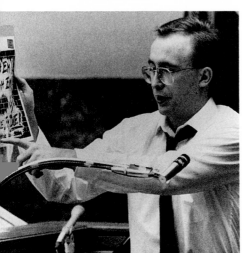

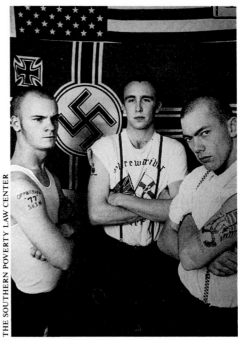

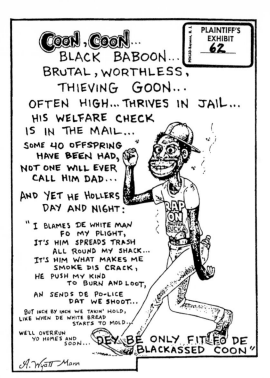

These plaintiff's exhibits helped convince the jury to return a verdict against the defendants. **Right:** Exhibit 1, the plaintiff's "smoking gun," tied the Metzgers directly to Portland skinheads. **Top right:** Exhibit 138 was sketched by a Portland skinhead minutes before Seraw was killed. **Above:** Exhibit 62 was like many produced by the Metzgers demeaning blacks. **Next page, left:** Exhibits 59 and 56 were distributed to skinheads by Mazzella to encourage violence. Exhibit 58 is a WAR recruitment poster. **Next page, right:** Skinheads pledged allegiance to WAR's Aryan Fighting Code, Exhibit 155.

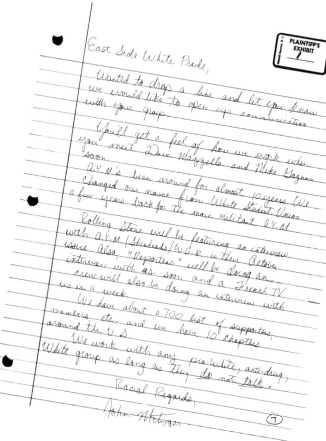

Aryan Fighting Code

ARTICLE 1: I am an Aryan. I serve the forces that guard my Aryan race. I am prepared to give my life in defense of my race.

ARTICLE 2: I am an Aryan. I will never surrender my mind to my captors. I will never betray other Aryan people.

ARTICLE 3: I am an Aryan. If I am incarcerated, I will remember at all times my duty as an Aryan. I will aid other Aryan prisoners, if possible. I will accept no special favors from my captors.

ARTICLE 4: I am an Aryan. As a political prisoner, I keep faith in fellow Aryan people. I resist any activity harmful to the Aryan race. I will obey lawful orders of superior officers at all times.

ARTICLE 5: I am an Aryan. As a racial political prisoner of war, I will answer only with my age, name and address when questioned. I will make no oral or written statements disloyal to my race.

Above: Richard Cohen, legal director of the Southern Poverty Law Center, assists trial consultants Robert Hirschhorn and Cathy Bennett with jury selection. **Right:** Elden Rosenthal questions Seraw's uncle, Engedaw Berhanu, about Seraw's early life. **Below right:** Judge Ancer Haggerty presided over the case with fairness. **Below left:** Morris Dees holds Henok Seraw at the counsel table as the jury's verdict is read.

ANCER L. HAGGERTY

Above: Center investigator Joe Roy shows the jury a video in which Tom Metzger encourages skinheads to commit violence. **Left:** A Portland SWAT team provided security at the courthouse during the trial. **Below:** Trial and security teams relax on the Columbia River Gorge during a weekend break. *Left to right,* Morris Dees, Sergeant James Hudson, Officer Paul Weatheroy, Larry Gibson, San Diego attorney James McElroy, Center staffers Linda Stringer, Danny Welch, and Beth Boyd, Officer Ed Brumfield, and Officer Wayne Baldassare.

Above: Seraw's father, Seraw Tekuneh, and uncle, Engedaw Berhanu, celebrate with Klanwatch director Danny Welch and Morris Dees at an Ethiopian restaurant in Portland.

Some of the trial team at the victory party: *Clockwise:* Morris and Elizabeth Dees; secretaries Linda Stringer and Sally Lane; San Diego attorney James McElroy and Center investigator Joe Roy; Portland attorney Elden Rosenthal; and ADL attorney Richard Shevitz.

the judge granted this, we breathed a sigh of relief, confident that he would rule the same way with respect to Mazzella.

All this maneuvering to prevent Metzger from knowing Dave Mazzella was our star witness would have been for naught in almost every other state in the union. Oregon, as noted earlier, has bucked the overwhelming national trend to compel the revelation of witnesses and most documents during the discovery period. The traditional argument for such disclosure is that it eliminates surprises and makes for a fairer trial. I'm not so sure.

I'm not in favor of hiding evidence from an opponent. But if I go out and dig up information that might devastate my opponent—and in this case we had found some documents, photos, and other material that we hoped would badly hurt the Metzgers—why should I reveal it to an adversary too lazy to do his own legwork? The purpose of a trial is to bring out the whole truth. White supremacists I have battled feel that they can lie with impunity. Their oath to the race supersedes their oath to the court. There is only one way to come close to getting at the truth with them: hit them with contradictions they can't anticipate.

My point is that you may be more likely to hear the truth (or see that someone is obviously lying) if you show a witness material for the first time when he is on the stand rather than reveal it to him in advance. There is nothing unethical about this. Oregon has chosen to follow this procedure.*

Danny and I arrived in Portland one week before the trial was to begin. Had the drug dealers, prostitutes, and bookmakers of the city been privy to police policy, they might have made special plans for the days ahead. The city had assigned virtually its entire drug and vice unit to provide security to our party. The first team of six plainclothesmen was already established in the hotel when we arrived.

By the end of our first day, we had transformed the common area in my two-room suite into a "war room," with a rented Xerox machine, a VCR, large cardboard blowups of key exhibits, and files upon files. This would be "trial central" for the foreseeable future.

*Many other states followed the same procedure for many years until they adopted the federal rules over the past twenty years.

I had barely settled in when I had to leave. After months of refusing to give a deposition, John Metzger, faced with the prospect that he would not be allowed to testify at trial if he continued to invoke the Fifth Amendment, had decided to break his silence. Elden and I flew down to San Diego. Accompanied by Jim McElroy, we listened as Tom Metzger gave a preview of his entire case by virtue of the questions he asked his son. The Metzgers, who constantly called for an end to the U.S. government, were going to put their faith in the free speech provisions of the Constitution.

On the same day that the Metzgers were wrapping themselves in the First Amendment, the ACLU finally filed a trial brief with Judge Haggerty. We had drafted our complaint as we do most complaints— broadly. Alternative counts ascribed different degrees of intent to the Metzgers. In one count, we alleged that the Metzgers had intentionally caused unlawful action. The ACLU acknowledged that if we could prove this, the defendants could indeed be held liable for damages resulting from their speech. In alternative counts, we alleged that the Metzgers' conduct had been negligent or reckless. The ACLU argued that liability could not be predicated on these theories:

> If liability can be imposed upon the basis of speech that is merely negligent or reckless, individuals or organizations with no intention of inciting imminent lawless action might restrict their speech in order to avoid potential liability. Thus, the threat of liability for negligent or reckless speech could have a chilling effect upon the exercise of First Amendment rights.

The ACLU went on to note that the U.S. Supreme Court in the 1969 decision *Brandenburg* v. *Ohio* had distinguished between abstract advocacy of the use of force, which constituted protected speech, and inciting imminent lawless action, which lay beyond the protection of the First Amendment.

This reading of the law was not new to us. We had faced free speech questions in earlier Klan cases, and from the time we had filed suit against the Metzgers, Richard had advised me what we would have to prove to win. My line of questioning at trial would be specifically tailored to demonstrate that the First Amendment did not protect the Metzgers' conduct.

The ACLU acknowledged that federal and state courts were split on whether negligent or reckless speech was protected by the First Amendment. Although the U.S. Supreme Court had not specifically ruled on the question, the ACLU pointed out that certain court decisions protecting speech turned on the absence of intent to incite lawlessness. In a 1973 case, *Hess* v. *Indiana,* a participant in an antiwar demonstration had been convicted of violating an Indiana disorderly conduct statute after stating "We'll take the fucking street later (or again)" as he stood at the side of a street that was being cleared of demonstrators by the police. In reversing the conviction, the Supreme Court had noted that the defendant did not appear to be exhorting the crowd to go back into the street and that his statement did not appear to be addressed to any particular person or group.

Our response to the Oregon ACLU's brief, filed four days later, said basically what I had said in my letter to the organization's executive director months earlier. "The plaintiff does not seek to impose liability on anyone for what they have said or written. Instead the plaintiff seeks redress for the brutal, racially motivated murder of Mulugeta Seraw." Our memorandum went on to explain that the Metzgers' words could be used as evidence against them to establish that they had acted unlawfully; the Constitution did not immunize the Metzgers simply because they had used words to carry out their plan.

We noted that our first theory of liability against the Metzgers rested on the concept that the Metzgers, through their agents, had substantially assisted in or encouraged the actions of Mieske and Brewster. This argument had nothing to do with whether the Metzgers made racist speeches or mailed inflammatory material to the members of East Side White Pride. We would prove that the Metzgers sent their agents to Portland to organize East Side White Pride and to spur its members to commit acts of racial violence. This was very different from the *Hess* case, where a single public statement was directed to no one in particular. Although the Supreme Court had held that "the teaching of the moral propriety or even moral necessity for a resort to force and violence is constitutionally protected," the Court has repeatedly emphasized that "preparing a group for violent action and steeling it to such action" is not.

Our second theory was civil conspiracy. The Metzgers (through their agent Dave Mazzella) and the Oregon defendants (Mieske and

Brewster) had agreed upon a common objective that clearly contemplated injury to others—the pursuit of white supremacist goals through violent means. As a result, Seraw was attacked. Nothing in the First Amendment prevented imposing liability if such a conspiracy could be established.

Our next two theories rested not on negligent or reckless use of speech by the Metzgers but on the negligent or reckless selection of agents Mazzella and Barrett to organize East Side White Pride. Oregon law was clear: a principal who recklessly or negligently engaged an agent with dangerous propensities was responsible for the foreseeable harm that followed. If, for example, the owner of an apartment building hired a maintenance man with a known history of sexual misconduct, he would be liable to a tenant victimized by the man. As long as Mazzella or Barrett could be held liable for their conduct in encouraging ESWP to commit violence, there was no First Amendment problem with finding the Metzgers liable. Liability stemmed from their conduct in selecting the agent, not from their words.

We felt that this point-by-point response effectively dismissed free speech questions raised by the ACLU and the Metzgers. Our argument to the jury, based on analysis of the law, would be simple: Under our Constitution, you have the right to hate but not to hurt, and you are responsible for hurt perpetrated by your agents. Facing a First Amendment challenge, we chose to take it head on. Our theme—as logical and easy to remember as "You can't shout 'Fire' in a crowded theater"—put the Metzgers' behavior in perspective.

We would not argue that all of the newspapers, hotline transcripts, and other writings and recordings that we hoped to introduce into evidence made the Metzgers liable. That did not mean, however, that they could not be presented to the jury. U.S. Supreme Court rulings made it clear that the fact that the Metzgers were free to express their racist views did not mean that those words could not be used against them. In 1982, the Court had overturned a civil judgment against the NAACP for its role in a seven-year boycott of white merchants in Mississippi beginning in 1966. The merchants argued that boycott leader Charles Evers's fiery rhetoric had led to violent acts that had occasionally marred the primarily peaceful boycott. The Court refused to hold Evers or the NAACP liable for his words, but it did say that "speeches might be taken in evidence that Evers gave other specific instructions to carry out violent acts or threats." Similarly, in our case, speech could be used to corroborate our allegations that Metzger had sent Mazzella to Portland specifically to lead East Side White Pride to commit violence. This, I had told the Oregon ACLU long ago, was all we were doing.

We were confident that Judge Haggerty would understand and agree with our reading of the law. Would a jury? We worried that if the Metzgers and the ACLU succeeded in characterizing this as a First Amendment case, some jurors might vote in their favor.

Portland's politics were hard to read. I had been told that many parts of Oregon were quite racist. A sizable number of Southerners had migrated to the state in the late nineteenth century. In 1945 one survey had listed Portland as "the most racist city north of the Mason-Dixon line" and, according to the *Oregonian,* "the city's entire power structure enforced into the 1950s a race caste system that was as obvious as it was rigid. Housing discrimination was part of the civic plan and written into duly recorded deeds." Robert Mathews, who had been shot and wounded in Portland by the FBI before their final confrontation in Whidbey Island, had been a hero to many in the Pacific Northwest. Also, skinheads had found Portland a mecca, and there had been some one hundred incidents of racial violence over the past two years. At the same time, the city also had a reputation for being somewhat liberal; it had elected a mayor who was famous for having posed as a "flasher" in front of a statue for the popular poster "Expose Yourself to Art."

Some liberal-minded folks might be disposed to adopt the ACLU's position at the drop of a hat—or jerk of a knee. Did this mean we should strive to keep "liberals" off the jury? True, they might disdain attacks on free speech, but wouldn't they also be most likely to abhor attacks on blacks and Jews and other minorities? And wouldn't they award more money to the family of an Ethiopian immigrant than "conservatives" would?

Another factor might also color the attitude of Portlanders. Jesse Jackson had called for a boycott of Nike shoe company, a major employer and economic force in the area. Jackson and others argued that blacks constituted a substantial percentage of those buying Nike products, yet the company's employment practices and commitment to the black community were deficient. Would this threat and Jackson's posturing push some white jurors closer to the Metzgers' corner?

No one on our trial team was sure of the answers to these and many other questions, but we sure wanted to know before picking the jury that would decide our client's fate. Enter Cathy "Cat" Bennett, a thirty-nine-year-old jury-and-trial consultant who might legitimately be called the mother of modern criminal law practice.

Cathy had been helping me pick juries since the mid-1970s. In those days, attorneys, myself among them, were suspicious, if not resentful, of the handful of people calling themselves "jury consultants." We trial lawyers were quite capable, thank you, of selecting jurors without the assistance of consultants or other interlopers who had never tried a case—or so we thought.

My eyes were opened when I helped defend Joan Little, a black woman accused of killing her white jailer in North Carolina in 1975. Joan claimed that she had only been defending herself from the ice-pick-wielding jailer when he came into her cell seeking sex. The case had received national attention, and with Joan facing the death penalty in a highly charged climate, we had employed consultants to survey the attitudes of those in the county where she was originally to be tried. The results of the survey had helped persuade a judge that Joan could not get a fair trial in the rural county. He moved the proceeding to Raleigh, where, we felt, we stood a much better chance. We had then employed the consultants to conduct a second survey, in Raleigh this time, to develop a profile of jurors most likely to be sympathetic to our case.

I had first worked with Cat, a tiny, attractive blond dynamo, in 1975 while representing Leon Banks, a black man who faced the death penalty in Georgia after shooting a white man, who left a young widow and four children. Cat quickly exhibited the best interviewing and listening skills I had ever seen. Even more important, although only twenty-four, she opened my eyes to dealing with clients.

After Cat's excellent work in picking a jury, the prosecution had finally agreed to accept a plea that would keep Banks out of the electric chair. Before leaving town, Cat said she wanted to visit him. I went with her to the small jail where Banks was being held. I had no plans to say good-bye to him, had no feelings for him as a person. I was just happy to have helped him avoid execution, as I do not support the death penalty.

Cat told Banks to take care, asked if there was anyone he wanted her to contact, and then suddenly put her arms around him and said, "Leon, I love you."

She was in no way condoning what Banks had done. But she was viewing him as a human being, not merely a client. Seeing this changed forever the way I interact with those I represent. No longer do I keep them at arm's length. Lawyers are trained not to feel. Cat taught me—and in the following years scores of other lawyers—to become loving, feeling human beings in court. This comes through to a jury.

Over the next several years, she helped me and other Center lawyers on several cases in which criminal defendants faced capital punishment. We got a number of people off on lesser charges and even won a few outright acquittals. By the time she helped us pick the jury in the Michael Donald case in 1987, Cat had become the nation's foremost jury consultant. She had assisted such diverse clients as the Native Americans at Wounded Knee, John DeLorean, and members of Hell's Angels.

In 1986, doctors told Cathy she had breast cancer. The disease had metastasized and she had been given little chance of surviving. Undaunted, she had continued working, pursued a number of "alternative" therapies, and moved from hectic Houston to more tranquil Galveston, Texas. We kept in close contact, and while I marveled at her will, I was not surprised by it, or by her survival. After taking the Seraw case, I called her and asked if she would help, if and when we went to trial. She agreed to work on the condition that she do so for free. This would not be the first time that Cat had assisted the Center and other clients at no charge.

Cat's husband, criminal defense attorney Robert Hirschhorn, frequently assisted her. Two months before the trial, I sent them a seven-page letter summarizing our case and explaining Tom Metzger's two defenses: first, that Mieske and Brewster were the victims and had themselves been attacked; and second, that the most Tom did in publishing his papers was to exercise First Amendment rights. "He says our claim that he sent agents to Portland to organize skins to overthrow the U.S. government is a joke," I wrote. "Naturally he misconceives our case, because we do not contend that he did any more than encourage violence and send agents to carry this out." I noted that the ACLU had intervened.

"I think a community survey is needed to determine racial attitudes, skinhead attitudes, etc. We can obtain other attitudes in the process." We would also want a questionnaire for those actually called for jury duty, but this would require filing a motion with Judge Haggerty, I noted.

In early September, Cat and Robert had sent me their proposed telephone poll. Callers would ask one thousand randomly selected residents of Multnomah County thirty-eight questions from four categories. The first set of questions concerned experience with jury trials. Had the person called ever served on a jury? Was it a civil suit or criminal case? Our pollers were instructed to terminate the interview if the respondent had been called for jury duty in the near future. Court rules forbid communication between parties and prospective jurors.

The second category dealt with what the pollers would describe as "some current issues in Portland." In reality these were issues relevant to our trial. The questions were designed to determine attitudes about free speech, skinheads, race, and immigrants. The respondents were asked whether they agreed strongly, agreed somewhat, disagreed strongly, disagreed somewhat, or had no opinion about such things as whether burning the American flag should not be allowed; whether the Portland police should devote more effort to controlling the skinheads; whether someone who encourages another person to commit violence should be held responsible for those acts; whether blacks were responsible for most of the violence in our society.

A series of questions about "the case in which a black Ethiopian was killed by three skinheads in Portland" followed. Had the respondent heard of the case? What came to mind when thinking of the case? Was it right for the family of the dead man to sue the leader of the white supremacist group? Was it right to hold that leader "responsible when he was not even there when the killing happened"?

The final set of twenty questions sought background information about the respondent. Did the person follow the news? What magazines did he or she subscribe to or read regularly? What was his or her favorite TV program? Movie? Was the person employed? What type of work? Had the person served in the armed forces? Any experience in the field of law enforcement? What was the highest grade of school completed? What was his or her marital status? Spouse's line of work? Did the respondent have children?

These background questions were important, for they would allow us to develop a profile of the individual who answered the earlier questions most to our liking. Thus, by asking key, but innocuous-sounding, questions to prospective jurors in court, and with a written questionnaire (if Judge Haggerty permitted it), we could in a relatively short time correlate it to the phone survey and make educated guesses about their feelings on the pivotal subjects of the trial.

The phone survey is only one element to be used in the jury-selection process. The body language of the individual provides clues, and there remains no substitute for good interviewing skills and the intuition born of years of experience. I would rely on the entire trial team, Center staff, and my wife, Elizabeth (an expert at reading people), in picking the twelve people to hear our story.

Our principal storyteller, Dave Mazzella, arrived from Jackson County jail three days before the trial was to begin. Public defender Orf had handled his release.

We installed Dave at a hotel about twenty minutes away from ours. He rented a VCR and watched movies endlessly until his girlfriend, Ruth, arrived from Medford. Then, according to Eddie Ousley, a rock-solid Center intern we assigned to protect our star witness, who had been in jail for months, Dave and Ruth devoted themselves to other pursuits just as endlessly.

I was happy that at least one of us could apparently distract himself from the worries of the upcoming battle. I had dinner with Dave forty-eight hours before the trial, and he seemed happy and confident.

If only that confidence had lasted.

———————————■———————————

What we are up against is so vile, what we are up against is so dark, what we are up against is so evil that it is not enough to come to a rally on one weekend, on one month, and to show solidarity and then to think our job is done.

—Congressman Les AuCoin,
at Portland rally for Dignity and Diversity,
October 7, 1990

CHAPTER THIRTEEN

October 9, 1990
■
Portland, Oregon

Tom Metzger rose slowly and moved to the center of Ancer Haggerty's courtroom. "I am a white separatist," he began. "I advocate radical ideas. . . . I'm not apologizing to anyone about our beliefs."

The forthright introduction jerked the twenty-two prospective jurors to attention on this Tuesday afternoon, the first full day of voir dire, the process by which the jury is selected.

"I'm going to talk to you like I would one of my customers over a cup of coffee or a beer," he continued, pushing his thumbs under the suspenders of his chocolate-brown suit. "Miss Scoles, do you believe in forced integration?"

The blond woman in seat number one paused, pursed her lips, and finally said, "No."*

"Miss Fedderson, do you think if we were all what used to be called

---

*This closed-ended question, requiring a yes or no answer, demonstrated Metzger's inability to use voir dire to learn what the juror really thought or how she might relate to his case. I don't fault Metzger for this; most lawyers lecture jurors, ask closed-ended questions, and learn little. He should have asked her how she felt about forced integration. Answering this open-ended question would have revealed her belief structure. Her body language while answering might have revealed even more than her words.

the 'U.N. coffee-colored brown man,' everything would be hunky-dory?"

"No, sir," said the sandy-haired woman in seat number two.

Each of the women queried was white. Indeed, there were no black jury candidates in the courtroom. There were no Jewish people either, and only three Asian Americans.

The Portland City Council had designated October 7–13 as "Dignity and Diversity Week." I wasn't expecting much dignity from Metzger, but I was hoping for more diversity in this first panel. There had been one black man and one Jewish man in the original group of twenty-five candidates brought in late Monday. Judge Haggerty had excused them, however, after each had stated that he would be unable to render a fair verdict because of his personal disdain for Metzger.*

Dignity and Diversity Week had begun on Sunday with a march that revealed a community's disdain for Metzger and boosted my confidence that we'd find sympathetic jurors. Some fifteen hundred Portlanders had taken part in a crosstown rally that included speeches decrying hate and prejudice, by Congressman Les AuCoin of Oregon and others, and a memorial for Mulugeta Seraw at the site where he was murdered. Mayor Bud Clark, Deputy District Attorney Norm Frink, and several city officials had marched with members of groups representing blacks, women, Native Americans, Jews, gays, environmentalists, and even antiracist skinheads.

Diversity was certainly apparent in this throng as it moved through the downtown area. Various marchers carried pictures of Dr. Martin Luther King and signs proclaiming, among other things: "Fight Racism with Militant Action! Smash the Nazi Skinheads"; "Columbus Was a Racist"; "Support Native American Land Rights"; "The Holocaust Must Never, Never Be Forgotten"; and "Women Against Racism." Surely, the irony of this last group's acronym was not lost on the crowd.

Police intelligence had indicated that as many as three hundred skinheads and neo-Nazis from out of town might come to break up the rally. Blue-helmeted riot policemen formed a ribbon of security on the marchers' right flank while twenty more officers on motorcycles

*Another prospective juror was dismissed because she was moving out of town in the next days.

provided protection on the left. A police helicopter hovered above the rally all afternoon, and a bomb-disposal unit and bomb-sniffing dogs stood ready if needed. The *Oregonian* noted that the 150 local and state officers constituted the largest police turnout for any demonstration or event in the city's history. About 100 policemen had monitored Elvis Presley's 1957 concert, and 90 had been assigned to a Run D.M.C. rap concert in 1987. Fortunately, the skinhead threat never materialized.

The march was featured prominently on the front page of the *Oregonian.* But this good news was tempered by two other articles on the same page. The newspaper reported that an interracial couple had been driven from its Portland home by threatening phone calls and racial slurs. Equally disturbing and alarming was the news from Louisiana that David Duke had polled 44 percent of the total vote and almost 60 percent of the white vote on October 6 in losing the race for the U.S. Senate to incumbent Bennett Johnston. Pre-election polls had not predicted such a strong showing. Many of those queried had apparently been willing to cast a ballot for Duke in the privacy of a voting booth but had been unwilling to tell pollsters that they would do so.

This reluctance to enunciate publicly what may be perceived as inappropriate political views or social beliefs did not surprise me, but it did give me pause. We would face a similar situation in questioning prospective jurors. In an open courtroom filled with the press, a black judge, and fellow citizens, few, if any, would admit that they agreed with a David Duke or a Tom Metzger.

I am a great believer in the American jury system. Most citizens called upon to render justice take their responsibility seriously and almost always attempt to act fairly. That said, I must note that I have witnessed countless prospective jurors lie, or at least shade the truth, when asked about personal attitudes. Some might admit that they oppose a policy like forced integration, but rare is the individual who will acknowledge that she is disturbed when she sees an interracial couple. In an open courtroom, those on the spot almost always give socially acceptable answers.

The attorney selecting the jury in a case with such sensitive issues must walk a fine line. It is important to learn the individual's true feelings, but it is equally important not to embarrass or antagonize that person while doing the questioning; he or she might end up deciding your client's fate.

Metzger lost points by creating extreme discomfort in the jury box with his pointed questions, but he did impress me with his understanding that a major purpose of this process is to educate prospective jurors about your case. "I don't believe in equality," he said. "I don't believe individuals are equal or that races are equal. We want to get that all out before we get into this case. What I need to find out is not whether you like a racist." The real issue, he said, was whether he had incited anyone to commit the acts that had led to Seraw's death.

He then invoked the cherished First Amendment. Should a video store owner be held liable if someone rented a violent movie and then "sliced somebody up"? he asked.

"No," answered the potential juror.

Should comedian Andrew Dice Clay be held liable if a fan assaulted a woman after hearing one of his sexist routines?

"No."

Should the Catholic Church be culpable if a parishioner who hears an antiabortion sermon goes out and vandalizes an abortion clinic?

"No."

These were effective, if bogus, analogies. If Metzger could persuade jurors that his role in the death of Seraw was really no different from the role of the club owner, comedian, or church, he would win. His role, of course, *was* different. Anticipating Tom's misdirection play, Elden Rosenthal and I had offered our view of the case when questioning the candidates earlier in the day. "I think I would be the first person to defend Mr. Metzger if somebody was trying to restrain his free speech," I had said in introducing myself. "This case is not about free speech, but about killing an innocent man by the incitement, encouragement, and even the direction of the third-highest agent of White Aryan Resistance."

I then asked several of the prospective jurors a series of closed-ended questions about free speech to frame our issues. Should free speech protect a person who encourages violence? Is there a line to be drawn between speech that is protected and speech for which one can be held responsible? I followed with an open-ended question to learn the jurors' beliefs and feelings. What would happen if we didn't draw that line? Cat sat next to Elden and me and passed follow-up questions.

The responses pleased me. Mr. O'Connor said a person crossed over the line when his words led to violence and physical damage. Mr. Johnson said, "With freedom comes responsibility."

Elden's voir dire was particularly impressive. He managed to elicit revealing information from the panelists, while at the same time establishing a bond that we hoped would last until the verdict. With each answer, I made notes on a grid that identified candidates by name and seat location. Fifteen occupied the jury box. The other seven sat in the first row of the gallery in the tiny courtroom.

As there were only eight narrow oak benches, four apiece on each side of a short aisle, the crush of spectators and reporters desiring entry could not be accommodated. The many individuals unable to find seating could, however, watch on two local cable-television stations carrying the proceeding in its entirety.*

The courtroom's walls were a striking green-orange-and-black marble. Judge Haggerty sat on a raised oak bench, the seal of Oregon above, his clerk seated at a desk below. The flags of the state and America stood behind him; the witness stand was to his immediate left; the two-row jury box to his far left. Two rectangular tables for the attorneys—one for us, one for the Metzgers—sat in the center of the courtroom. I had made certain to take the one nearer the witness stand and the jury box. In Oregon, attorneys must conduct their examinations seated. I therefore wanted to be as close to the witness as possible. I also wanted to establish personal contact with the jury, get a better view of jurors' body language, and pick up things they were saying.

Our table could comfortably accommodate only Elden, Engedaw, and myself. When the trial began, Joe Roy, responsible for maintaining our exhibits, would sit in a chair behind me. Cathy Bennett took

*Although the cameraman and sound technician were unobtrusively positioned on a short platform along a wall, I feared that their mere presence would make the jury worry about publicity and treat the case in an out-of-the-ordinary fashion. Since the trial, a number of factors, including the televising of the William Kennedy Smith trial, have changed my mind about cameras in the courtroom. Television affords the public the best way to see how our justice system does or doesn't work.

this seat for jury selection. We could have made room for Richard
Cohen and Jim McElroy, but we did not want the presence of so many
lawyers to create sympathy for the defendants. Richard and Mac
squeezed in with my wife, Elizabeth, and the rest of our team—Danny
Welch, ADL attorney Richard Shevitz, and Center staffers Linda
Stringer and Beth Boyd—on the front bench allotted to our party.

The Metzgers' team, too, had a bench. Behind the leader of WAR
and his son sat not lawyers, but "bodyguards." The burly Carl
Straight was joined by Harry Vaccaro, Rick Cooper, and Wyatt Kaldenberg. Vaccaro, an intense, red-haired young man, sported a blue
tattoo on his neck. National Socialist Vanguard director Cooper appeared an unlikely mentor to skinheads. A graying man of average
size, he looked almost meek watching the proceedings from behind
thick-lensed glasses.

Kaldenberg was the house "intellectual," a former Trotskyite who
wrote much of the WAR newspaper and penned many of the tabloid's
most offensive drawings and poems. Dark-haired and corpulent, he
hardly looked or carried himself like an Aryan master. He could keep
neither his glasses on his nose nor his pants around his waist. Each
time he bent over or turned, the gallery was treated to a view of his
naked rear end. But inept as he appeared, Kaldenberg, too, could be
violent. He had broken Geraldo Rivera's nose during the televised
fracas involving John Metzger and Roy Innis, the black director of
CORE, the Congress of Racial Equality.

To the Metzgers' side, along the wall directly across the room from
the jury box, five Portland detectives sat watching for any signs of
trouble. Other officers, part of a crew of twenty stationed in an adjacent room, moved in and out regularly. Security on the street and in
the halls was even tighter.

On this morning the police had carried Richard, Elizabeth, and me
from the hotel to the courthouse sandwiched in the middle of a three-
car caravan. To avoid detection by anyone scanning police radio
bands, the drivers used an elaborate code when speaking to one another and home base.

The main entrance to the Multnomah County Courthouse on
Southwest Fourth Avenue faces a lovely park graced with ginkgo
trees. This urban oasis is the perfect place to spend a lunch hour
. . . or lie in wait for the attorneys opposing a hero of the radical right.

The city, already trying to shade itself from the spotlight brought on by the murder and now the trial, was not about to let anyone from our camp or, for that matter, the Metzgers' entourage get hurt.

As our car approached the courthouse, we saw dozens of riot police standing like centurions between the park and the building. Mounted policemen cantered along Fourth Avenue while helicopters whirred overhead. Sharpshooters dotted the rooftops of several nearby structures. Motorcycle police were also represented. I hadn't seen so many bikes since my annual spring trip to the Daytona Beach motorcycle races.

Despite this show of force, we had sped past the Fourth Avenue entrance to a small door on the Fifth Avenue side of the eight-story stone courthouse. There, a half-dozen members of the police bureau's Special Emergency Response Team stood alert. They wore combat fatigues and wide-awake looks and carried submachine guns.

"Let's move," said our driver as he pulled up to the entrance, and we were out of the car and into the building within a few seconds.

A private, metal-enclosed elevator usually reserved for prisoners took us up to the fifth floor, where a secured corridor inaccessible to the public led to the courtroom. The windows across the corridor from the courtroom were covered with white butcher paper, apparently to block the view of anyone in or on nearby buildings. Others in our party, the Metzgers, Judge Haggerty, and the jurors—all of us prisoners of this dangerous climate of hate—would eventually use the special entrance and elevator.

Those not directly involved in the case could not simply stroll into the courtroom. Some on our staff, as well as spectators, reporters, and others, had to wait in line down the hall from the courtroom, then pass through two metal detectors and endure hand frisks and seizure of any objects that looked dangerous.

These measures paid off on the first day. Danny, who left the courtroom frequently to talk with the police and make his own security checks of the hallway and street, reported that there had been a confrontation in a fifth-floor corridor between skinheads supporting Metzger and those from SHARP—Skinheads Against Racial Prejudice. Insults were traded, but a host of riot police called in from the street separated the rival gangs before violence erupted.

The police also arrested two skinheads for carrying concealed weapons—a knife, brass knuckles, and a spring-loaded gun. A third skin-head was arrested on an outstanding warrant. Three weeks earlier he had tried to carve a swastika into the skull of a SHARP member, the police said.

All 151 prospective jurors ordered to appear at the courthouse on Monday afternoon had observed the police presence, and the first panel of 25 randomly selected candidates had been frisked prior to entering Judge Haggerty's courtroom. Before beginning his question-ing on Tuesday, Metzger would move that the entire panel be dis-missed because they had been prejudiced by exposure to such intense security. Judge Haggerty denied the motion.

After arriving on Monday, the jurors had filled out questionnaires designed by Cat and Robert and approved by Judge Haggerty and the Metzgers. Intended to speed up the selection process, the two-page survey was unlike our previous telephone poll; we did not ask ques-tions about attitudes on race or this particular case. We did, however, seek personal information, as we had in the telephone poll. In what part of Portland did the candidate live? What was his or her marital status and armed forces and employment history? What magazines did he or she read, and to what clubs did he or she belong?

As a result of the telephone survey, we had a rough picture of the kind of juror we preferred. The answers had been fed into a computer and cross-referenced to determine what demographic facts correlated with attitudes about free speech and other key subjects. When sex, age, education, race, employment, and marital status were factored in, an even clearer pattern emerged. A person who did not believe that flag burning should be considered a form of protected speech, our computer analysis showed, would not be favorable to Metzger's First Amendment defense. For our purposes, males would be slightly better jurors than females. Younger men, college-educated men, and men in supervisory positions would be preferable. Women with prior jury experience and those who watched the news regularly would be desir-able jurors. Those in clerical or sales jobs and married women were less appealing to us. Interestingly, the survey showed that a woman who was unable to name a favorite movie would probably be an undesirable juror.

I should stress that cues from a survey are helpful only to a point. In this case, for example, a young college-educated man who supervised others and detested flag burners might have turned out to be the worst juror we selected. Cat has taught me over the years to keep probing. Good interview skills are critical in jury selection, and that's why I have never selected a jury in a major case without expert help.

As the prospective jurors had filled out their questionnaires in an empty courtroom, we had argued pretrial motions, many of which were designed to prevent Tom Metzger from carrying on as he had done at depositions, at previous hearings, and in his pleadings. Noting our fears of a mistrial, Elden asked Judge Haggerty to keep Metzger from making speeches when examining witnesses, as he had during depositions. I also asked the judge to prevent Metzger from making the kind of "wild and unsubstantiated claims" that had characterized documents previously filed with the court. Judge Haggerty granted our motion requiring the Metzgers to refrain from irrelevant, gratuitous references to the Center, the ADL, and me. Our fund-raising efforts, endowment, and involvement in past cases were also ruled off-limits, as was my personal and professional history.

In handling these motions, the judge had shown himself to be judicial. He was firm yet fair and understanding of Metzger's lack of legal training. A broad, stocky former college athlete with receding black hair and a thin mustache, forty-six-year-old Ancer L. Haggerty was living refutation of many of the Metzgers' racist arguments. He had grown up in Portland and attended Oregon University, where he was an all-league football lineman. After graduating in 1965, he joined the Marines. As a first lieutenant he was injured in Vietnam while rescuing others under fire, for which he earned the Purple Heart and Silver Star. When he returned to the United States, he was the nation's most heavily decorated black officer.

After graduating from Hastings College of Law in San Francisco in 1973, Haggerty had spent four years as a public defender in Portland before joining one of the city's biggest firms, where he represented insurance companies and other corporations in civil suits. He had been a judge since 1988, one of only two black jurists (out of thirty-four) in the county.

Metzger had a short explanation of Haggerty's long list of achievements. On his telephone hotline he described the judge as an "Uncle Tom." He also told the press that Haggerty had been placed in his position of power to relieve white guilt. The judge had not responded.

Judge Haggerty's calm but commanding presence was also evident during Tuesday's jury selection. He betrayed no emotion as Metzger espoused his racist philosophy. When Metzger finished, the judge reiterated the rules for choosing the twelve jurors and two alternates who would render a verdict in *Berhanu* v. *Metzger*. There was no limit to the number of jurors that either party could strike from the panel "for cause." This requires demonstrating to the judge a sufficient reason why the individual should not be permitted to serve—anything from a previous relationship with one of the parties to the inability to rule fairly because of racial prejudice or preconceived notions based on pretrial publicity.

Many observers had thought that there would be an epidemic of such challenges. In fact, there were none after Judge Haggerty dismissed the two gentlemen on Monday afternoon. Our jury would therefore come from the thirteen men and nine women in this initial panel.

How would we determine the twelve jurors and two alternates from these twenty-two? Under Oregon law, each side could dismiss three potential jurors without explanation. Those sitting in seats one through twelve would be our jurors unless excused by these "peremptory challenges." Those sitting in seats thirteen and fourteen would be the alternates unless they moved up in position owing to the peremptory challenge of any of the first twelve.

Late Tuesday afternoon, Judge Haggerty sent the Metzgers to one room on the fifth floor and our trial team to another to determine our challenges. Cat, Robert, and I wanted as much input as possible from those in our party. The previous evening we had all gathered in my hotel room to go over the questionnaires filled out by the panel. Elden had provided helpful information about the candidates' neighborhoods, the businesses where they worked, the schools their children attended, and the organizations to which they belonged. Based on his insights and other information gleaned from the surveys, we had been able to consider the pros and cons of those on the panel before questioning even began. We had also been able to tailor questions to determine if our initial impressions were accurate.

Cat had asked everyone to take extensive notes during the questioning and to watch for telltale body language when a candidate was speaking or listening to a fellow candidate. At lunch we had begun discussing whom we might want from the panel. I was particularly interested to hear what the observant Elizabeth had to say, and she brought to our attention revealing movements and responses that could prove important in making the final cut.

As expected, none of the panelists had indicated support for Metzger's beliefs, but some clearly seemed more sympathetic than others. Now, with forty-five minutes allotted for this final conference to pick the jury, Cat asked everyone to rate each panelist on a scale from one to five and to list the three whom we each would strike.

All of the people of Asian extraction impressed us. We felt they would all abhor the Metzgers' anti-Asian ravings. Miss Nguyen was a Vietnamese boat refugee. She would have particular sympathy for an Ethiopian immigrant murdered in America, we reasoned.

Others on the panel were equally appealing. Mr. Johnson, a fifty-three-year-old program assistant at a local cemetery—the man who believed in "freedom with responsibility"—had also said that he thought that the quality of life in Portland had improved as the city became less segregated. Mr. O'Connor, a thirty-nine-year-old project manager at Intel, had articulately described that side of the line where speech is not protected. One of two professional men on the panel, he seemed foreperson material to me. He looked as if he wanted to be on the jury as much as we wanted him there. Unfortunately, he was not positioned in the first twelve seats. He would move up only if our challenges and those of the Metzgers' opened up the five seats ahead of him.

As we compared our ratings, we realized there were five panelists who troubled us in varying degrees. We all agreed that juror number eight, a large man in his early forties who did not work because of an old football injury, had seemed the most sympathetic to Metzger. The woman in seat four also worried us. When I had read her questionnaire on Monday night, I had thought she might make a good juror; she worked with terminally ill children and contributed to Greenpeace and local police benevolent societies. On the downside, she indicated that she read *Astrology World* regularly. Reliance on the stars was not a quality I coveted in this jury box. During questioning she had revealed herself as a "survivalist," somewhat wary of outsiders. Robert Mathews and others on the radical right had derived significant support from survivalists. Mulugeta Seraw might be considered an "outsider." This woman was too unpredictable for my liking.

After much debate we settled on our third challenge. Juror number ten was a fifty-year-old truck mechanic whose wife worked for the Bureau of Indian Affairs. We had hoped his wife's position had sensitized him to the problems of minorities. Surprisingly, however, when I had asked him if he had ever witnessed discrimination against blacks, he had said no. He was either insensitive or lying.

We assumed the Metzgers would strike the three Asian Americans from the panel. But they surprised us. They challenged Miss Nguyen and Miss Lee, a twenty-three-year-old unemployed photographer who had recently graduated from college. Their third challenge, however, was not Mrs. Wilkinson, a Japanese American grandmother. Instead, they excused Mr. Hall, a thirty-four-year-old white truck driver.

While Hall had seemed attuned with our side philosophically, I was not terribly sad to see him excused. I had asked several panelists if they would be willing to award significant punitive damages if merited. Such damages had the potential to break Metzger financially and to send a message to other merchants of hate. It was important not only to win this case but to win big. Hall, more than any other candidate, had expressed reservations about punitive damages.

Judge Haggerty announced the challenges in the traditional fashion—without indicating which side had excused which panelists. Our jury was set. Three women and nine men, among them Mr. O'Connor, would begin hearing the case the next morning. Under Oregon rules, a party in a civil case does not need to win all twelve votes to prevail in a civil suit. We would have to convince only nine.

I went back to the hotel with my police escort, worked out in the hotel gym with my police escort, showered and changed into a pair of jeans while my police escort waited outside my room, and then went down to the gourmet restaurant in the lobby with Elizabeth, Richard, Cat and Robert, and my police escort.

The trio of armed officers took a table near ours and ordered soft drinks. They were on duty. I selected a bottle of wine for our table. In a sense, I was on duty, too. I was to give one of the most important opening statements in my career in less than twelve hours. I hoped a few glasses of chardonnay and a nice dinner with such dear friends would relax me enough to figure out what to say, for at this moment I honestly had no idea what I was going to tell the jury. "I've been so immersed in this thing for so long that tomorrow seems almost anti-climactic," I confessed after finishing my first glass of wine too quickly. "I can't seem to get psyched."

Elizabeth put her hand on mine and said, "It will come."

Cat nodded. "It always has."

I drank another glass of wine and hoped that they were right.

This case won't be easy to prove because there are many elements that need to be demonstrated in linking the leaders to the acts of their followers.

—Professor Caroline Forrell, University of Oregon Law School, quoted in *The New York Times,*
October 12, 1990

CHAPTER FOURTEEN

October 10, 1990
■
Portland, Oregon

"Ladies and gentlemen, back in November of 1980, Mulugeta Seraw left Addis Ababa on an airplane. . . ." So began the trial that had grown from a single newspaper article clipped by Danny Welch almost two years earlier.

I had stayed up until three in the morning outlining my opening statement, experimenting with several introductions before deciding to begin with Mulugeta. His wrongful death was what had brought us here, not the desire to test some abstract principle about free speech. A murder, a racially motivated murder, had occurred, not merely the distribution of fliers or the delivery of speeches. I wanted the jurors to know this from the outset, wanted the spirit of Mulugeta to inhabit the courtroom until they rendered a verdict.

I told the jury about Mulugeta and his uncle, Engedaw, then moved from our table to the jury box and described the night of the murder. "Mieske took that baseball bat, and he slapped him beside the head, full swing, a swing that had the force that would knock a ball over the center field fence." I lifted my arms and spread my legs as if holding the weapon over the prone Mulugeta. "Mieske stood over him with that bat and hit him with such a force that the doctor will tell you that it took the whole top of his head off." Whoosh! I chopped down with my imaginary bat.

Juror Johnson winced.

I explained that if Mieske and Brewster had not admitted that they killed Mulugeta for racial reasons and if the Portland police had not found some critical evidence, this would have been just another murder case and this jury would not be sitting in Judge Haggerty's courtroom on this day. "But that evidence led a trail right back to this young man, who in the chain of his organization works directly under his father. This young man acting for his father set upon a course of action that led to the murder of my client."

I pointed to John Metzger. He grinned.

We'll see how you're smiling in a few days, you smug little bastard, I thought.

John's father had acquitted himself well during jury selection. He may have shocked some of the jurors, but he had not sounded totally unreasonable. He had painted himself as a separatist, a supremacist, but had insisted he did not encourage violence. He was, he said, a simple businessman exercising his constitutional rights. It was time to pierce this public persona. "Tom Metzger is a pathetic character," I said. "I felt that many of you were having feelings that this man is speaking out on an unpopular cause, and that people have the right to speak out on unpopular causes. *We agree.* But there's more to it than that. There's a private side of this man that you will see in this trial. You're going to hear from David Mazzella."

I looked at Tom out of the corner of my eye to see his reaction to the news that Dave was on our side of the fence. His head snapped back and he swallowed . . . twice.

Mazzella, like so many other impressionable, disaffected kids, had fallen into Metzger's "cult," I continued. "You have to have an enemy to attack, so they picked out a target that was the darkest of the mud people, black people. They also don't like Jews . . . Japanese . . . anybody Asian. . . . And so they begin to brainwash and educate these kids. And Tom calls it 'free speech.' "

Mazzella would testify how Tom instructed him to use random

violence against blacks and Jews. "Tom Metzger told him, 'David, you teach violence 'cause that's what it takes to turn skinheads on.' That's not what Tom Metzger says in public, but that's what he told David Mazzella."

I shook my head, then made eye contact with Mr. O'Connor. He did not look away. I would be directing much of my attention to this potential jury leader.

The evidence would show that the Metzgers had considered Dave their best organizer, had sent him to Portland with fliers and educational tracts to organize the skinheads. Mazzella met with Mieske, I said. "It isn't like IBM sending a salesmen in. It's not like they have an office. They don't check in with the chamber of commerce. They dress up like skinheads and go out on the street and they get a little respect."

How did they get respect? Mazzella, the Metzgers' agent, would explain.

Mr. Johnson's words provided a closing. "One of the jurors summed it up yesterday best: when you talk about free speech, it's freedom with responsibility." I paused, then added, "In America we have the right to hate, but we don't have the right to hurt."

The Metzgers had done a lot of hurting. I asked the jurors to return a large verdict. "One so big that there's going to be a wall ten million dollars high that's going to stop Tom Metzger from coming back into this state, so big it will put him out of business."

John Metzger spoke next. He said he wanted to use his opening statement to explain how he became involved in racial matters. The self-portrait he drew was both chilling and sad.

John had grown up in his father's shadow, a dark shadow occasionally lit by a burning cross. At the age of eight Tom had enrolled him in the Klan Youth Corps. "Nothing wrong with that." John shrugged to the jury. "Never did anything illegal. Just had fun. Went to some meetings. Played out in the grass."

By junior high school, deeply influenced by his father, he had begun to "glimpse the big picture." Fascinated by history, he started questioning what his teachers taught, what was in the books. "Different parts of the Civil War, World War Two, World War One. It just seemed strange," he said, unbuttoning his gray sport coat and moving toward the jury.

John's history teachers told him to be quiet. Tom, however, encouraged him, providing literature that brought the big picture into focus. By ninth grade, John said, his high school "couldn't convert me on the idea of race, because I think it's an insult to the intelligence of everyone here that all races are equal."

Tom was not John's sole mentor. As a freshman, John began communicating with Greg Withrow, who had already formed the White Student Union in Sacramento. "Greg inspired me. . . . I became more concerned about the issue of race. No one was really representing the other side because of the feeling of white guilt."

John created the country's second chapter of the White Student Union at his high school. "I was the one who had the guts to go out and present my ideas," he explained.

While he found peers receptive to his ideas, he had difficulty with the establishment. Fallbrook High School forced the group off campus. After high school, John worked first for Hughes Aircraft, "until they suspiciously laid me off," and then at a nuclear generating site, until "all of a sudden they bumped me off."

Our lawsuit was further evidence of such persecution, he claimed. War Youth did not even have any members. "We use the word 'member' as a fictitious name." Vice president—Mazzella's title—was also "a fictitious name." War Youth was "just a bunch of young kids getting together."

John insisted he had no agents and did not believe in violence. He asked the jury to consider motive. "My life is fine. Why would I just go out and tell somebody fifteen hundred miles away, or tell what they allege as agents of mine, 'Hey, let's get a black man'?"

There was no evidence to link him to the murder, he said. This was an attack on the Constitution and freedom of speech, "harassment because of my beliefs." After urging the jury to be open-minded, he closed by asking a rhetorical question: "Race is very important. If it wasn't, why would Charles Lindbergh be interested in race? All of the various famous people down through history. Jack London, famous author . . ."

And as John spoke, I saw a young blond boy sitting on his father's lap, hearing this nonsense, believing it gospel because daddies are never wrong. Tom Metzger had corrupted the sons and daughters of many men and women. Perhaps that did not bother him. But this was the legacy he would have to live with, win or lose this case: he had made a monster of his son as well.

"I'm Tom Metzger, evil one," Tom deadpanned to the jury. He then presented himself as a model citizen, married to the same woman for twenty-seven years, with five daughters and a son, and a grandchild on the way, proprietor of a small TV repair shop. "Nobody ever sent me to prison. Nobody ever found me guilty of a crime." This was true, although he was currently facing criminal charges stemming from a cross-burning incident in Los Angeles County.

Metzger then described his transition from Republican supporter of Barry Goldwater to John Bircher to radical. "Radicals go to the root of the problem," he explained. Most people, organizations, and political movements wasted time by "talking about problems and wringing their hands" instead of doing something.

Metzger had done something in 1971 when the Internal Revenue Service came to audit his books. "I said, 'No. . . . You're killing this country. You're robbing the people. You got us in Vietnam, and I don't like all my friends coming back in body bags. So I'm not going to pay any more income tax while this war is going on.'" Several older jurors had served in the military. I wondered if Tom's opposition to the war might be as distasteful to these men as his racism.

Metzger claimed that nine IRS agents with guns had visited him. Later, while he was leaving on a family vacation, agents had seized his home. "So I began to hate the very system that we call government. It seemed like about everything they didn't like I was beginning to become interested in."

Soon Metzger was part of a "minuteman-type" group of about fifty that aided San Diego County small businesses targeted by the IRS. These minutemen would form a protective circle around the business establishment, singing songs of protest, and the IRS would usually back off.

Four years later the tax rebel had become a Klansman. "I met a young man named David Duke. Perhaps you have heard his name." Duke, just twenty-five at the time, was already Imperial Wizard of the Knights of the Ku Klux Klan. Metzger was "impressed with his talents . . . his knowledge . . . his youth. . . . He convinced me that for the race, for the nation . . . and all of these problems, maybe we ought to all get together."

In 1978, Metzger and his friends were patrolling the California-Mexico border for illegal aliens. "You've got to understand," he told the jury, "someone who comes across the border has more rights than you." The federal government sued him, he said, but he won the right to continue the patrols as long as he did nothing illegal.

By this time he was "being infiltrated by police officers . . . being followed about everywhere I go. Everything I do is monitored. . . . They wanted any excuse to get Tom Metzger, so I decided to go into politics." After running unsuccessfully for the board of supervisors in San Diego County, he decided to run for Congress in 1980. "I had a lot of issues like immigration," he said. He won the Democratic nomination. "Fifty-five thousand 'agents' went down and pulled the lever for Tom Metzger. I won that primary as a Klansman. I never hide. I'm out in the open with what I am."

Such openness had led to numerous attacks, he claimed. Progressive Labor Party members had attacked him and Duke. Anti-Klan groups had thrown rocks and stones. During his run for Congress, a man jumped up at a Democratic central committee meeting and tried to assassinate him. The man was arrested, but released the next day on his own recognizance, Tom said. "Can you imagine if a skinhead or Klansman . . . would . . . try to pull a gun and kill a candidate for office. It would be world news. That guy would be so far back in the jail, you would have to pump air to him through a hose. . . . You see there seems to be two kinds of law in this country."

Elden leaned over and whispered. "This guy is good. He's charismatic. Look at the jury."

The jurors were indeed spellbound. Mr. Carter, a forty-five-year-old factory worker, had moved up to the edge of his seat. Mr. Reed, a seventy-six-year-old man in ill health, had slumped through much of my opening statement. Now he sat erect.

Motorists passing a terrible traffic accident are also spellbound. "It's early, Elden," I said.

Metzger had "put the Klan to rest" after losing the general election in 1980, and had created in its place the White American Political Association. "We said . . . 'We don't need these oaths . . . these robes. . . . We just need . . . the minds of people.' " This had evolved into White Aryan Resistance. After acknowledging his racial beliefs, Metzger said, he had been able to "sit down with any black person, Asian person, anybody else, and talk." People from all over America, Japan, and Europe came to speak with him about mutual problems, he said, adding that he had met with delegations of blacks who also believed in separation of the races, and he had joined with black separatist Louis Farrakhan to fight for the rights of Native Americans.

Of course, Tom spent more time with skinheads than blacks, Native Americans, and Asians. He insisted, however, he had not organized them. "We heard people saying skins were being organized, but after a short while we found out that's impossible." Skinheads had their own ideas, chose their own leaders, moved around.

"To have people who are youthful and sometimes even undependable and say to them 'We want to change the government and now here is what we want you to do: load your truck with baseball bats and get some steel-toed boots and . . . go to Portland and find a black person or something and kill him and this will be our form of revolution' . . . I think I'm more incensed at the insult to my intelligence than anything else in this case."

Did the jury really believe he could "press buttons and have brainwashed kids in Portland" do his bidding? "It's all nonsense. Sometimes I can barely get somebody around the house to do something."

This levity lasted only briefly. "We'll fight it out right here," he told the jury. "Whatever you decide, fine. It won't make a bit of difference in what I do politically in the future because I live in a little house on a little street. WAR doesn't have a big war chest. If I have to live in a trailer someplace in the hills or in a tent down by the sea, I'm still going to do exactly what I do now."

In my opening statement, I had noted that Metzger had paid homage to the revolutionary, criminal Robert Mathews by naming a trailer/meeting hall in his memory. Now, Metzger looked angrily at me. "And one closing thing," he said, "Robert J. Mathews was one of the finest men this country has ever produced. . . . I don't make judgments. He and his men obviously broke the law, and they paid for it. But I understand why they did it. . . . I'm not ashamed for any man who stands up and fights the system and maybe has to die doing it."

Six policemen led our group down the corridor to a special elevator that took us up to the sixth floor. We moved quickly through a suite of county offices to the conference room that would serve as our dining hall for the entire trial. Our security people and the police had said it would be too dangerous to eat out. Elden's wife, Margie, joined us to provide moral support. Through the conference room's large window we could see Mount Hood.

Elden's secretary, Sally Lane, who helped us tremendously throughout the case by keeping us straight on many of the arcane points of legal practice unique to Oregon, had apparently bought out a local delicatessen. Sandwiches, chips, sodas, and gourmet cookies were piled high on a long table. I hadn't eaten much in the morning. Now, my opening behind me, I ate well.

A discussion of Tom's presentation consumed much of the lunch period. Linda Stringer, who had run a quick errand before joining us, reported that the media and the spectators were surprised how skilled Tom was. Most in our group were, too. I wasn't. Tom had been making speeches, rallying the troops, moderating his own television show, for years. He was a strong communicator.

He was not, however, a lawyer. I suspected that would become obvious when witnesses began taking the stand. Whether his inexperience in the courtroom would work to his disadvantage was not so obvious. Certainly his ability to make proper objections, to exclude evidence that a seasoned trial lawyer might be able to exclude, would be impaired. On the other hand, by representing himself he reinforced his strategy of appearing to be just an ordinary citizen whom the government, the Center, the ADL, and Morris Dees were devoting extraordinary effort to destroy because of his unpopular views. In short, he was the underdog facing not only the two trial lawyers at the table, but that benchful of aides behind the table and the unseen hands of federal, state, and local governments.

In his opening statement he had asked the jury of his peers—common men and women—to put themselves in his shoes. "This is a stacked deck anytime you defend yourself. And I know they say, 'Well, you had the choice. You made your choice.' But if you were sued for ten million dollars, which law firm would you get and pay a hundred grand to defend you, cash up front?"

Jurors often develop great sympathy for underdogs. Elden and I would have to be careful, while prosecuting our case to the fullest, not to appear to embarrass or overwhelm the Metzgers with our abilities or resources. Elden had skillfully prepared the jurors for this during the selection process, asking if they would not be biased against us because Metzger was representing himself, and if they would understand that our client had the right to expect us to put forth our best effort on his behalf. All those he had questioned had said they would understand. Still, I wished Tom did have a lawyer with him in the courtroom. The presence of an attorney would not only reduce sympathy for him but lead to a shorter and better-conducted trial and make our victory (if it came) sweeter.

Was his lack of money the real reason? I don't think so. In our lawsuit in San Diego charging Metzger with fraudulent conveyance of his house to his wife, Jim McElroy had determined that the Metzgers' home was worth at least $125,000. Tom had no mortgage. Our analysis of his bank records showed he had deposited over $8,000 each month in various accounts. He could afford to retain a talented trial lawyer. Indeed, he had found competent lawyers to help him with his pleadings, motions, and briefs.

A large ego, not a small bank account, motivated the director of WAR to defend himself. I think he felt he could beat our team, beat me in particular, just as, in his eyes, he had beaten others with whom he had debated on national talk shows. Victories in the Donald case and other Klan cases had brought notoriety and acclaim to the Center and its lawyers; Metzger wanted to be known as the man who knocked me off my saddle. If he did, his stock would rise even higher, not only with his followers but with other white supremacist leaders. Quite honestly, if he did win, my effectiveness and the Center's would be severely damaged. My ego is not as large as a lot of people think it is, but it's big enough so that I didn't want to be branded as the lawyer who lost to that racist who didn't even have an attorney.

Win or lose, Metzger wanted the spotlight. He did not have the constitution to sit quietly while a lawyer pleaded his case. Because of the tremendous media attention, he could speak to a national audience every time he did the things a lawyer does—jury selection, opening statements, examination and cross-examination, and closing arguments.

Everyone on our team realized that by bringing to light Tom's actions, we were turning a spotlight on him as well. None of us relished giving him greater notoriety and a bigger audience. We felt, however, that if we could expose him for what he truly was, then that audience would appreciate the threat, want nothing to do with it, and fight to stop it.

When Ken Mieske took the stand late in the afternoon on this first day of the trial, we knew much more about him than we had at his deposition. He was born in Seattle in 1964 to an unmarried mother who had already given up one child for adoption. After being shuttled between relatives and friends, he was adopted at the age of two.

His new mother found him slow—behind developmentally and unable to feed himself. When he was four, doctors determined that Mieske was hyperactive and suffered minimal brain dysfunction. They prescribed the drug Ritalin to calm him down.

Life in the new household was not particularly healthy. Mieske reported that he had been physically and verbally abused. At thirteen, he was placed in a group home by his own choice. Two years later he ran away, and in 1982 he ended up in Portland with Cody Wallis, the thirty-two-year-old rock promoter.

Mieske also told Oregon corrections officials that he had started using marijuana at the age of eleven. Eventually he had experimented with cocaine, and he had used amphetamines on a regular basis from

1984 or earlier to 1986. At the time of the murder, he was taking Antabuse. Because this drug causes vomiting and other ills when mixed with alcohol, it is often given to deter those in substance-abuse programs from drinking.

In private conversations with us, Wallis described the Mieske that he first met as tough but charming. "He seemed kind of lost. He wasn't happy." Mieske had long hair and "was into Led Zeppelin." Wallis gave him a place to stay and job in the kitchen of the Crab Bowl restaurant. Mieske was not a good worker. "He was lazy and smoked a lot of pot."*

Wallis was living with a woman at the time, but was "figuring out my own sexuality." Ken was straight, but on the street, where he had lived, words like "gay" or "straight," Wallis said, "weren't cool to use, but if you were tight with somebody, sex wasn't a problem either. That can happen." Mieske called Wallis Uncle Cody.

After a year in Portland, Mieske began to get into the punk scene, becoming a fan of the Sex Pistols and other groups. He started going through a rebellious phase with Wallis, too. The two exchanged blows when Wallis chastised Mieske for failing to return his car on time. "He just flew into a rage that I'd never seen before," Wallis remembered. "I realized he could really get crazy." Wallis suggested Mieske find another place to stay. About this time, Mieske was arrested for cocaine possession.

During this period, Wallis never saw Mieske display any signs of racism. "Ken liked gore, *Nightmare on Elm Street* stuff. He liked music that offended and assaulted you, not physically, just shocked you. But he wasn't a racist."

Only when Mieske was released from prison after his second burglary conviction did Wallis see racist tendencies. "I think he became involved in the Aryan Brotherhood in jail. He was really screwed up when he got out." In the world of rock music, Wallis said, the line between racism and performance art was sometimes difficult to distinguish. "The next thing you could do to thrill everyone was wear Nazi things and talk about killing Jews, and he got into it."

*Wallis never testified at trial. He did, however, speak with us.

Wallis gave Mieske William Shirer's *The Rise and Fall of the Third Reich.* "I thought he'd find it interesting, and see how wrong he was. He found it interesting, all right. He thought it was totally cool, wild, and radical."

Two months before the murder, Mieske was implicated in the stabbing of a security officer at a Safeway store. When the police refused to believe Mieske's denial of involvement, he became hostile and demanded to be taken to jail. Police reported he calmed down only after four or five emotional outbursts.

After hearing of the Safeway incident, Wallis, a former police officer, asked Mieske to meet him for coffee.

"Listen, Ken," he said. "This is way beyond anything you've ever been involved in. If somebody stabs a guy and you're around, you could go to jail for murder."

When Wallis expressed his disgust with Mieske's skinhead friends, Mieske told him his friends were only into white pride and would never hurt any black people. He also indicated that he didn't want to get too involved with the skinheads because they were too radical and crazy.

Wallis saw a ray of hope. "I said, 'Great, Ken. Take Julie [Belec] and leave town, because this is getting out of hand. You are going to get in a fight where someone is hurt bad, and you're going to be blamed.'"

Three weeks later Dave Mazzella arrived in Portland intent on providing direction to loose cannons like Mieske and the others in East Side White Pride. Soon Mulugeta Seraw was indeed hurt bad, and Ken Mieske was blamed.

The Oregon Corrections Division conducted a presentencing investigation after Mieske pleaded guilty to murdering Mulugeta. Advised by his attorney not to answer questions about the crime, Mieske told the examining probation officer, "It was horrible. It shouldn't have happened. I'm not a violent person, and I'm not into hate."

The officer noted that Mieske seemed to be trying to tailor his answers to please her. She then described him as above average intellectually, able to express himself well, "a bright, articulate, even thoughtful young man." He was, she concluded, "typical of individuals who are relatively sensitive, thoughtful, imaginative, and pleasant in their interpersonal style. These people are not very aggressive by nature and exhibit reasonable self-control."

Was the probation officer talking about the same young man who had clubbed Mulugeta to death? She offered a possible explanation for this profile, which she acknowledged was "not typical of individuals who act out in an antisocial manner." Mieske had "obtained an elevation" on a scale called Overcontrolled Hostility. This scale had been derived by comparing inmates who had been convicted of homicide or attempted homicide but who did not have histories of repeated assault with inmates who did have histories of repeatedly aggressive and assaultive behavior. "Data suggest that most people who have been involved in crimes of murder tend to overcontrol their anger for long periods of time until the moment of the murder, when there is an explosion of anger into violence." Was this the true Mieske? A time bomb that had finally exploded?

In her summary the probation officer had written: "Mr. Mieske responded in a cooperative manner, exhibiting a social demeanor. He answered questions candidly." This clearly was not the same person whose deposition I had taken. As Ken Mieske entered Judge Haggerty's courtroom, I had no doubt which version we were going to see. Indeed, if the Mieske I was expecting didn't reveal himself to the jury voluntarily, I planned, to quote Tom Metzger, to push some buttons.

Ken Mieske carried himself like a young power lifter. He strode smugly to the witness stand as if he had a steering wheel built into his torso. His starched white shirt could hide his tattoos but not his ego. The chip on his shoulder had apparently grown as dramatically as the shoulders themselves. Burly and long-haired, he looked as frightening as I had hoped he would. The jury should have no trouble envisioning him destroying a car and then a human being with a baseball bat.

Mieske was our seventh witness of the day, the first whom I would question. Presenting a case is a bit like putting together a puzzle. Elden had begun putting in the pieces by briefly questioning the officers who had conducted the murder investigation, arrested the perpetrators, and seized weapons, literature, and other material while doing so. Ken

Death was our first big piece, an essential link in the chain leading from Tom Metzger's headquarters in Fallbrook to the murder site at Southeast Thirty-first and Pine in Portland.

As a defendant, Mieske had the right to stay in the courtroom for the entire trial and mount a defense with or without counsel. He had, however, chosen to come only for his testimony. He had written to us that he had no interest in attending; he did not want to miss his prison school classes. Apparently he believed that even if he lost, there was nothing we could get from him; he had no money and was already serving a lengthy prison term. It is also possible that the Metzgers asked him to stay out of the courtroom because they didn't think it would look good to the jury if they sat next to their murdering co-defendant for the length of the trial.

Plaintiff's Exhibit 1 had been our key document since long before we filed our lawsuit. If the Portland police had not found the letter from John Metzger to Ken Death, and if Larry Siewart had not told Danny about it, we might not have had the confidence to move forward so aggressively. I began by asking Mieske if he had ever seen the letter.

"I vaguely remember seeing it from the past. You know, I was getting a lot of mail," he explained.

The "candid" Mr. Mieske was already contradicting himself. At his deposition he had claimed that he had never seen the letter. Now, less than two minutes into the examination, I had the opportunity to expose him as a liar bent on protecting the Metzgers. I asked the clerk to provide the witness with a copy of the deposition, then asked Mieske if he wanted to change his previous testimony.

"Well, I vaguely—you know, now that I have thought about it, I did see it, but, you know, I vaguely remember reading it. . . . I've gotten a lot of mail between then and now. So, you know, you can't expect me to remember every letter I read."

"Yes," I said, my disbelief obvious.

"Between here and 1988, *sir*," he snarled.

As I had hoped, he seemed to have little interest in controlling the hostility toward me that had been so evident at the April deposition.

I didn't think for a minute that Mieske's memory had improved. I showed him a copy of the visitation records at his prison. Interestingly, Rick Cooper, Metzger's ally in Portland, had come several times. Just a few weeks before Mieske's deposition, they had visited for two hours. Had Cooper told Mieske that he had talked with Tom about Mieske's being a witness?

No, Mieske said.

Had Cooper told him that John's letter was a major piece of evidence and that he should deny seeing or reading it?

No.

Cooper had also visited Mieske a few weeks before this trial started. Mieske acknowledged that they had discussed the lawsuit at that time. Again, I planted the notion with the jury that Cooper had suggested how Mieske should testify. "Didn't he in fact tell you this time that it was going to look bad if you denied having seen this letter, because your girlfriend, Julie Belec, testified at her deposition that you read it and took it to East Side White Pride and read it?"

No, Mieske insisted. He explained that he had learned what Julie said through the motions and "paperwork" we sent him, not through Cooper. When I reminded him those documents contained no such information, he backtracked.

I pressed forward. "But I thought you just told the jury she said in her deposition that you had gotten this letter and read it and showed it to East Side White Pride."

His face grew red. "You're putting words in my mouth," he snapped.

All the jurors had been leaning forward to hear Mieske. Now, several retreated, repelled, I hoped, by his animus.

From John's letter about Mazzella, I moved to Mazzella himself. Mieske testified that Dave had come directly to his place upon arriving in Portland in early October 1988. He again contradicted his deposition by admitting that he had talked to Tom Metzger on the telephone after Dave had called Fallbrook that very first day.

His answers to my next questions made it clear that he had come to court to save Tom Metzger by destroying Dave Mazzella. He acknowledged that Dave had White Aryan Resistance fliers when he arrived but denied that Dave had come to organize East Side White Pride into a tight-knit skinhead group. Indeed, he said, Dave had come to only one or two meetings of the group during his entire stay in Portland. Although he admitted that Mazzella might have gone to meetings when he was out of town or in jail briefly during this period, Mieske wanted "to make that clear for the record . . . Mazzella didn't organize nothing."

We would get to the murder itself, but before doing so, I wanted to further establish the relationship between Mieske and the Metzgers and Mieske and Mazzella.

Earlier in the day we had introduced into evidence pertinent phone records of Tom and John Metzger, Dave Mazzella, Mieske, and the county jail where Mazzella and Mieske had been held after the murder. Mieske now agreed that he had called Tom from jail shortly after the murder and had also talked with John in the days after the arrest. These were unlisted numbers, I noted. How had Mieske come by them?

Mazzella, he said, had given them to him.

"You and Dave were pretty good buddies, weren't you?"

"Toward the end, yeah. Before this stuff happened."

Good buddy Mazzella had given the Metzgers' literature to East Side White Pride. I handed Mieske a document headed "Clash and Bash" and asked him to read it to the jury. He refused. Judge Haggerty, at my request, instructed him to do so.

Minutes earlier Mieske had testified that he considered black people to be subhuman, "Half ape, half man." The judge had betrayed no emotion. Now, Ken Mieske, high school dropout and prison inmate, looked icily at Ancer Haggerty, law school graduate and judge. "I don't want to read it. Throw me in jail. I don't care." He paused, then said quietly, "I'm not that good a reader in the first place, so—"

I interrupted. "I don't mean to embarrass you. I'm sorry."

And I was sorry for a moment . . . until Mieske the tough guy reemerged. "Oh, I'm not embarrassed," he chuckled.

"I didn't realize that was a problem," I said.

"*You* got a problem. *I'm* not embarrassed."

I read from the document, an Aryan Youth Movement paper:

White students and youths who are fans of both heavy-metal and Punk Rock music are experiencing a phenomenon across the nation. It's called "bashing," a sport in which "hunting parties" of White youth seek out non-White individuals and break their bones, while other White youths go out and confront government officials in several ways. . . . The AYM [Aryan Youth Movement] and WSU [White Student Union] encourage white youths to enjoy their music and to take caution in choosing a "bashing" partner.

Mieske could not recall if Mazzella had read this paper to East Side White Pride members or taught the message. He also did not know whether Mazzella had circulated another Aryan Youth Movement training flier that I now showed the jury:

We feel that the most important project in America today is to create a new wave of Predatory Leaders among Aryan Youth. Our Enemies understand only one message: That of the knife, the gun and the club on the campus or in the streets.

We shall continue to encourage "sporadic incidents" on school campuses and neighborhoods across America while simultaneously rebuilding the hunter-killer instincts in our youth.

"Encourage sporadic incidents." This was exactly what the Metzgers' agent, Dave Mazzella, had done.

Although Mieske could not remember these documents, I noted, the police had found other WAR material on the wall above the bed he shared with Belec. By now the jury did not believe his denials. I showed him and the jury two framed drawings. In one, a WARskins offering, a skinhead wielding a bat or club stared out threateningly under a banner reading: "Join White Aryan Resistance: White Power." In the second, bearing the words "White power. White Aryan Resistance," a skinhead stood with his boot on the chest of a supine black man. For good measure, the skinhead held the long end of a banner with an Iron Cross to the man's throat. Mieske claimed the drawings belonged to Belec.

Judge Haggerty had said we would break for the day at five o'clock. As the hour approached, I wanted to pursue one more line of questions. "Wasn't Mazzella constantly telling you that he was taking orders from Tom and John Metzger as to what he was doing and what he was passing out up here and what he was teaching East Side White Pride?"

"No."

"Well, didn't you consider him just a *toy* or a *tool* of Tom and John Metzger?"

No, Mieske said. Mazzella had come to Portland to escape his girlfriend and the police in California and had then "leeched off of all of us."

The police had given me several pieces of correspondence they had secured with search warrants. I showed Mieske a letter he had written to skinhead Clark Martell in Chicago a few months after the murder. "Did you tell him that 'John and Tom Metzger don't want to believe me about their *toy* Dave Mazzella'? Did you write that?"

"Right," Mieske answered with a so-what shrug.

I told the judge I had no further questions for the day.

The next morning's *Oregonian* described my examination of Mieske as "confrontational, if not hostile." A few people in our party reported that some in the courtroom were surprised that I had come on so strong after delivering my opening statement in a comforting, non-aggressive drawl. "Maybe you should tone it down a little, Morris," said Richard as we discussed the next day's witnesses. I was ready to, anyway. The true Ken Mieske had already revealed himself.

That same Ken Mieske was back on the stand Thursday morning. Less combative, I began by demonstrating that the Metzgers had not disassociated themselves from the murderer once he was arrested. Mieske, when confronted with phone records, acknowledged that his two post-arrest phone conversations with Tom and John had lasted a total of thirty-two minutes—time to discuss much more than the right to remain silent. Mieske also noted that he had written the Metzgers from prison with ambitious plans for organizing skinheads into three hundred units along the West Coast and elsewhere.

I still had to establish that the Seraw murder was racially motivated. We moved to the night of November 12. Mieske said that in the hours before Mulugeta's death, he had been among those passing out literature Mazzella had brought from California. Remarkably, he claimed that he had not bothered to read the material.

I asked who had been standing on the street after the group had been kicked out of Nick Heise's apartment just minutes before the murder. Mieske looked at the judge. "Can we please hold on a minute? . . . Do we have to go over this? I don't really feel like talking about the murder, if that's where he's trying to get at."

"You are required to testify," said Judge Haggerty.

Mieske turned back to me. "Well, I don't see what you are getting at. I mean it's done, and I don't feel like discussing the murder scene."

I ignored him. As I presented Heidi Martinson's and Steve Strasser's story of the confrontation, the account accepted by the police, Mieske disagreed with many of the facts.

He maintained that Kyle Brewster had not referred to the Ethiopians down the street as "niggers," nor had he suggested "messing them over." This version was either "a plot by Martinson and Strasser" or words put into their mouths by the police. He suspected they had changed their stories to escape prosecution.

Mieske said that when the two cars had faced each other bumper to bumper, Mulugeta "had told us to calm down and he walked off to his apartment." After that, as the cars finally began to pass, "[the Ethiopians] were yelling at us and flipping us off, and we were yelling at them and flipping them off." As Patti Copp drove away, Brewster pulled the emergency brake, but only after Antneh and Tesfaye had "stopped their car and jumped out and pulled their coats off and started walking toward our car."

I didn't believe this suggestion that the two Ethiopians were spoiling for a fight. Hadn't Brewster initiated the fight by pulling the emergency brake and getting out and attacking Mulugeta?

"He didn't attack Seraw," insisted Mieske.

Mieske testified that Strasser had followed Brewster out of the car. Then "I said, 'Fuck it,' and so I grabbed the bat and I went to Tesfaye and started beating his car."

"So you went down to that car, and you and Dave Mazzella had discussed clashing and bashing with bats in the East Side White Pride meeting, hadn't you?" I said.

"I don't believe so."

"You didn't think—"

Mieske shrugged. "I'm sure he told us about some of the fiascoes he got down in California and Nevada and whatever."

I showed him pictures of the damage he had done to the car, knocking out the back and side windows, headlights, and taillights.

"Aren't you going to show this? I did that, too," he smiled, proudly pointing to the bumper that had been knocked loose from the car's body.

"When did you go up and hit Mr. Seraw in the head with the bat?"

"When he came down and attacked Kyle."

I lifted my eyebrows and looked at the jury. "Oh, *he* attacked Kyle."

"Yeah." Mulugeta, Mieske said, had grabbed Kyle Brewster from behind and started choking him. Brewster had appeared lifeless and out of breath when Mieske arrived to rescue him.

"So Brewster was unconscious?" I asked.

"Yeah, Kyle was out. He only came to after I hit him in the shoulder with the bat by accident when I swung at Seraw."

"So it was self-defense, is that what you are saying?"

"For Kyle's behalf, yeah."

The second swing had connected with the true target. Mieske said he had hit Mulugeta from the side, knocking him unconscious.

"Isn't it true Mr. Brewster was punching Mulugeta and Mr. Antneh and Mr. Tesfaye had driven off, and you had nothing else to do, so you ran up and hit Mulugeta from the blind side with the bat?"

"No, that's not true."

Julie Belec had told the police otherwise.

"She's lying," Mieske spit out, putting her into the company of Martinson and Strasser.

Mieske denied swinging at Mulugeta on the ground but admitted he and Strasser had kicked him even though he was already unconscious. Why?

"Because everything was happening so fast . . . there was a lot of hostility."

Hadn't Mazzella taught him about kicking people in the head?

"I'm sure he talked about it," said Mieske.

This was an important admission. I paused to let it sink in with the jury. How had he come by the steel-toed boots he used to kick Mulugeta?

He had purchased them from Mike Gagnon, the other skinhead named in John Metzger's introductory letter. Several jurors made notes.

The day after the murder Mieske had spoken with Mazzella. Then he had gone to the beach to burn the bat.

"Why did you do this if it was self-defense?"

"Well, at the time all the media reports were saying it was an unprovoked racial attack. . . . That scared the hell out of us."

I reminded Mieske that in pleading guilty to the murder, he had said to a judge in open court that he had killed Mulugeta Seraw because of his race.

His lawyer had advised him to do so to avoid federal prosecution, Mieske explained. "I didn't want to say that I killed Seraw because of his race, but that was part of the plea."

"So you're telling us that you were lying to the judge?"

"Yeah."

"Well, how are we to believe what you're saying now?"

Mieske ran his hand through his long hair and threw his head back. "It's up to you whether you believe my statements or not."

"The reason you said you killed him for racial reasons was that when you looked up the street and saw him standing on the side of the street and you all said, 'There's a nigger. Let's go get him.' That's the reason you made that plea, wasn't it?"

"I think you should take that back."

I didn't.

I wanted to leave the jury with a final vivid impression of the killer—the lyrics of a song, in his handwriting, found by the police. He refused to read it to the jury. I did.

> *Victims all around me*
> *I feel nothing but hate.*
> *Bashing their brains in*
> *Is my only trade.*

Senseless violence is the only thing I know.
Piles of corpses never ending, watch them grow.
Kill my victims for pleasure and for fun
Beat them over the head. Shoot them with my gun.

Line them up against a wall.
Shoot them. Watch them die.
I love to hear the agony
They vomit scream and cry.

Mulugeta's uncle Engedaw shook his head. I put my hand on his shoulder and sat down.

Twenty-four hours earlier Tom Metzger had told the jury that skinheads are a misunderstood lot. Now his task was to show that Ken Mieske had been misunderstood. He did a surprisingly good job.

"Mr. Mieske," he began, "we're going to slow this down and try to get these answers as clear as we can. . . . Did Tom Metzger ever tell you to get into fights and hurt nonwhites?"

"No, he didn't."

"Did Dave Mazzella say to you that Tom Metzger ordered nonwhites to be physically attacked?"

"No, he didn't."

What about Rick Cooper? Mieske said he had no knowledge that Cooper had any connection to White Aryan Resistance. Rather, he understood that Cooper operated a wholly separate entity, the *National Socialist Vanguard Report.* He believed Cooper visited him in prison to report his side of the story.

Had Mazzella really come to Portland in his capacity as vice president of Aryan Youth Movement? Mieske reiterated that Dave had journeyed north not to organize for the Metzgers but to escape his pregnant wife and his police troubles. When Metzger invoked Dave's past involvement with the KKK, the obliging Mieske testified that Mazzella often discussed his membership in the American Klan, wore his robes in Portland, and "gave everybody applications to join the Klan. . . . He was pushing more on this Klan than WAR."

Whatever Mazzella's affiliation, Metzger argued, he had not exerted any influence over the Portland skinheads. Mieske testified that East Side White Pride was just a group of young people who hung out together. He insisted that Mazzella never had any control over the group. Mazzella and Barrett, he said, had told him they were quitting WAR and wanted to join East Side White Pride. However, the group's members had refused to allow them to join because they didn't know them well enough.

Elden leaned over and whispered, "This is too pat."

I couldn't read the jurors' faces. Could they see that Mieske was doing all he could to convey that Metzger was not involved?

Metzger moved on to the phone call he had received from Mieske after the murder. He argued that he hadn't even known who Mieske was when he called collect. "Didn't you yell into the phone, 'I'm the guy who was in the fight with the Ethiopian'?"

"Right."

Mieske said that when the group met on the afternoon before the murder to make plans to distribute literature, members also vowed to stay out of trouble. "We were sick of all the violence being created. We said, 'Let's just try to avoid fights and quit getting into confrontations with people that run their mouths when we walk by.' We were going to show people we were peaceful."

But what of the fight? Metzger inquired.

"It was spontaneous, a spur-of-the-moment deal," Mieske said with apparent sincerity.

"Do you believe if it had been whites it might have been the same outcome?"

Mieske nodded. "It's usually the way it is. That's the first time we ever got involved with a minority group."

I made a note of this as Metzger continued. "No plan to go out and hunt Ethiopians?" he asked.

"No."

"Dave Mazzella didn't get you all fired up to go out and hunt nonwhites?"

"No, he didn't."

Mieske again explained that with the federal authorities threatening prosecution, his lawyer had persuaded him to plead guilty to state charges and admit the murder was racially motivated. "The pressure got to me. I was sick of the finger being pointed at us like we were evil people and [the Ethiopians] were just innocent people sitting there. . . . I was boxed in."

"And so do you feel you were screwed?" asked Metzger.

"Yeah."

"And you're still being screwed?"

"Yes, I do."

Mieske the victimizer had become Mieske the victim . . . if his testimony was to be believed. Because we had witnesses to add to the doubts created during my earlier questioning, my redirect examination was brief. I wanted to emphasize one important revelation: "You said that this attack on Seraw was the first that you had made on a black person and that East Side White Pride had made on a black person, didn't you?"

Mieske agreed, replacing the polite, calm voice used to answer Metzger with the hostile, biting tone he had used on my direct.

This was a key admission: *Until Mazzella came to Portland and started teaching the Metzgers' ways, there had been no racial attacks.*

One more thing puzzled me. If Mazzella had quit WAR when in Portland, why had Mieske and his fellow skinheads gone out on the night of the murder to distribute Aryan Youth Movement fliers Mazzella gave them?

Mieske clumsily explained that Mazzella wanted to get rid of the papers because they were taking up space in his van.

"Oh, I see," I said skeptically.

"He just didn't want to throw them away."

The order of witnesses is critical in a case such as this. Mieske was an angry, physically imposing murderer with every reason to lie to the jury. Now it was time for the petite young girl who, despite her feelings for Mieske, would, we hoped, tell the jury the truth.*

---

*Although we had not expected Julie Belec to be available for trial, and we had taken her deposition expecting to introduce it into evidence, she testified in person.

With her frizzy blond hair pulled back, Julie Belec looked like a younger version of the actress Carol Kane. She wore white this day—a white blouse, a white jacket and short white skirt, and white stockings. The blue tattoo on her calf was barely visible through her hose. The Iron Cross around her neck was more noticeable. I sensed she was trying to send two different messages. She wanted the jury to think she was an innocent. She wanted Mieske, the Metzgers, and all fellow travelers to know she remained loyal.

Mieske had written to her from prison. In one particularly tortured letter, he had chastised her for cooperating with the police and characterized her as a "filthy fucking liar." But in the next sentence, he had proclaimed his love and promised to forgive her if she forsook the "Fag-Balled Punk Rocker" she was seeing. She could make up for her sins by becoming Mrs. Ken Mieske.

Julie had not accepted the proposal, but at her deposition she had admitted that she continued to love him. Still, she could prove him a liar on several points, most notably with respect to the letter from John Metzger and the murder itself. Had Mieske received the letter? I asked.

"Yes, he did," she said quietly.

"What did he do with it when he received it?"

"He read it, and he showed it to me. . . ."

So far, so good, I thought. Julie was telling the truth instead of trying to protect Mieske or the Metzgers. What about the WAR literature framed on the wall over the bed in her apartment? "Whose property was that?"

"It was mine," she said.

Her answer surprised me. *She wants to go over to the other side. Get her back on track.*

"Didn't you tell me at your deposition that it was also Ken Mieske's?"

"Well, I can't say exactly whose they were, because we both had fliers and we both put them on the wall."

I showed her a third WAR drawing from the wall, which read GET OUT JEW PIG and showed a marksman aiming at the head of a curly-haired, hook-nosed individual.

"That was ours together, I guess," she reluctantly acknowledged.

Her desire to help the defendants was apparent. *Put it in perspective.* Did she still love Mieske?

"Yeah, I do. I have known him for a long time. . . ."

From Mieske to a member of Hitler's inner circle, Rudolf Hess. "Are you a fan of his?"

"Yeah. I have read a lot about him."

And the Metzgers. Did she believe in their teachings?

"Well, I don't know exactly everything that they believe in . . . but I'm sure some of it is similar."

Now we could go on to the murder. Rather than just ask her to describe what happened, I would hold her to her police statement. I reminded her that she had told the police that she had answered their questions truthfully and had indicated there was nothing else she could recall.

"Now," I continued, holding up the statement, "did you tell them at that time that while Kyle Brewster was fighting with Mr. Seraw, Ken came out of his blind side where he couldn't see and hit him over the head?"

"Yes, if it says that I did in there, I did."

"And then you further said, 'Seraw goes down and Ken hits him two more times while he was on the ground'?"

"Yes," she said quietly.

Brewster, she said, was not hanging lifeless when Mieske came to his aid. Instead, he was punching Mulugeta. But she added that Mulugeta had his hands up and was fighting back.

"And then Ken comes up from the back side and slaps him across the head?"

Julie made one last effort to help her love. "Yes, in Kyle's defense."

Metzger's cross-examination was brief. Julie appeared happy to testify that Mieske had never told her that the Metzgers had suggested he make unprovoked attacks and kill people. She also stated that Mazzella had never told her he was sent to Portland to teach anyone to kill people.

Why had someone been killed that night in November? Mieske had insisted that a spur-of-the-moment fight having nothing to do with race had erupted because the Ethiopians were blocking the street. We called our next witness to put that lie to rest.

Heidi Martinson had been nervous all week about testifying. She had made a new start and didn't want to relive her painful past—particularly on television for all in her hometown to see. On the Sunday before the trial, I had asked Cat Bennett to assure her that she could survive this trauma. Then I had spoken with her and her new boyfriend, Goggles Flynt, to pledge that we would do all we could to make the court appearance painless. Accordingly, as Heidi walked hesitantly to the witness stand, giving our table a forlorn look as she passed, Elden told the court that the witness would prefer that her face not be televised. Judge Haggerty ordered the cameraman to focus elsewhere during her testimony.

Elden wisely took Heidi slowly through her actions on the evening of the murder. She seemed to have calmed down a bit when he came to the first critical question. Had Kyle Brewster said anything about seeing a person up the street?

"He indicated that he had seen, as he put it, 'a fucking nigger' up the street. After he said it a couple of times, then we acknowledged it."

Mulugeta was standing outside the car when the vehicle driven by Patti Copp pulled up, Heidi said.

"Was there room to drive around Mr. Antneh's car?"

"Yes, sir."

Instead, she said, Patti's car had stopped, and Brewster had begun yelling, then jumped out and started the fight. Climbing out of the car to find her boyfriend, Steve Strasser, Heidi had seen Mieske down the street. Her description called to mind the movies of Sam Peckinpah, in which death is presented in slow motion, bathed in light that belies its ugliness: "I had seen the back of Ken Mieske's baseball cap on backwards and I knew it was him and the way the light was shining on him I couldn't see anything in front of him, but I saw the bat come back twice. . . . It wasn't like a baseball bat. It was like I could see the tip of it come back into the streetlight." She motioned up and down. "Like this, not side to side."

Elden fractured this luminous, eerie, almost dreamlike sequence. "Like he was chopping wood?"

"Yes, the same sort of motion."

Engedaw leaned back in his chair and sighed deeply.

During the day, Tom Metzger had surprised us by filing his own lawsuit at the courthouse. The two-count complaint named six defendants whom Metzger claimed were jointly liable for the death of Mulugeta Seraw. These six, he argued, should therefore pay his damages if the jury in our case found him liable.

The complaint alleged that Tilahun Antneh and Wondwosen Tesfaye were responsible because they had intentionally blocked Mieske and Brewster from proceeding down the street, "conspired to enter into a street brawl . . . shouted racial epithets . . . challenged Mieske and Brewster to a fight . . . attacked . . . and acted with malice and racial hatred," thereby causing the death of Seraw.

Messrs. Mazzella, Gagnon, Barrett, and Strasser were also responsible, charged the complaint. These four individuals claimed to be "agents" of Tom Metzger. Count 2 stated: "Although this is untrue, this defendant recognizes that injustices can happen in courts, particularly to defendants who hold unpopular views and must appear before biased and incompetent judges. . . ."

Metzger went on to claim that Mazzella, Barrett, Gagnon, and Strasser were hired or retained by the Portland police "as informants or agent provocateurs" and that any action taken by these individuals which led to the damages claimed in our suit against the Metzgers "was taken while these individuals were in the employment or acting as agents of the City of Portland."

In light of the day's testimony, the assertion that Antneh and Tesfaye had precipitated the confrontation seemed ludicrous. More important was the claim that Mazzella and the others were agent provocateurs of the city. In effect Metzger was saying, "I agree that Mazzella provoked Seraw's death. I agree he was acting as somebody's agent. But he wasn't *my* agent. He was Portland's." He had previously made this same assertion in a complaint filed against the city itself three weeks before the trial. We intended to use this. We would be delighted to let the jury hear all the evidence and decide whether Mazzella was working for their fair city or for the Metzgers.

When our trial team gathered after court for Thursday's postmortem, we all agreed that the last two days had gone well. We had engaged the jury by showing the horror of the crime. We had demonstrated that it was racially motivated. We had established that John Metzger had written Mieske about Mazzella and that Mazzella had arrived in Portland and immediately called Tom Metzger. But we still needed to establish that Mazzella, as the Metzgers' agent, had encouraged Mieske and friends to commit racial violence. Our case still hung largely on the testimony of one young man. The time had finally come for Dave Mazzella to take the stand and tell his story.

After dinner, Jim McElroy and I drove to the hotel where Dave was staying. In a small conference room, the three of us prepared for the next morning's testimony.

"Please state your name," I said.

And Dave froze. It took him half a minute to say his name.

"Dave, what did Tom Metzger tell you about . . ."

Again, silence. Then, finally, "Well, I met him, you know, and he made me vice president—"

I interrupted. "Dave, I asked what Tom told you."

All color had drained from our star witness's face. Trembling, he sat before me terrified, his eyes like those of a deer caught in a car's headlights.

"Let's take us a little break," I said.

With our police guard a few yards behind us, we walked silently around the hotel grounds under a starlit sky. When we returned to the conference room, I spoke sternly. "We've come this far together, Dave. You've told me your story casually before without any problems. What's going on here?"

What was going on was ego. Dave was worried about how he was going to look on television. Consequently he had what I can only describe as witness block, the courtroom equivalent of writer's block. The words just wouldn't flow.

Prying those words out one at a time tonight would serve no purpose. "Dave, just get a good night's sleep. I'll come back early in the morning and we'll go over things then."

I returned to my room and reviewed the questions I had prepared for him. I felt like an accompanist practicing for a performance knowing the singer has laryngitis. Still, the review was helpful. I telephoned my singer to inform him I had decided to revise the music. The sequence would be easier for him to follow; the questions would be simpler. "I'm sure it's gonna be all right," I said confidently.

Of course, I wasn't sure. I tried to sleep but couldn't. Elizabeth, awakened by my pacing, mumbled that I should try counting sheep. Instead, I counted other possible witnesses who might rescue our case if Dave bombed.

Michael Barrett? Based on the affidavit that we had filed and my hints, the newspapers had long speculated that we would call Barrett. Both Metzger and Judge Haggerty had indicated that they expected to see him in court. But we had never thought he would make a good witness. We had been content to rely on Mazzella, who knew more and—until this night, at least—spoke better. Danny had tried to locate Barrett before the trial just in case he was needed. The disappointing, but not surprising, news was that he was homeless and had apparently last been seen in a crack house. *Scratch him.*

Pete Gibbons? We had him with us in Portland, but I was hoping not to use him. He could shed some light on the private side of Tom Metzger, testify that Metzger encouraged violence and ran WAR with the hopes of making big money. Pete, however, had left WAR before the murder. In addition, by putting a police informant on the stand we would give credibility to Tom's repeated cry that the authorities were out to get him. Finally, Pete's girlfriend had just left him and he was not in the best emotional condition. *Use only if absolutely necessary.*

Greg Withrow? Through our friends at the ADL, we had made contact with the Metzgers' former associate. He had called us a few days before the trial, and we had brought him to Portland for a last-minute debriefing. He still had an ax to grind with the Metzgers, but that could cut both ways. He might come off as someone willing to convict them at all costs, just as Mieske was willing to save them. Also, his knowledge of their recent affairs was negligible, and he struck me as even less stable than Gibbons. *Scratch him.*

Steve Strasser? A big question mark. As Mazzella's roommate in Portland, he could probably provide a fairly strong link to the Metzgers. But would he? Although he had seemed relatively sympathetic to our case in correspondence, he was clearly reluctant to get involved. He had never returned the affidavit I had sent him. Living in the same prison system with Brewster and other skinheads—a system in which word traveled fast—he was understandably frightened about bringing down Tom Metzger. He wanted to do his time, mind his own business, get out of prison, and start anew without having to look over his shoulder. *Reserve judgment.*

Barrett. Gibbons. Withrow. Strasser. At this point, Dave Mazzella remained our best hope. That frightening thought kept me awake most of the night.

Observers said in the first two days of the trial Metzger had succeeded in getting his main point across: that he and his son are being sued not because of anything they have done, but because of the things they have said.

—*The New York Times,*
October 12, 1990

CHAPTER FIFTEEN

October 12, 1990
■
Portland, Oregon

Tom Metzger stood by the defendants' table sharing a joke with several reporters. He had been cultivating the media all week, holding press conferences at the end of each day's testimony, granting private interviews, exchanging confidences during recesses. There is a fine line separating what a lawyer can and cannot properly tell the press during a jury trial. Since Metzger was pandering to the media, our team had decided not to comment on the proceedings until there was a verdict. We did not want jurors or the public to view us as a countergroup to Metzger and WAR.

I sensed that Tom struck the reporters with whom he was now laughing as a kook, harmless and surprisingly amiable. Addressing jurors rather than skinheads, separated from his technology—the cable TV show, the newspapers, the hate hotlines—he might seem a little like the Wizard of Oz *after* Toto opened his curtain—human and vulnerable. There was no outward indication that he was a hate-monger, much less an advocate of violence. Central casting would not have sent this short, squat man with the cheap suits and cheaper toupee to play the leader of White Aryan Resistance. No, Tom Metzger would have been sent to play a . . . a TV repairman.

Our job today was to show that evil need not look like Ken Mieske.

Could Dave Mazzella convince the jury that Tom and John Metzger had done more than just *say* things?

I had called Dave before breakfast and assured him again that all would be well. There was no need to meet, I said. McElroy would accompany him to the courthouse.

Dave had sounded calmer, and as I was doing my sit-ups in the room, I'd almost convinced myself that the worst was behind us, the "witness block" was over. Two hours later, as I watched Metzger and the press joking in the courtroom, McElroy came up to me and whispered, "Morris, Dave's a basket case."

I looked at my watch. The day's proceedings would start in a few minutes. "Well, he's got about half an hour to stop being a basket case. He's on right after the Hatch deposition."

Tom Metzger laughed loudly. I wondered if he knew the trouble we were in.

After Judge Haggerty explained that Walter Hatch's testimony should be considered just as if he were on the witness stand, we positioned a television monitor in front of the jury box and turned on the videotape of his August deposition. At this point, jurors would see only my brief examination of the *Seattle Times* reporter. If the Metzgers wanted to play their lengthy, tedious cross-examination, they could do so when they put on their defense after we rested.*

A handful of questions and answers made our point that Dave Mazzella was sent by the Metzgers to Portland.

"What, if anything, did John Metzger tell you concerning the organizing of skinheads in Portland, Oregon, by White Aryan Resistance?" I asked.

"I think the newspaper story makes it clear that what he told me was that they had a member of their organization, a Mr. Dave Mazzella, who had gone to Portland to organize skinheads."

Hatch said John had told him that Dave held the position of vice president in his organization. John had also said that he was surprised by the success of the recruiting drive in Portland.

---

*Metzger had agreed to this sequence. He had the right to play the lengthy cross-examination immediately but apparently thought that it would bore the jury and make him look silly.

Had Hatch and John discussed the Seraw murder, which had occurred only three weeks earlier?

Yes, said the reporter. John had suggested that the media had not
given an accurate picture of the killing. If the skinheads had acted in
self-defense, John argued, the death was justified.

Hatch testified that John had also said that he would send WAR
Youth organizers to Seattle, too, if requested.

"Did he tell you whom he would send?"

"Yeah, he said he would send Mazzella or another organizer to
Seattle, if that was requested of him."

Finally, Hatch's article had noted that John had said that skinheads
did not use drugs and did not assault others without provocation.
Hatch confirmed that John had then said: "Skinheads these days are
deadlier than the skinheads of two years ago. They're more disciplined, more kosher, if you will."

Enter the deadly skinhead. Dave Mazzella, erect as a soldier, marched
quickly to the witness stand without looking at the Metzgers or the
thugs behind them. Judge Haggerty's words to Dave reminded me
how courageous this twenty-one-year-old had been to first approach
us with his story and then agree to tell it in court.

"If you testify, you have to understand that any privilege you might
have not to testify against yourself would be waived," advised the
judge. "And since the event involved a homicide, there is no statute of
limitations. . . . I want you to be aware that your testimony could be
used by either the State of Oregon or the U.S. Government if they
chose to bring a criminal matter against you."

Softly, but clearly, Dave told the judge he understood this and
remained willing to testify.

We knew he was willing, but was he able? Before Dave's last-minute
case of nerves, I had planned to let him tell his story as a writer might.
The facts would unfold slowly but surely, building to a dramatic
climax. Now, uncertain how well or how long he would hold up, I was
more than willing to sacrifice drama. The first five questions would be
critical.

Judge Haggerty nodded for me to proceed. I saw Danny cross his
fingers and Mac take a deep breath. Dave slumped in his chair, his
thumbs twitching nervously. He looked uncomfortable in his white

shirt and navy blue tie. When I asked him to state his name, he spoke almost inaudibly. I moved to the stand to place the microphone in front of him, then backed away so the jury could, for better or worse, see him.

Q: In November 1988, Dave, when Mr. Seraw was killed, were you the vice president of WAR's youth division?

A: Yes, I was.

Q: In that capacity, did Tom and John Metzger instruct you to teach skinhead recruits to commit violent acts against blacks and Jews and other minorities?

A: Yes, they did.

Q: Did these instructions include the commission of physical violence?

A: Yes, they did.

Q: Were you sent to Portland by Tom and John Metzger in October 1988 to organize East Side White Pride?

A: Yes, I was.

Q: Now, Dave, while you were in Portland, did you teach and direct East Side White Pride members to commit violent acts against blacks and other minorities in the Portland area?

A: I did, several times.

Boxers need to land a punch or two before they can truly get over their prefight jitters. Witnesses are the same way. With each response, Dave's voice grew stronger and he sat a little higher in his chair. His confidence was returning.

It was understandable that Dave, who as a child had been shuttled among mother, father, and grandparents, none of whom seemed to want him for long, had grown up to crave and need attention. He had received it for a while from the skinheads who had looked up to him as a leader and from the great Tom Metzger himself. He had relished "performing" on national talk shows. Now, he sat before the cameras again. His fears of the previous evening dissipated; his instinct as a performer returned.

The first five questions had been like the true/false section on a test. Now we were coming to the essays. We began with Exhibit 1, the letter from John Metzger to Ken Death. Dave explained that before leaving Portland he had known that John had sent the letter. He also knew that the letter had been shown at a meeting of East Side White Pride, "verifying my position of who I was."

Why had he gone to Portland?

At the Aryan "Reich 'N Roll" Festival in Oklahoma earlier in 1988, the Metzgers had met members of Portland's POWAR, who had told them that "a lot of people in Portland were interested in white supremacy" but that there was conflict with another skinhead group, East Side White Pride. A few months later, both Tom and John had suggested he go to Portland to recruit skinheads—this was one of his major responsibilities as vice president of WAR's youth division. The Metzgers had given him WAR literature to take up north. Later John would send more fliers and newspapers used to recruit and train the Portland skinheads.

Dave reiterated that upon arriving in Portland, he had immediately proceeded to Ken Death's place. From there he had called Tom Metzger. During their five-minute conversation, Tom had told him: "Make sure you guys stay out of trouble, and stay in touch with me."

At first glance Tom's admonition appeared to hurt our case. But Dave explained that he knew from his past dealings with Metzger that "stay out of trouble means basically don't get caught."

We continued the narrative. Dave told the jury the same thing he had told the Portland police shortly after the murder. When he first saw East Side White Pride he was "really depressed."

Why?

A lot of the members were into drugs and had drinking problems, he said. "They were unorganized. They didn't have enough direction." Knowing his connection to the Metzgers, the group had greeted him enthusiastically and "things started moving along."

Dave looked at the jurors as if they were old friends and then matter-of-factly explained, "With skinheads, it's all about respect.

Skinheads will only respect someone who is violent and who will kick some ass." To earn respect, provide direction, to move things along, he had acted quickly.

On his first night in town, Dave and several members of East Side White Pride had gone to Rocky Butte, a popular place in northeast Portland where young people hung out and drank. After announcing, "Hey, there's a nigger," Dave had assaulted a black man. Mike Gagnon, Ken Mieske, and others had joined in the beating.

In light of Mieske's testimony, this was important. I wanted the jury to know who had initiated Mulugeta's killer into the ways of racial violence. "Mr. Mieske testified that he had never attacked a black person. He said he had attacked some white persons before. But after you attacked this black person he followed suit. Is that correct?" I asked.

"Yeah."

Still "hyped up" from the Rocky Butte incident, the skinheads had moved to Laurelhurst Park, just fifteen minutes southeast of the courthouse. There Dave had walked up to another group of people and singled out a young Hispanic man. "I said, 'Why don't you get down on your hands and knees and kiss my boot.' And he kind of hesitated. By that time Ken Mieske was standing by him and saying, 'You had better get down on your hands and knees and kiss some boot.' So the guy got down on his hands and knees and I kicked him in the teeth."

Mrs. Wilkinson, the Japanese American juror, recoiled. I wanted that disgust for Dave to be transferred to, or at least shared with, the man who had pulled the strings. "Had you done this type of thing many times before as an organizer for Tom and John Metzger in other places?"

"Yes," Dave said. So, too, had young people working under him.

Metzger was well aware of these incidents, Dave said. Dave sent him "[newspaper] articles of what happened, like report cards." He had done this, for example, after people he recruited attacked a black woman in San Jose. Metzger apparently gave him high marks, for as the incidents increased, "my position in the organization was moving up."

But did Metzger really sanction such violence?

Yes, Dave said. Metzger had once believed in the political process, but he had abandoned that for a more militant posture when White American Political Association became White Aryan Resistance. I asked him to read a portion of an editorial from Tom's WAR newspaper:

> There is a change, however gradually, from the conservative gibberish, and hobbiests are falling by the wayside. Those that are with us now and who are joining are the white mean machines we have really needed for years. I do not hear the usual crying in the beer halls, only honest casualty reports.

Was Dave trying to generate casualty reports?

Yes, he said. Metzger "wanted people that could act out their part, and that part was kicking ass."

Dave was by no means the only organizer acting out his part. There were many, including Mike Barrett, he said. Each operated in different chapters.

How did Metzger react to the casualty reports? "A lot of times when we did things . . . attacked somebody, I told Tom and he said . . . 'Good job' or something like that. After incidents started happening more often . . . he said, 'Well, don't tell me about it. I don't want to know.' "

Long before sending Dave to Portland, the Metzgers had known of his violent behavior and his arrests for assault. Rather than boot him out of the organization, Tom counseled him to take the Fifth Amendment if arrested. Dave recalled an incident when he and others had been arrested shortly before they had planned to use bats and chains to break up a Martin Luther King Day rally in Fontana, California. Eventually, John Metzger had come, with Dave's father and another WAR member, and bailed him out of jail. Tom had later chided him—not for planning a violent act, but for failing to carry a glove and baseball so that any bats the police saw would have appeared legitimate.

I showed Dave an Aryan Youth Movement newspaper featuring an article that read, in part, "Dave Mazzella has had heavy contact with the skinhead scene, recruiting very good and aggressive youths." Dave was described as Aryan Youth Movement's vice president.

John Metzger was president of Aryan Youth Movement. Tom

Metzger held no official title in the organization. I didn't want the jury to think this let the father off the hook. Who ran Aryan Youth Movement? I asked Dave.

"They tried to fool everybody and make it seem like John controlled it, but it was basically Tom."

I looked over at the Metzgers. John leaned back in his chair, amused, if not smug. Tom leaned forward, attentive, if not concerned. Behind them, Carl Straight gave Dave the evil eye. Elizabeth later told me this went on all day.

We now moved to the hours preceding the murder. At the East Side White Pride meeting on the afternoon of November 12, Dave had talked about setting up phone lines for WAR and passing out the Metzgers' papers. The group had also discussed committing "sporadic . . . random violence . . . physically assaulting minorities." Dave again turned to the jury: "The bottom line is physically assaulting, attacking people, making things happen. I mean things just don't happen by themselves."

Dave described leaving Nick Heise's apartment shortly before the murder. Steve Strasser eventually told him what had happened on the street. Later a "freaked-out" Mieske had called. "I asked what happened and he said, 'Shit, it's just a fucking nigger's dead. That's all it is.' " Engedaw closed his eyes and lowered his head.

Dave testified that he had called Tom Metzger the next day, November 14, to notify him what had happened. Metzger told him to keep his mouth shut and wait and see what transpired. Nervous, he had called John the following day. Based on these conversations, he had told Mieske, Strasser, and other skinheads to remain silent.

Judge Haggerty, impassive throughout Dave's testimony, looked at the clock and announced it was time for the morning recess. The jury left the room. Dave moved from the witness stand to our table. "You were sensational, buddy," I said. "You—"

One of the Metzgers' henchmen slapped a piece of paper into Dave's hand and announced, "You've been served." Dave held the complaint that Metzger had filed the previous day, naming him agent provocateur.

I was furious. You do not serve a person in the courtroom when he is in the middle of his testimony as long as there are other ways to do so. Metzger could have served Dave by registered mail. He could have served him in the hallway after all his testimony was over. This was a blatant act of intimidation. Two thoughts ran through my mind: How could I use this to our advantage, and how could I get back at Metzger for doing this?

When Judge Haggerty called the court to order fifteen minutes later, I set about turning the incident to our advantage. I asked Dave if Metzger or one of his agents had approached him.

"Yes. They tried to sue me. Just tried to slap a lawsuit on me."

I turned to the judge. "I think Mr. Metzger needs sanctions for doing something like this with a witness on the stand," I said angrily. I asked permission to introduce the complaint into evidence so the jury could see that Metzger was alleging that Dave Mazzella was working for their city, not WAR. Judge Haggerty said that he would rule on this later and asked that I move on to other areas.*

We had covered Dave's time in Portland adequately before the recess. I wanted to show how the Metzgers operated, shamelessly appealing to alienated kids.

"It was like a whole different world once I entered Metzger's world," Dave now testified. "I'd walk down the street and I would look at blacks and they all looked like monkeys and I would look at Asians and they looked, you know, disgusting . . . nothing looked real. They looked like bugs. You could step on 'em. These people didn't matter in this world."

I paused to let this telling testimony sink in with the jury. Metzger had clearly borrowed a page from Adolf Hitler. Der Führer calculatedly portrayed the Jews of Germany as subhumans, creatures who could be killed without the qualms that would ordinarily accompany the exterminating of a fellow human being.

Dave said Tom had been "a second father" to him. "I was willing to die for him and his beliefs and for WAR."

---

*When we argued this before the judge later that morning outside the jury's presence, Metzger insisted that he had no intention of intimidating Dave. He explained that this just seemed like the best way to serve Dave because "people sometimes disappear in the night." I again vented my anger. I noted Metzger had said things in his opening statement that he knew were off-limits by previous motion. "He's not a naïve babe in the woods. He brought this document in to intimidate this man." I said the complaint should be introduced because it was relevant to punitive damages because it showed Metzger's unrepentant nature. The judge said he would not allow it into evidence, but I could question Mazzella or Metzger about it and argue about it in my closing argument. That was fine with me.

Their relationship had been close. Dave described visits to the Metzgers' home and Tom's role in his wedding. When he recounted how Metzger had made him prove his wife-to-be was actually white, several jurors frowned. We were stripping away Tom's public front. I couldn't wait to get him on the stand.

Dave told of meetings at Metzger's Mathews Hall, where Metzger wore a small side-arm, Yasser Arafat–style. The WAR director would put imprisoned Order members on a speakerphone to exhort the assembled, most of whom were teenagers. "All of the skins were pretty excited about that," Dave said.

I didn't have too many more questions. To reemphasize that Dave had stayed in touch with the Metzgers from Portland, I showed him an ink drawing of a black man with a bullet in his head. The caption read: NIGGER GET OUT. Dave explained that he had been preparing to send this picture by Nick Heise to the Metzgers for their newspaper when the Portland police arrested him. He had, however, communicated with the Metzgers in other ways from Portland. He had copies of two letters he had sent John.* Phone records that we would introduce into evidence substantiated that he had made numerous calls, too.

We knew Tom would question both Dave's veracity and his motive for testifying. Dave's statement to the Portland police helped our cause immeasurably. Just four days after the murder, long before he met me, long before our lawsuit, Dave had described himself as the Metzgers' "spokesman," and he had told of the assaults at Rocky Butte and Laurelhurst Park.

Talking to the police after you're arrested is very different from voluntarily calling the Anti-Defamation League. I wanted Dave to tell the jury why he had come forward in the summer of 1989, told his story, and agreed to testify.

He took a deep breath before answering. "I didn't feel right about everything I have done in my life. I did a lot of bad things, a lot of evil things, and I wanted to come clean." He knew about the ADL because Tom Metzger frequently mentioned it in his publications.

"Were you made any promises for testifying?" I asked.

"No."

---

*Dave had made copies of much correspondence before sending it.

"Were you given any money?"

"No, I wasn't."

Not wanting to hide anything from the jury, I asked Dave to describe his arrests since he had moved to Oregon in the fall of 1989. The jury was probably wondering whether Dave had been turned on to violence by the Metzgers or was just a young man who was prone to such behavior. I hoped they realized that it really didn't matter. Dave's testimony made it clear that the Metzgers knew he was committing acts of violence, rewarded him for it with a vice presidency, and continued to utilize him as a major recruiter.

One final question to emphasize this. I showed Dave a magazine article published shortly before the murder. Dave had told the interviewer, "Instead of verbally assaulting people, we skinheads physically assault them. We don't take shit. We're like a big stone you can't push."

Q: Did Tom Metzger, you being the vice president of his group, tell you not to make those kinds of statements or not to carry forth those kinds of activities?

A: Not at all.

"Oh, boy." Tom Metzger sounded as if he had just been struck with a pretty good punch . . . and knew it. "Thank you, Morris," he said facetiously. He put his glasses on, then adopted the posture and tone of a teacher confronting a wayward student. "Good afternoon, Mr. Mazzella."

Dave was not intimidated. "How ya' doing, Mr. Metzger."

Violence. Metzger began by asking Dave if they had beaten anybody up after their first meeting on the *A.M. San Francisco* show.

"Nope," Dave said.

"Sounds like you're saying we were beating people up all the time."

"Occasionally."

Occasionally? Metzger held up a letter I'd never seen in which Dave apparently claimed he had beaten up eighty people in his first four days in Portland.

Dave explained that he meant that all the skinheads in his group had combined to beat up something close to that number.

Metzger was incredulous. "Sounds like a real reign of terror, huh?"

"Yes, it was."

I stood up and asked that the letter be introduced into evidence, *for our side.* I wanted the jury to realize that this communication didn't hurt Dave; rather it corroborated his testimony. Somewhat surprised, Metzger said he had no objection.

Wrinkling his brow, the WAR director continued. "And you're saying I taught you how to do these things?"

"Yes."

"Where did I teach you to do these things?"

"At your house."

They quibbled about how many times Dave had visited the house. Dave said about twenty-five times; Metzger said no more than six or eight. They quibbled about where in the house Tom had taught him to hurt and kill. Dave said he had done so everywhere and offered to draw a floor plan.

"Did I teach you in front of my wife?" Metzger wondered, looking to the jury for affirmation that this would be ridiculous.

"Yes. Your wife is involved, too," Dave said. He explained how the Metzgers had encouraged and rewarded violence.

The roles were shifting. Dave was now lecturing Metzger. It reminded me of when my oldest son stood up to me and for the first time didn't back down.

Metzger asked Dave if he had ever seen any skinhead boots, baseball bats, brass knuckles, or knives in the house where he supposedly taught him to do violence.

"It's not what you showed. It's what was said," Dave explained. He reiterated that after he and his companions committed violent acts, Metzger would commend him for "a good job," and that Metzger never told him to cease this violent activity.

Metzger registered surprise that Dave was no longer doing it. "You have turned over a new leaf?"

"Uh-huh."

But hadn't Dave admitted that he had been in several fights since the murder? And wasn't he still involved in the racial movement, organizing skinheads in Medford?

Dave denied he was organizing, but acknowledged he had hung out with racial groups. "Southern Oregon is a racial area . . . you couldn't get around it," he explained.

"You mean you *had* to hang out with these racial people?"

Metzger was scoring some points. Dave's involvement in racial activities on his own after Portland did not negate his activities in Portland on behalf of the Metzgers. This line of questions did, however, raise questions about his credibility . . . until Dave provided a rather poignant explanation. He admitted that he didn't have to spend time with skinheads and other racists. Unfortunately, he had done so in the midst of personal problems—he wasn't getting along with his family and he had lost his job. "It was so easy to go back to what I was," he confessed. "It felt like I had a family when I was sitting around people that thought like I used to think, and so I did it for a while."

Metzger showed Dave the latest issue of his WAR newspaper, directing his attention to a particular drawing. When Dave offered that he no longer subscribed to the tabloid, Metzger retorted, "Naughty, naughty."

Metzger grew serious. Pointing to a stack of papers piled high on his table, he said, "We'll let everything hang out here, Dave." And he meant it. For much of the afternoon, he showed Dave newspaper after newspaper and asked how specific articles, editorials, photographs, and drawings taught him to do violence.

The folly of this line of questioning was evident. It was as if Ken Mieske had defended himself by citing black people whom he had *not* killed. Dave was patient yet quick in responding to this mock First Amendment defense. He acknowledged when a particular offering did not encourage violent behavior, but he also pointed out the subtle ways the Metzgers delivered their message. Example: an article in which Metzger railed about immigration did not encourage violence, but the accompanying illustration dehumanized blacks and Hispanics. "People look and they think that's how they all are like." If you saw enough of these degrading drawings month after month, you began to feel that the minorities depicted were like bugs to be squished—the Hitler legacy.

Metzger showed him a drawing of a Martin Luther King Day parade getting blown up. "Did *you* ever blow up a parade?"

"No," Dave answered, "but I went to a Martin Luther King holiday and got arrested."

The jury was tiring of this. Judge Haggerty had announced they could take notes during the trial. Until this afternoon, almost all had been writing regularly, but with each new article, another juror quietly tucked away pen and paper.

Metzger handed Dave a photograph from his paper that showed Mickey Mouse standing at Disneyland next to a bunch of children giving the Sieg Heil salute. "Did Mickey Mouse teach you to kill people too?"

"No, but it legitimizes what you're preaching. . . . I got involved with you when I was young. Some impressionable person like myself sees something like that—it's just part of your whole plan, Tom. It just legitimizes what you preach is all it does."

As the afternoon wore on, Metzger finally moved from the newspapers to Dave's motive for going to Portland. Hadn't Dave told a reporter in September 1988 that he was thinking of moving to Milwaukee because of better job prospects?

"That's what I told her, but basically I was recruiting people. I wanted to recruit people." He added that because WAR had begun communicating with a skinhead group in Milwaukee, he had thought about going there to organize. Then Tom had phoned and "you guys suggested that I go to Portland."

Metzger asked if this was the same phone call in which "I told you to stick with your wife, take care of your baby, keep your job, and stay."

"No," Dave said, and explained that he was already separated from his wife and didn't have a job.

"Did we give you any money to finance your trip to Portland? Any credit cards?" Metzger asked.

"No. We were talking about self-sacrifice. . . . We recruited people without asking for money. You used to preach to everybody: 'We are not in this for bucks. We do this because we are proud of our race.' "

Metzger pushed Dave to admit that WAR was a loose association of like-minded people, not a formal organization with members. But Dave said that characterizing WAR this way was a front.

"What kind of front?"

"We were talking about public front and private front. In public we say things that are a bunch of half-truths and lies, leading people to believe that we are not violent. And in private we talk about beating people up and hurting people and how to get away with things and stuff like that."

Dave admitted passing out a WAR paper that stated, "We are not violent. We do not believe in illegal activities of violence." Metzger again suggested that he only condoned violence in self-defense. Wasn't it legal to defend yourself if you were attacked on the street without provocation?

Yes, Dave said. But earlier in the day, during my questioning about the assault on the black man at Rocky Butte, Dave had poked a large hole in Metzger's holier-than-thou self-defense argument. Trying to start a fight by calling someone "nigger" or some other epithet was standard WAR operating procedure. Metzger instructed his followers to aggravate people, Dave had explained. "We drive by and say, 'Hey, nigger,' and they get pissed off and flip us off, and we'll go back and kick their ass, and in our minds we feel it's justified because they flipped us off, even though we started it."

This sounded much like Ken Mieske's version of the confrontation with the Ethiopians.

Metzger now asked Dave a question that must have been on most jurors' minds. Had Dave been charged with any criminal offense in connection with Seraw's death?

No.

Had he been named in any civil lawsuit?

No.

"But you were the guy that was supposedly beating up people?"

"But it wasn't my literature. I didn't kill anybody, and I didn't print the material that was passed out."

"But you said you got these people all excited to go out and kill people."

"Yeah, for the organization . . ."

Of course, it shouldn't matter whether Dave had been named a defendant or not. If the jury determined he was the Metzgers' agent and had done what we said, the Metzgers should be held liable. Still, the fact that Dave had somehow escaped criminal and civil charges suggested some kind of deal must have been made. The jury would have to decide if they thought Dave was lying to save his own skin.

As the clock approached five, Metzger returned to the murder. "Did you tell anybody at Nick Heise's, 'Now that the party's over, let's really get down and do it. Go out and find a nonwhite and kill him or hurt him'?"

"No, I didn't."

"So as far as you knew everybody was just going home?"

"Yes . . . but most of the people that day were pumped up from passing out literature and stuff like that."

Had they planned the fight at Heise's?

No, Dave said.

What had they talked about?

Dave said they had played quarters and talked about the movement. Then Heise had drawn the picture of the black getting shot through the head.

I didn't know this. I had never asked Dave *when* Heise had drawn the picture. *Only ten or fifteen minutes before the confrontation with the Ethiopians, a skinhead had succinctly encapsulated the Metzger philosophy as taught by Vice President Mazzella.*

Metzger returned to the newspapers. As he asked Dave to go through the entire stack and single out which ones had incited him to kill, the jurors grew restless. I'd had enough. I objected to going over the same ground we had just been over. Judge Haggerty overruled the objection and the examination of newspapers began anew.

"Anything here that would drive you over the edge?" Metzger asked in reference to one paper.

"None of this drives me over the edge. You just add it together. It's like a puzzle you put together."

Metzger shook his head. "Tom Metzger in his living room, with his wife, John Metzger, little kids, driving you into this feeling that you must go out and kill and hurt nonwhite people or Jews?"

Dave sounded like the brainwashed kid his mother had lost years earlier. "You see, I had to build respect for the movement and that was part of my job."

Judge Haggerty said this would be an appropriate place to stop. I couldn't have agreed more, nor could the jury and the rest in the courtroom. I suspected that the cable television station's ratings had dropped considerably as the day wore on.

The jury was not sequestered. The judge cautioned the jurors not to discuss the case with friends or relatives over the weekend. They were not to listen to radio or television or read any newspaper articles. This is a standard admonition in most cases. I suspect some jurors take it to heart and others do not.

I thought our case was going well enough so that nothing that appeared in the media could do us any damage.

Some forty-eight hours later, after reading a column written by Phil Stanford in the *Oregonian,* I was not nearly so confident.

Justin is a Sharp—that's the non-racist [skinhead] faction. . . . This is Justin's story:

He's sitting in [the Confetti Club] . . . it's about 1 A.M. Saturday morning when this blond guy comes up and sticks out his hand.

"Hey, brother," he says.

"Who are you?" says Justin.

"Dave Mazzella."

Now this is news.

By now, Justin says, he recognizes Mazzella from the TV news. So he decides to ask him some questions. For example: Is he still an Aryan? The guy says "Yeah." In fact, he says, he's been doing some organizing in the Eugene area on behalf of the Klan. . . .

Morris Dees is able to state categorically [that] Mazzella was miles away where Dees says he is being kept under constant watch by his own security people. . . .

So who was it? Will the real Dave Mazzella please stand up?

—Phil Stanford, Portland *Oregonian* columnist,
October 15, 1990

CHAPTER SIXTEEN

October 15, 1990

■

Portland, Oregon

Dave Mazzella had been nowhere near the Confetti Club. He had expressed no desire to go there. Why would he? After testifying against Tom Metzger, he would have been taking his life in his hands to enter one of Portland's most notorious skinhead hangouts. Even if he had been foolish enough to want to stroll down memory lane, we wouldn't have been foolish enough to let him. We had instructed Eddie Ousley, the Center intern who was acting as Dave's bodyguard, not to let Dave leave his hotel room, and he had not.

Still, Phil Stanford's Monday-morning column sent a scare through our camp. On Friday Dave had looked jurors in the eye and told them that his skinhead days were behind him. He had also denied Tom Metzger's allegations that in November 1988 he was, in effect, a free-lance racist, working for the Klan as much as he had been working for WAR. If the jury now determined that Dave was still up to his old tricks and was pushing the Klan, the credibility of his powerful testimony on Friday would be in jeopardy. Since our case depended in large part on this testimony, we had to put out this unexpected fire as quickly as possible.

"I'm sure Tom will try to bring this up during cross-ex," I said to Richard Cohen and Jim McElroy before leaving for the courthouse.

"Objection, relevancy," Richard said.

"Exactly," said Mac. "What difference does it make what Dave was doing two years *after* the murder? He could have shaved his head, tattooed his ass with swastikas, and lockstepped naked down Broadway, and it wouldn't be relevant. Judge Haggerty should not let the jury hear this crap."

"That may be moot," said Richard.

He was right. Yes, the judge had cautioned the jury not to read the newspaper. But, in all likelihood, at least one of the fourteen would have seen it. If that was the case, he or she might very well share the information with fellow jurors. Yes, the column noted that I said that Mazzella was in his room that evening. But a juror could be forgiven for thinking *What else would Dees say?*

"These things never go as smooth as you hope, do they," I said. "One minute it looks like Dave is so nervous he won't be able to say anything. Then he gets to the stand and hits a home run. And now this."

"Never underestimate old Tom Metzger," said McElroy.

Mac had dealt with Metzger on a day-to-day basis. I knew what he was getting at. There were only a few explanations for Justin's account. Justin could have been a Metzger sympathizer who wanted to discredit our star witness and therefore fabricated the story. That seemed unlikely. Stanford had noted that others had also seen the young man claiming to be Mazzella. It was more likely that someone had actually represented himself as Mazzella. We had no information as to whether this impersonator was operating on his own to help Metzger or someone on the Metzger team had put him up to it, but we had our ideas. I suspected that before the day was over, we'd know even more.

About the Confetti Club incident, Stanford had written: "Something fishy is happening here." We saw the first evidence of that when we arrived in the courtroom. Metzger's right-hand thug, Carl Straight, was not his usual self. For some reason he had dyed his hair black. Someone in our group suggested that one of Straight's colleagues might have mistaken Carl's head for a boot and proceeded to use dark polish on it! Or perhaps Straight had done something over the weekend for which he now did not wish to be recognized.

As I contemplated whether Straight could have been party to some Confetti Club chicanery, Judge Haggerty entered the courtroom. Metzger asked that before the jury was brought in, we once again discuss the relevance of charges "filed in another state that these people have been guilty of suborning perjury and possible bribery."

Of course, neither I nor anyone else from the Center had ever been found guilty of such acts. But ever since we had filed our lawsuit, Tom Metzger had attempted to put the spotlight on me, the Center, and the ADL. It was *our* conduct, he alleged, that was unethical, if not illegal. Before the trial, Judge Haggerty had granted our motion to keep out references to the behavior of the Center, the ADL, and myself in other cases. They had nothing to do with this trial, he ruled. Now, Metzger suggested that because Mazzella had met with me in Southern California and elsewhere, "we need to get into that."

Judge Haggerty told Metzger that anything discussed by Mazzella during my direct examination was fair game, but "allegations or accusations that certain witnesses in other jurisdictions and other cases may have been promised something for testifying falsely are not relevant to this case." That should have ended this ploy but it didn't. And Metzger's persistence, if not his adherence to the judge's ruling, would lead to some major problems before the week was over.

We had thought Metzger would immediately launch into the Confetti Club affair when the jury entered. Instead, he waved Dave's statement to the police after the murder in the air and argued that it proved Dave a liar. How? Because Dave had told the police he had been to the Metzger house "a thousand times." Because Dave had said he'd heard the story of the murder repeated "fifty times in five days." Add to this Dave's letter to his friend stating that he had beaten up eighty people during his first few days in Portland and, Metzger said, you had proof that Dave could not be trusted to tell the truth.

Dave's explanation that he had merely been using "figures of speech" seemed quite plausible, and I sat back expecting another boring exchange, but Metzger got back on track and began to score some points. He wondered if Mazzella had admitted committing all those assaults when Detectives Hefley and Nelson had questioned him four days after the murder.

No, Dave said. "I was trying to watch my rear end, too."

"So you didn't come clean?"

"Yes, but not to the full extent. . . . I was caught between spouting the party line and doing what was right."

Metzger scratched his head. "But if you were telling them everything you knew about the Seraw attack, were you my agent then?"

"No. I was trying to do what was right."

"Mr. Mazzella, when you went to the Safeway parking lot a few hours before the murder, did you not tell everyone not to bring weapons downtown the night that you were handing out newspapers?"

Dave acknowledged he had told the skinheads to leave their weapons behind.

"Were you acting as my agent, John's agent, when you said that?" Dave admitted he was.

The police statement provided more ammunition. Metzger noted that Detective Nelson had asked Dave if he had gotten "East Side White Pride straight on the skinhead ways, the way you have been taught by the Metzgers." Dave had responded that "the Metzgers don't teach about the skinhead ways."

Dave remained calm. He looked directly at Metzger and said, "Well, skinheads is a culture, and then *you* direct the culture into violence."

Metzger asked if Dave had told the detectives that he and Mike Barrett had been sent to Portland "for the purpose of training anyone to beat or kill nonwhites or Jews?"

Dave rightly said that he hadn't been asked that question.

But why, if he had turned over a new leaf, hadn't he volunteered that information? Metzger asked.

Dave reiterated that he had still been caught between doing the right thing and remaining loyal to WAR. "You don't just turn the switch off overnight," he explained.

"Because you were brainwashed?"

"Yes. I believe that's what happened, yes."

"In my living room?"

"Your living room. Everywhere. Yes."

Metzger moved on to Dave's motive. "Are you now operating as a paid agent provocateur of any agency of government—federal, local, or state?"

"No, I'm not," Dave said forcefully.

Perhaps, then, he was working for us. "Did you ever receive any money from the Southern Poverty Law Center, Mr. Dees, or anyone connected with his organization?"

"No, I haven't."

Metzger now said he wanted to discuss the night of the murder. Noting that Dave and the skinheads had distributed WAR papers outside the Confetti Club, he asked about the establishment's clientele. When Dave said he had never actually been inside the club, Metzger seized the opening. "Isn't it true that on this very Friday night at twelve o'clock to one o'clock in the morning, you were in the Confetti Club?"

"No."

"And isn't it true that you were recruiting for a Klan group in Eugene, Oregon?"

"No, it's not. I'm under twenty-four-hour watch right now."

Judge Haggerty, who, understandably, had mistakenly thought that Metzger was referring to the night of the murder, now asked, "How would that be relevant?"

Metzger explained: "The relevancy is we will present witnesses that this man, while a star witness—"

I stood up. "Your Honor, I object."

"—was in that club recruiting for the Klan."

This was inappropriate, and Metzger knew it. "He's going to tell the jury something totally irrelevant," I said. "I ask this be heard outside the presence of the jury. This is just a cheap shot."

Judge Haggerty acted decisively. He sustained my objection and added that Metzger would not be allowed to bring in witnesses to testify about Dave's conduct in the last week unless it pertained to specific statements by Dave that had relevance to this trial.

Our "punishment" for successfully shutting off this area of inquiry was an attempt by Metzger to return to the papers he had shown Dave on Friday afternoon. "We want Mr. Mazzella to indicate which articles in the papers incited him to violence or mayhem or murder."

"I thought he already did that," said Judge Haggerty. Bless him.

Metzger asked a few more questions, and then gave the floor to his son. John went over much of the same ground covered by his father. Repeating that he and his father had "limited contact" with Dave, he wondered: "In that short amount of time, we sat you down and thoroughly programmed you to be some kind of violent person?"

Dave was patient. "Like I said, the papers, everything supports everything. When I did acts of violence, I was condoned for it until these attacks became more numerous, and then I was told not to tell you guys about it. . . . Just do it."

John closed with his strongest piece of evidence, a letter Dave had sent to a friend after arriving in Portland. "I'm really glad I made the choice to come here," he had written.

"*You* made the choice," John stated.

"No, I didn't," Dave responded. "I made the choice after I got up here, yeah, that's what I wrote the guy. It was suggested I come up here. When I wrote that, I had made the choice. You guys suggested it, and I said, 'Okay, I'll come here.' "

John moved to an easel by the clerk's desk that held large sheets of paper for our use. "Dave Mazzella," he wrote in large letters with a Magic Marker. "I'm real glad I made the choice to come here."

John nodded to the jury, secure, apparently that he had just destroyed our case.

My redirect examination of Dave was brief. To counter the letter John had just introduced, I asked Dave to look at Exhibit 1 again. The message was clear. John had written Ken Mieske that he was sending his man Dave Mazzella to Portland.

In the Donald trial, we had shown the jury a Klan newspaper that featured a drawing of a black man with a noose around his neck and the caption "All whites should work to give blacks what they deserve." The newspaper had predated the lynching. The position of the man's head in the drawing had been eerily like that of Michael Donald's when he was found hanging on Herndon Avenue. This piece of physical evidence had made a tremendous impact on the jury.

The "NIGGER GET OUT" drawing by Nick Heise that had taken me by surprise on Friday had similar potential. Dave now testified that he had directed Heise to draw the black man with the bullet through his head. They planned to send it to Metzger.

"Approximately how long before the murder was this drawing done?"

"I would say about ten or fifteen minutes."

There remained one last item to clear up. Had Dave been working for the KKK in Portland at the time of the murder? I showed Dave a letter he had written Tom Metzger some time before Mulugeta's death.

Dear Tom,

Well, I've had enough of the American Klan. I've finally gotten the picture. . . . I'm sorry I did not totally listen to you before. . . .

The Metzgers followed my redirect examination with several more questions. Finally, midway through the afternoon, after almost two days on the stand, Dave Mazzella was dismissed. He would return before the trial was over.

I had wanted to repay Metzger for serving Dave with the complaint in the courtroom on Friday. The time had arrived. "I call Carl Straight."

The bodyguard with the newly dyed hair stood up. "I haven't been subpoenaed."

Joe Roy walked over to the bench behind the Metzgers' table. As he handed Straight a subpoena, I said, smiling, "We have one for you."

Dressed in a dark shirt and a blue blazer a few sizes too small, the man known as "Bonecrusher" and "The Enforcer" sauntered to the witness stand.

"Are you an investigator for WAR?" I asked.

"Oh, I investigate things, yeah." He nodded, as if giving me a warning.

"Now, in your role as a WAR associate, is one of your duties to train people like Mr. Mazzella and Mr. Barrett to do violence?"

The cool Mr. Straight accidentally knocked the microphone. "Whoops. Excuse me," he said. Then he answered the question. "I don't train anybody for anything."

I asked for a yes or no answer.

"No," he said.

"Your Honor, at this time I would like to impeach this witness by a prior inconsistent statement. To do so, I would like to show a piece of video."

Straight sat up. "Could I have a drink of water?" he said, bored by the entire proceeding.

Judge Haggerty dismissed the jury so that he could see the video-tape first. We provided the judge and the Metzgers with a transcript.

"That was part of a television show," Tom Metzger said after reading the document. He objected to the videotape: "Prejudicial. Misleading. Irrelevant."

Judge Haggerty overruled the objection. "You can play the tape," he said.

In 1988, Mazzella, Barrett, and Straight had appeared on Morton Downey's talk show. The jury now saw a portion of that program. The tape began with Mazzella introducing himself to the audience as vice president of Aryan Youth Movement. Michael Barrett then identified himself as the leader of WARskins.

Downey now turned to Straight. "All right. You, sir. You with the whole head of hair."

"Oh yeah, I'm Carl Straight, White Aryan Resistance, and I train these people how to break bones and crush skulls."

From the witness stand there came a loud sigh. Carl Straight had been trapped by his own words. "Whoo," he said.

"I have no further questions of this witness."

Tom Metzger's cross-examination was, wisely, brief. After Straight said that he had appeared on the Downey show three or four times, Metzger asked, "And how many times were we coached by Morton Downey to be as wild and crazy as possible to make a good show?"

"Probably every time." Program directors at all talk shows always asked him to be "as wild and woolly as possible," Straight claimed.

Had he ever held organized training sessions to teach anyone how to break bones and skulls?

"No."

Had he ever been arrested for breaking bones and skulls?

"No."

Straight displayed an "I showed them" waltz as he returned to his fellow bodyguards. They smiled and gave him the thumbs up, as out of touch with reality as he was.

We called John Metzger as our next witness. Only weeks before the trial began, we had seriously contemplated dropping John from the lawsuit either before or during the trial. We had thought the jury might feel sorry for him and that we might score points by dismissing him because he was obviously operating under the influence of his father.

When preparing for a trial, I make a list of all potential witnesses and what we hope to elicit from each of them. The list also includes a brief description of every witness, similar to the Cast of Characters page at the beginning of a Russian novel. Dave Mazzella, for example, was "brainwashed teenager, repentant WAR official." Carl Straight was "Metzger's tough-talking aide." I had originally described John as "the misled son to be pitied," but by the time the trial began, "pompous brat" was more apt. He was the kind of kid who hides behind his daddy's coattail, runs out and spits at you, and then scurries back to safety. His smug facial expressions and his evasiveness at his depositions had so alienated me that I had no intention of letting him off the hook.

My initial questions were framed by two newspaper articles that quoted John on the subject of the skinheads. He acknowledged that five months before the murder, in June 1988, he had told *The New York Times,* "I pat myself on the back a little for organizing them. We have been able to influence them and fine-tune their perceptions."

I trusted the jury remembered that during Tom's opening statement and his cross-examination of Mazzella he had argued that the skinheads could not be organized or influenced.

The jury was already aware of the second article. What had John meant, less than three weeks after the killing, when he told *Seattle Times* reporter Walter Hatch, "The skinheads these days are deadlier than the skinheads two years ago"?

Without a script, John was less articulate. "I think they were deadlier, 'deadlier' was the word. Maybe it's too strong of a word. But 'deadlier' to me was they were more effective in combating a lot of the problems they were seeing in their community."

He admitted that he had something to do with this transformation. "Once I got to talk to them and filled in with suggestions . . . I felt they were deadlier. They weren't an easy target anymore." Now, when attacked, they would fight back in self-defense.

Did fighting back in self-defense require exercising any self-restraint? At his deposition a few days before the trial, John had answered yes. Now I showed him something I had held back at the deposition—a transcript of an interview with John played over one of the Aryan Update hotlines. Asked if there was a right to "attack back with everything we have got," John had responded:

Not only every right, every obligation. But you can go ten times further. . . . We are like Viking berserkers. If someone attacks you, they are trying to kill you and they are trying to hurt you, everything you believe in, and when you're doing right or when you're not doing anything and someone attacks you, go for it. Go for gusto. Destroy them. Anything you have to do. Poke their eyeballs out. Beat the hell out of them. Who cares what you have to do. . . . I would rather be tried by twelve than carried by six.

What exactly was a Viking berserker?

"Someone who's not going to take it anymore. They are just tired of being attacked. They defend themselves . . . a lot of them very properly."

"Deadlier" meant self-defense. "Viking berserkers" meant self-defense. What of the Aryan Youth literature Mazzella had taken to Portland that called for creating "a new wave of predatory leaders among youths"?

John explained: "They should go out and install telephone lines or their own newspapers. They should be predators. . . . They shouldn't just sit around at home like quite a few of them have."

Mr. O'Connor's head had been down as he took notes on his yellow legal pad. With this incredible answer, he looked up.

"So that's what 'predators' means?" I asked.

"Everybody I think would take that in their own way," John said, his eyes narrowing. "I know what you're implying, but it's totally implied the other way."

And what was the implication of the article in the Aryan Youth Movement literature about "Clash and Bash"?

John said his predecessor, Greg Withrow, had been responsible for this.

But why had John continued to print it after Withrow departed?

Because, unlike some folks, he would never censor free speech.

In another article John himself had written, "Violence along with intelligence and unity was soon the white man's only avenue of escape from the cesspool of nonwhite hoards."

He explained that this was a fictitious article written in 1988 to imagine the world in 1991.

"It was kind of like *The Turner Diaries,* a recipe of how white people could maintain their identity and destroy and kill nonwhite people," I said, referring to the manifesto for revolution that had inspired Robert Mathews and the Order.

John shook his head. "You're taking it completely out of context."

Of course, if printing newspapers was all John and his father had done, they would not have been defendants in this case. We had to establish how they carried out their philosophy. I returned again to Exhibit 1. John explained he had written the letter to Ken Death and East Side White Pride "to open up communication" and to get the group away from their feud with the other skinhead faction in Portland, POWAR.

What had he meant by writing that East Side White Pride would get "a feel" for how Aryan Youth Movement worked when they met Mazzella and Mike Gagnon?

"Mazzella and Gagnon, you know, had ideas that were similar to mine on race," John responded lamely.

Was Mazzella his vice president when he went to Portland?

"No."

But hadn't he told Walter Hatch after the murder that Dave was v.p.?

No. Hatch, like most media people, was biased against him and was lying.

We wanted to make it clear that the Metzgers had known about Mazzella's propensity for violence before sending him to Portland. John acknowledged he had known about Dave's record of assaults and had even bailed him out of jail after he was arrested carrying weapons in Fontana on Martin Luther King Day.

At his deposition, John had said he agreed with his father's assessment that Mazzella was a "loose cannon." Why then had John failed to warn East Side White Pride of this in his letter of introduction?

John denied that this was a letter of introduction, then looked at the jury and explained, "Obviously I give people a chance." He added that it would also have hurt his [John's] pride, because people looked up to Mazzella.

Exactly! And that was why sending Dave to Portland to recruit made good sense.

John was tripping on his own words. Almost every question I had asked him was precipitated by something he had said or written. Now I showed him a letter composed by him and his father that said WAR had enjoyed a "very successful year in 1988." John acknowledged success was measured in part by increased donations via the mail.

In his opening statement, John had asked rhetorically why he would have wanted to be involved in the murder of a black man fifteen hundred miles away.

"When you get a lot of attention nationally about your activities, your mail increases. Is that right?" I asked.

Yes.

Did he solicit money frequently?

"Probably not quite near as many requests as your organization does."

Judge Haggerty quickly sustained my objection to this improper response.

John knew what I was getting at. The Metzgers made a pretty nice living off their hate business, and the murder in Portland had elicited a great deal of free publicity.

When Tom Metzger asked John if he owned a baseball bat, I thought: *He needs one, with all the softballs Daddy is throwing him.* No, he didn't own a bat. No, he had never been arrested for violent activity. Yes, he published a newspaper and helped produce a cable show, as was his right.

After several more lobs, Tom finally tried to rebut some of the points established during my examination. Referring to the letter to Ken Death sarcastically as "the great document," father noted that it was not illegal. Son agreed.

What had John meant in the letter when he described Aryan Youth Movement as "militant"? Tom answered for him. Didn't that mean "We want to be right out in the open and the hell with it"? Again John agreed.

More softballs about John's Spartan life-style—he didn't have a fancy apartment or new car—and Tom was done.

It was noon. Judge Haggerty said we would break until one-thirty. That was fine with me. I wanted a little more time to prepare some hardballs for my next witness: Tom Metzger himself.

DEES: Tell the jury who you would consider "mud people."

METZGER: You could use mud. You could use Third World. You can use any term you want.

DEES: Well, would a Jewish person be mud?

METZGER: Some of them would be even a little worse than that.

—Examination of Tom Metzger,
October 16, 1990

CHAPTER SEVENTEEN

October 16, 1990

■

Portland, Oregon

For months Tom Metzger had been telling anyone who would listen that the Anti-Defamation League, the Southern Poverty Law Center, and Morris Dees were involved in a conspiracy to bring him down and would use all their resources to do so. I don't think he had any idea how good those resources were, how thorough our investigation had been. By the time he finally took the witness stand on Tuesday afternoon, I had read literally everything he had ever written or published from cover to cover, had read transcripts of every message he had sent out over his hotline, and had watched videotapes of his "Race and Reason" shows. Having done so much homework, I was probably more familiar with his words than he was.

Metzger had told the jury that he was going to let it all hang out, that he had nothing to hide. There was not, as we "conspirators" alleged, a secret side to him and his organization. We'd see how open and honest he was. After asking a few harmless questions about where he lived and operated his business, I went for the quick kill.

Q: Mr. Metzger, have you ever told or suggested to skinheads that they should use violence?

A: No, I haven't, unless it was in self-defense.

Q: So you have never told them that they maybe ought to kick a little ass then unless it was in self-defense?

A: In self-defense.

I turned to Judge Haggerty and asked for permission to play a videotape to impeach Metzger's testimony.

Unbeknownst to the defendants, Danny Welch had obtained a somewhat grainy tape from the Aryan Fest held in Oklahoma a few months before the Seraw murder. The jury, who had been through this exercise before when we impeached "Bonecrusher" Straight, looked anxiously at the monitor. There they saw a casually dressed Tom Metzger, microphone in hand, interviewing young skinheads.

Tom Metzger: What should they do when they wake up?

Skinhead 1: Become a skinhead, quit drugs . . .

Tom Metzger: Quit drugs.

Skinhead 1: . . . get pride in their race, get pride in themselves.

Tom Metzger: Maybe kick some ass once in a while.

Skinhead 2: Yeah.

Tom Metzger: You ever do that?

Skinhead 3: Oh, on occasion. You need to react every now and again, I guess.

Tom Metzger: How about over here?

Skinhead 4: Oh yeah.

Tom Metzger: Oh, every day probably, huh?

When the tape was over, several jurors picked up their notepads and began writing. Metzger, dressed in a gray three-piece suit, pushed his glasses up and sat back ready for the next salvo. It came as quickly as the first.

At that same Aryan Fest had he made a speech to the assembled skinheads and others, in which he said: "Do you know why Jews are afraid of skinheads? Because the skinheads kick ass."

Metzger explained he had been referring to acting in self-defense.

The entire speech had been reprinted in one of the WAR tabloids. I asked him to look over the paper and point out where he mentioned anything about self-defense.

There was no such mention, he acknowledged after a painfully long pause. "And the reason for that is that I had spent hours and hours with these young people . . . before I ever made the speech, and they were all instructed on obeying the law and not getting your ass in jail because it didn't help the movement." He added that while he had not said anything about self-defense in the speech, he had "not called for imminent violence either."

We'd get to that. I showed him the WAR newspaper in which he'd referred to "the white mean machines now joining the movement."

Yes, he said, skinheads were part of this group.

And what were the "honest casualty reports" mentioned in the same issue?

"Coupled with 'mean machine,' 'casualty reports' means: we win and the opposition loses. People like you get defeated. People like us win."

The text adjacent to the call for casualty reports had not chronicled courtroom victories over people like me. Instead, Metzger had reprinted a newspaper article describing numerous attacks and killings by skinheads from coast to coast. He shrugged these off. Skinheads were no different from people in any other group. Some among them committed crimes and killed, "just like Republicans, Democrats, Catholics, Baptists . . ."

Our Klanwatch division, which collects information on numerous hate groups, had long monitored Metzger's telephone hotlines, taping each day's offering. Now we played a tape that featured reports about other violent crimes allegedly committed by skinheads. Why had he broadcast this information?

Skinheads were getting a bad rap, he explained. They couldn't get good lawyers. "Many times they're innocent. . . . I like to tell other young people that that's the case."

I didn't believe this. "Isn't it a fact that violence committed by skinheads goes hand in glove with your recruiting skinheads to join up with your group?"

Metzger sat up. "That's not true," he insisted. "I tell people not to break the law and use violence unless you're being attacked."

How, then, did he explain his hotline message about skinheads he believed had been railroaded in Milwaukee? Again, we played the tape. "Is the message this," Metzger inquired on the recording, "that if you are going to get ridiculous sentences for minor offenses or protecting yourself, then why not go all the way and hurt them bad? Maybe you've got nothing left to lose."

Metzger turned to the jury. "If you can't depend on the law anymore for any rights at all, what chance have you got? That's what I was saying."

I was getting angry now. "So you just take the law in your own hands, and in the case of Mr. Seraw, if you happen to meet a black in the street, to quote your son: you'd rather be tried by twelve than carried by six?"

"That's a totally different situation."

I looked at Juror Johnson. "Is it?"

I asked Metzger if he had done an investigation of the Seraw killing before the lawsuit was filed.

He said he had tried but had been hampered because he could not afford to buy the police reports.

"Well, didn't you put on your tape, for the other skinheads to listen to, that Mr. Mieske did a civic duty to kill Seraw?"

"I don't recall any such statement."

Again, we were more familiar with Metzger's words than he was. We played the tape.

There was a point to all of this besides showing Metzger to be a liar. I summarized what we had heard over the last hour. "Now you tell them they got to kick a little ass. Then you make a speech and say, 'The skinheads kick ass. The Jews are afraid of them.' And then they hear you saying, 'Don't get mad. Get even.' Do you think they might put that together and think that Tom Metzger may think they ought to do some violence?"

Metzger threw up his hands. "Well, since the entire public listens to my phone messages, I guess everybody is going to run out and kick ass every time Tom Metzger says something from Fallbrook."

"I see." I turned my back and walked casually back to my table.

"You give me a lot more credit than I deserve."

I played one final tape, the recorded message from WAR's hotline that precedes Chapter 1. Metzger had interviewed Rick Cooper, who was now sitting behind John Metzger. After hearing Cooper talk about the growing number of skinheads moving up to Portland, Metzger had responded: "It all sounds great, Rick. . . . And, unofficially, the fights and attacks against the race-mixers and some of the race traitors and the racial scum has been picking up because of the new warriors moving into the area." He had then sounded a note as ominous as it was prophetic: "But I'm sure there will be more on that later. When it comes out, it will be all at once." Three weeks later the Portland skinheads had killed Mulugeta Seraw.

Who were the new warriors who had moved to Portland? Barrett? Mazzella? "Mr. Metzger, there's no doubt in your mind, is there, that Dave Mazzella was your agent sent up here as vice president of the youth section of your organization to organize this town?"

Metzger shook his head. "No," he said emphatically. "I don't send anybody anyplace."

The answer provided the perfect opportunity to bring up Metzger's lawsuits in which he claimed that Mazzella had been hired by the Portland police as an agent provocateur. "Wouldn't it be to your financial disadvantage to admit the obvious, that Mazzella was your agent, because if you admitted that, you'd lose your ten-million-dollar claim against the city of Portland?"

Yes, he admitted.

Metzger said he understood that an agent provocateur is someone who provokes somebody, kills somebody. Now for the critical query: "You're not questioning whether Mazzella provoked Mieske and Brewster to kill Seraw. You just said he did it as the agent of the city of Portland. Is that correct?"

"That may be possible, and we're going to see about it as the time rolls on. Another civil trial, Mr. Dees."

Fine. The jury could decide whose agent Mazzella was—Metzger's, or theirs, as citizens of Portland.

At the afternoon recess, our trial team marveled at how slow Metzger had been to pick up on our strategy. Time after time, he had denied making a particular statement or writing a particular article, only to be caught in a lie when we pulled out a videotape, hotline recording, or newspaper. Metzger's people must have finally alerted him to this during the break. He was considerably more cautious the rest of the afternoon.

"Mr. Metzger," I began when the trial resumed, "have you been with skinheads where weapon training took place or shooting of guns or anything of that nature?"

I could imagine him thinking *What are you going to show me now?* "Probably," he sighed.

He was damned if he did, damned if he didn't. I reminded him that at his deposition he had said he didn't recall any such meetings.

Over the next few minutes, I showed him nine different photographs of himself and John and others engaged in training with AK-47 assault rifles. My personal favorite featured a young armed skinhead with a Confederate flag tattooed on his neck.

Our friends at the ADL had obtained these photos, taken in the desert outside Phoenix. Our information was that the Metzgers had been training with a skinhead group called Arizona White Battalion. Metzger, however, insisted, he had just gone out for a friendly day of shooting cans as the guest of a WAR associate named George Miller. Skinheads had participated, but so had survivalists, a middle-aged bookseller, and others. The guns were not his.

But he did have pistols. I showed him a photograph taken at Mathews Hall. Metzger was holding up a .45 handgun. Rather than deny my summary of what he told those gathered, he said he wasn't sure what he had said. We played the tape, which we had purchased thanks to an advertisement in the WAR newspaper. "Learn a few things about this and don't worship, like the conservatives, a piece of paper [the U.S. Constitution]. A piece of paper won't save you, but this can." At this point Metzger raised the pistol in the air, then continued, "And it can convince a lot of your enemies to do right, too. Let them conform to our law."

Pistols can convince some people; guerrilla warfare carried out with explosives can convince a whole lot more. "Do you make available to

skinheads any kind of training information on how to make explosives?"

I could not have asked this question two weeks earlier. We'd had no
idea the Metzgers were selling U.S. military training manuals until I'd
stumbled upon an advertisement in the latest WAR newspaper while
flying back to Portland from John's October 4 deposition. One of our
private security guards in Portland, Larry Gibson, had some local
military contacts, and within twenty-four hours he was able to secure
the same manuals the Metzgers were selling. Joe Roy then took them
to a local photo enlarger who helped prepare our exhibits, and by the
time the trial started we had blowups of how to blow up a city.

The material was frightening. Here was instruction on everything
from how to make bombs in cans and bottles to how to destroy
highways with fifty-pound charges. One page taught the "Demolition
of a Superstructure." I tried to personalize this for the jury. "Is that
something like the Morrison Bridge that crosses the river?" I asked,
referring to the bridge less than a mile from the courthouse.

Metzger said he didn't know. He said he had never sold any of the
manuals, had never even read them, and had certainly not tried to
demolish anything. "If I tried something like that, I would blow
myself up," he said, laughing.

In his opening statement, Metzger had described Robert Mathews
as a patriot who tried to live within the system but had been chased
by the IRS and then finally snapped and became involved in guerrilla
underground activities. "Is that what you're doing now?" I asked.

"Well, if I'm a guerrilla, you would know it. But I'm not."

Metzger had shown Mazzella a seemingly endless series of carefully
selected articles from the WAR newspaper. We, too, had a number of
articles and drawings we wanted the jury to see. I handed them one by
one to Metzger and asked him to describe the picture and then read
the text. Then I passed them to the jury box.

One drawing featured a nasty caricature of a black man confronting
a white man. Metzger read the black man's lines with an exaggerated,
stereotypical delivery: "Well, look at this shit. A mother-fucking skinhead. Look here, boy. I got something you can skin. Why don't you
skin my motherfucking ass?"

In the next frame, the white man responds, "As you wish, melon
breath," and skins him with a knife.

"Do you have drawings that you show these skinheads that depict the black person as less intelligent, for example, or being basically criminals or baboons?" I wanted to remind the jury of Mazzella's testimony that Metzger had constantly demeaned and dehumanized his enemies to remove any scruples that people might have about doing violence to them.

"Yeah, certain black people . . . not the entire race . . . I can take you out here in Portland and find you some people that act just like that and look just like that."

Judge Haggerty remained as inscrutable as he had been since the first day.

The "Coon, coon, black baboon" drawing was perhaps the most dehumanizing of all. At the bottom of the drawing was the warning: "He's coming to a neighborhood near you unless you take steps to prevent it right now." Metzger explained the drawing: "It means that type of Negro may be taking over your neighborhood, gonna rape your wife and kids and loot your house."

"Is that kind of like Mr. Seraw?" I asked.

"Doesn't mean every black. Has nothing to do with Mr. Seraw."

But hadn't Metzger suggested that Seraw had a criminal record and that Mieske had done a civic duty killing him?

Metzger frowned. "Mr. Dees, seven percent of the people in this town commit fifty-seven percent of the crime, and they happen to be black. And that's a fact."

Another drawing showed a side view of a black man's brain under the heading "Let's answer the scientific question. What's on a nigger's mind?" Large sections of the brain were captioned *crave for watermelon; crave for drugs, alcohol, pussy, gold chains, and drumbeat;* and *criminal behavior.* A tiny section labeled *responsibility, vocal skills, intelligence, hygiene, logic, proportion,* and *creative skills* carried the parenthetical explanation "must be viewed through microscope."

Metzger said he thought the drawing was funny. Then he stated, "I can take you within a mile of here and find someone who acts just like that and happens to be black." He added that he knew white people like that, too.

Did he ever portray them in his publications?

"I have attacked white people quite a bit," he said, then stared coldly at me. "In fact, some of my worst enemies are white people like you."

We had no illusions that these drawings made the Metzgers liable for Mulugeta's death. We had never argued that they did. "You have the right to hate," we had acknowledged at the trial's outset. Still, the drawings were important, for as the U.S. Supreme Court had ruled in 1982, a defendant's speech can be taken as evidence that he or she "gave specific instructions to carry out violent acts or threats." The drawings were relevant because they supported Mazzella's claim that the Metzgers had sent him to Portland to organize East Side White Pride to wreak havoc.

Metzger had published these drawings for everyone to see. I wanted to move behind the closed doors of his organization now. WAR infiltrator Pete Gibbons had told us that Metzger sometimes hooked recruits to a lie detector. We had touched on this briefly with John Metzger, who had insisted that he had never seen his father conduct a full session on what they called "the box." Judge Haggerty had overruled Metzger's objection to my questions.

I returned to the topic. "There's no such thing as a lie detector," Metzger explained. He said he had used "stress evaluators." He had "hooked up two or three young fellows," taking them down to his basement and putting rings connected to wires on their fingers.

Did Metzger designate those who passed his stress test as "special operatives" and then send them around the country? He had mentioned these "special ops" several times on his hotline.

Metzger smiled. "A couple of times I have referred to them on the telephone, to make you upset more than anything else, because I know you're listening."

Judge Haggerty sustained my objection.

It was almost time to adjourn. I wanted to finish with Metzger by day's end. Returning once more to Mazzella, I asked if Metzger had known about the young man's violent tendencies. Yes, he said.

Had he encouraged Mazzella to take a van full of skinheads and baseball bats to the Martin Luther King Day rally in Fontana?

No, he had explicitly discouraged him from attending and had chewed him out after his arrest for being stupid.

But on his hotline he had portrayed Mazzella as a victim.

"No matter what publicly I said so we didn't look so bad, I gave him holy hell," Metzger insisted.

I jumped on the answer. "So you got a public and private side? You said—"

He interrupted me. "No, no, no, no, no."

Why had Metzger talked to Mazzella on so many occasions after he allegedly became disenchanted with the skinhead? They had communicated while Dave was in Portland both before and after the murder.

"It wouldn't be the first person that I wasn't entirely happy with who called me on the telephone," he explained.

Mazzella had also written him with recruiting plans after the Portland police released him from jail following the murder. Metzger said that by that time he was through with Dave.

Because he had snitched?

"I found out he was unreliable. The same way you'll find out he's unreliable." He smiled as if to suggest something was afoot.

There was one last area to cover—financial records. We hoped these would remove any sympathy the jury might have for the Metzgers by demonstrating that Tom conducted his hate business for personal gain. It's one thing to encourage young people to hate out of some sense of duty, but quite another to line your pockets at the expense of ruined lives.

Although he portrayed himself as a humble TV repairman, Metzger appeared to be making a comfortable living from WAR. Bank records showed he deposited almost $100,000 a year into his two bank accounts, one personal, one for WAR business. Less than 20 percent of these deposits were cash, but John Metzger had earlier testified that at least 70 percent of WAR's proceeds came in that form.

Metzger said he commingled the funds in the two accounts. Sometimes he paid personal expenses out of the WAR account. Indeed, he had paid his old nemesis, the IRS, about $4,200 from the WAR account.

I showed him the bank statements we had subpoenaed. In the WAR account, there were records of two checks totaling $260 paid to Oasis Hair Styling. These were for barber services, Metzger said.

Is that a personal expense? I asked. "Is this some hairstyle that you had so you would look better for WAR?"

"Probably." After a few more questions on this subject, he looked at me impatiently. "I bought a hairpiece. You know a lot of people here could use one. I got one."

"Yes."

Metzger had paid doctor bills from the WAR account and had deposited WAR money in his personal account as well. "It went back and forth like that sometimes," he said. "It's all mine."

The director of WAR grew increasingly restless with these questions. "You admitted this could be introduced into evidence? Did you agree?" I asked.

"Might as well," he said. "It will all be turned over to the feds anyhow, won't it?"

"No further questions."

I didn't know if the IRS would be interested in his financial dealings. Maybe another audit, some twenty years after the one that had turned him against the government, would do what we would not be able to do here, even if we won—put Tom Metzger behind bars.

I slept well for a change. The FBI had just arrested forty-four-year-old Mark Sommes in San Diego for mailing the threatening letter to me after the federal courthouse bombing in September. More important, the Dees/Metzger confrontation, which had been building ever since we had filed suit, had gone well. Thanks to all those who had helped prepare materials for the examination of Tom Metzger, we had stayed one step ahead of him all day. We had revealed a disgusting public side and a sinister private side that, we all believed, went a long way toward proving him guilty.

---■---

I think the hate crime law is a clear statement as to what the people in Oregon will tolerate and what they won't. They tolerate diversity, Mr. Metzger.

—Multnomah County District Attorney Michael Schrunk,
cross-examined by Tom Metzger,
October 17, 1990

CHAPTER EIGHTEEN

October 17, 1990
■
Portland, Oregon

"Mr. Metzger, Mr. Dees interviewed you at length yesterday on your two bank accounts."

The person cross-examining Tom Metzger on this Wednesday morning was . . . Tom Metzger. Yellow tablet of questions (and presumably answers) in hand, Tom was wearing the dual toupees of lawyer and client.

Metzger's appearance on the witness stand brought to mind a story of another self-interrogation. Some years ago a well-known Chicago trial lawyer named Max Wildman represented himself in a minor case arising out of a traffic accident. Like Metzger, Wildman asked himself a series of questions. "State your name." "Max Wildman." "State your address." He answered again. "State your occupation." "Attorney."

Whereupon the playful lawyer interrupted himself and said, "Mr. Wildman, would you please speak a little louder. I'm having a hard time hearing you."

Metzger apparently had no trouble hearing his questions on a variety of subjects covered during direct examination.

On the subject of commingling funds in his two bank accounts, he explained that he carried only one of his checkbooks to work. Sometimes he would have the wrong checkbook, but he would always straighten things out at the end of the day. "Nothing sinister," he said.

On the subject of firing a gun in the Arizona desert, he said he was not a gun enthusiast and had very few weapons, all legal, primarily for home defense. He had taken target practice only a few times during the year the Arizona pictures were taken.

He added that the photos we had shown of his private activity demonstrated he was under constant watch even though his activity was legal. "Everything that Mr. Dees and his friends are doing underlines the fact that there's almost no such thing as privacy anymore."

He insisted that he had not trained skinheads or other people for violence. "I wouldn't even know how to train them," he said, adding that it would not be illegal to educate people in self-defense. He had not trained people in weapons demolition or guerrilla tactics, either. The military manuals that he had just begun selling in the WAR newspaper were available from several sources other than his organization.

What about the drawings in his newspaper? These were protected by the First Amendment. "I don't ask the government what I'll print. Never have. Never will."

We also learned that he had once been a member of the NAACP and that his family, supposedly, lived on a budget of $1,200 per month.

I was impressed with one question and answer.

Q: Mr. Metzger, are your primary weapons ideas?

A: Yes. That's all I have ever used, the art of changing people's minds and putting ideas in their heads through legitimate means—television, newspapers, telephone machines, fax machines, any legal way that anyone else does the same thing.

The man who answered this was for a moment the same almost-reasonable-sounding individual he had been when introducing himself to the jurors ten days earlier. But when cross-examined a few minutes later by his son on the same theme, he sounded an ominous note. "When we're stopped from publishing a newspaper, stopped from putting out TV shows, when we're stopped from having phone machines, I've been very clear about it—at that point all bets are off, and I can't tell you what I might do then."

Metzger had been foolish to allege that Dave Mazzella was the city of Portland's agent. We felt confident that Mazzella's testimony and the other evidence we had presented demonstrated that Dave was clearly working for the Metzgers and WAR. Elden's concise, skillful examination of the next two witnesses served to eliminate any doubts, except perhaps those in the minds of conspiracy theorists. Both Portland Chief of Police Richard Walker and Multnomah County District Attorney Michael Schrunk took the stand and swore that Mazzella was not their agent, that he had never been in their employ, and that their respective agencies had never conspired with me and the Center to bribe Mazzella to participate in this lawsuit.

District Attorney Schrunk was particularly impressive during cross-examination when Tom Metzger sought to establish that hate-crime laws opened up a "Pandora's box." Schrunk responded: "What you are saying is we can't crawl up inside someone's head and decide why he or she committed the act. The answer is yes." Schrunk then turned to the jury, the people whom he represented in his position. "But when there are overt manifestations of racism, that's something that people in Oregon, certainly this district attorney, will not tolerate."*

From the outset, we had made a conscious effort to remind the jury that we were all here because Mulugeta Seraw had died. When opportunities arose to invoke his name during Metzger's testimony, I seized them. Was Mulugeta "mud"? Was Mulugeta the type of person Metzger was presenting in his "Coon, coon" poem or "What's on a nigger's mind" drawing?

Engedaw's presence at our attorneys' table helped immeasurably in keeping the focus personal rather than abstract. Here was a family

*Metzger's claim that Mazzella was an agent provocateur was so outrageous that some might have thought that it was foolish to waste the time countering it. However, this provided us the opportunity to show the jury that Schrunk and Walker, the two highest symbols of law enforcement in Portland, were allied with us. It also afforded the opportunity for Schrunk's eloquent remark.

member, a person deeply affected by the wrongs done his nephew. His presence humanized Elden and me, allowing us to be seen as lawyers representing a client rather than as self-anointed crusaders out to destroy the Metzgers.

Juries rightly wonder when a party to a lawsuit apparently doesn't feel that it's important enough to come to court. At great sacrifice, Engedaw had taken unpaid leave from his position as a social worker in Oakland to be with us. What must Engedaw have felt when he heard Mieske and the Metzgers testify? Quiet and dignified throughout, Engedaw told us only that he wanted justice.

Engedaw and Mulugeta's father, whom we had flown in from Ethiopia when the trial started, would be our final two witnesses.* Before their emotional testimony, however, we wanted others to paint a picture of Mulugeta. Mieske and Metzger had tried to distort that picture, suggesting he was responsible for the fight that led to his death and may also have been involved in criminal activity. Dr. William J. Brady, a Harvard-trained pathologist and former Oregon state medical examiner, dispelled the notion that Mulugeta had been the aggressor in the confrontation. All of the marks on his hands and arms revealed that he had only been defending himself, said the doctor, who had performed or supervised autopsies in violent death cases for over twenty-five years. There were none of the telltale signs that would have indicated he had struck blows with his fists or choked anyone.

Unfortunately, Dr. Brady's testimony about the blows to Mulugeta's skull and other parts of the body was unavoidably graphic. The autopsy photos he presented to prove his points were not for the squeamish. Engedaw, who had sat stoically while Mieske had described the murder, now turned away, his eyes filled with tears. When we broke for lunch, we suggested that Engedaw stay out of the courtroom until Dr. Brady finished his grisly testimony. Thankfully, Engedaw agreed and therefore avoided hearing how Mulugeta had been struck with the bat while on all fours. The jury, however, did hear this, and several members were clearly angered. We hoped that if the

*Mulugeta's father neither spoke nor understood English and was in the courtroom only on the day he testified.

jurors ruled our way, this testimony would drive up any punitive damages they might award.

Many of our lunches in our courthouse retreat had been surprisingly relaxing. After taking a few minutes to settle down from the pressure and excitement of the morning session, I'd been able to unwind for an hour or so before turning my attention to the afternoon. I'd look out the window at Mount Hood, usually wishing I was there instead of in court. Or I'd visit with Elizabeth, dreaming about where we would really vacation once the trial was finally behind us.

With Elden responsible for the remaining witnesses, I should have been able to take it easy on this day. Instead, I grabbed a sandwich and then huddled with Danny Welch to discuss disturbing news. For days we had been speculating about whom Metzger would call as his witnesses after we rested our case. We assumed that he would put Mazzella back on the stand. Now came word that Metzger was probably going to call one or more of the skinheads who had known Dave after he had moved to Medford a year after the murder. Dave's girlfriend, Ruth, who was still with him in his Portland hideaway, had received a phone call from her sister that these Metzger sympathizers had been contacted by the defense. Presumably they would testify that Dave had remained active in the white supremacy movement.

Dave continued to insist he had left the movement and had merely socialized with skinheads and other racists, whose admiration of him gave him a sense of self-worth. I believed him. But would the jury? If they determined that he was lying about his current beliefs, they might reasonably conclude that his powerful earlier testimony, so critical to our case, had been untruthful.

The timing of this new threat to our star witness's credibility could not have been worse. Earlier in the day, the *Willamette Week,* Portland's free newspaper weekly, had run a cover story about Dave titled "Can This Man Be Believed?" The subheading read: "If Morris Dees' case against hatemonger Tom Metzger depends on Dave Mazzella's testimony, he's in trouble."

The article repeated the eyewitness accounts that Dave had been at the Confetti Club and had identified himself as a Klan sympathizer/

organizer.* The writer also suggested that Metzger's cross-examination of Dave raised serious doubts about our claim that he had been instructed by Tom and John to commit or incite violence. If this was the perception in the jury box as well as in the media, we really were in trouble.

I was to meet with Dave after dinner to prepare him for Metzger's questioning. As our lunch break ended, we determined that Danny should talk with Dave and Ruth immediately to figure out which skinheads might be coming from Medford to help save their hero, Tom Metzger. Armed with names and background information, Danny could then call his sources in law enforcement to learn as much as possible about these potential witnesses. That would be essential to me when I cross-examined them.

Dressed in a blue suit and blue tie, Engedaw was again composed by the time the clerk swore him in as our twenty-third witness. He described for the jury life in Gondar province, Ethiopia, and noted that he had first seen his nephew Mulugeta as a newborn. He recounted his own journey to the United States and then detailed how Mulugeta had written and asked to join him. They had lived together in Portland until he had moved to the Bay Area. They had remained close after this and had last seen each other only a few months before the murder.†

Elden addressed Engedaw gently. "None of us lawyers or parties or jurors ever knew Mr. Seraw. I would just like to ask you a few questions about what kind of fellow he was. Okay?"

Engedaw's lip trembled. He took a deep breath and said, "Sure. Sure."

Engedaw said that he had never seen his nephew intoxicated and that he had not been a drug user. Elden then asked him to relate a

---

*We never learned the identity of the imposter.
†Three other witnesses testified between Dr. Brady and Engedaw. A fellow employee from Avis and an Avis supervisor told the jury that Mulugeta was a peaceful, intelligent, honorable young man and an excellent worker who had been honored as Employee of the Month. Then, in order to provide a means for the jury to calculate damages, an economist testified that Mulugeta, if he had lived, would have earned the equivalent of approximately half a million present-day dollars over the course of his lifetime.

story about Mulugeta on the soccer field. Engedaw's eyes moistened. Again he took a deep breath. In a quivering voice, he described Mulugeta as a good player. "One of his opponents tried to tackle him but fell down. Mulugeta could have scored very easily a goal but decided to pick his opponent up instead of scoring a goal. I thought he was crazy to do that." He laughed weakly.

How would Engedaw describe him to somebody who had never met him?

"Very easygoing, always had a smile on his face. He was kind and respectful of people . . . especially elders. And he was hardworking and eager to learn and eager to make other people happy." Mulugeta had been particularly proud of his widowed father and had tried to help him and the family that remained in Ethiopia financially whenever he could.

Some months after the case was over, I received a letter from Cygnette Cherry, the teacher at the school where Engedaw had worked as a custodian. She described him as "special," an "angel." This was the man whose life had been so senselessly ended by the bat-wielding maniac Ken Mieske, pumped up after a night of passing out the Metzgers' literature, instructed how to provoke a fight with blacks by the Metzgers' agent Dave Mazzella.

Elden asked Engedaw to relate one last story to the jury.

Engedaw nodded. "In 1987, Mulugeta came to Oakland, where I lived, because he hadn't seen my daughter for a year or so." He stopped to dry his eyes. "She was only two years old then. And he insisted on buying her lots of clothes, and I told him she would outgrow everything before, you know, she could wear everything she already had. But he insisted."

Engedaw paused again. The handkerchief was of little use now. "Mulugeta said, 'I want to buy my niece all kinds of clothes.' And I couldn't stop him. He was very—you know—I couldn't stop him doing that, and he was really happy to do it."

Engedaw Berhanu, father, uncle, swallowed hard several times before finishing his story in a broken voice. "And sure enough, my daughter remembered him every time she would wear one of those clothes, and she was"—one last swallow—"she still remembers him."

Through my tears, I could see the tears in several jurors' eyes.

* * *

Mulugeta's father, Seraw Tekuneh, had entered the courtroom before Engedaw's testimony. A slight man, he looked even smaller in his brand-new loose-fitting black suit. A halo of white hair ringed his dark, balding head and a gray beard framed his stoic face. This was a man who had lost his wife in childbirth and lost one child from natural causes. Now he had come halfway across the world because a second child had died from unnatural causes that were completely foreign to his experience. Earlier in the week, Elden, accompanied by a police officer assigned to protect him, had taken Seraw Tekuneh to the cemetery where Mulugeta was buried. All three men had cried at the gravesite.

Mulugeta's nine-year-old son, Henok, whom we had also flown in from Ethiopia, sat next to his grandfather wearing a blue windbreaker, dark slacks, and gym shoes. Neither visitor understood English. An interpreter sat with them on the bench behind our table.

When Seraw Tekuneh took the stand, Elden asked him to describe his son's work on the farm as a young boy. "Mulugeta was very industrious. I saw a lot of promise in him." And how did he do in school? "He was a very hardworking student."

When Mulugeta decided he wanted to follow Engedaw to America, he asked for his father's support. "I offered him my blessings and also I gave him five hundred Ethiopian dollars to help him in his schooling efforts." Seraw Tekuneh explained that he had taken out a loan from his Seventh-Day Adventist organization. "I borrowed, since my son needed money."

The two had experienced difficulty in communicating once Mulugeta left. There was no regular postal service in Seraw's hamlet.

Had Mulugeta ever been involved in fights?

The father shook his head. "He was a well-disciplined child. I raised him carefully. All of my other kids never really got involved in fights like this, and I've been very proud with my kids in general."

Elden asked Seraw Tekuneh if there was anything else he wanted to tell the court or the jury about his son.

Mulugeta's father thought for a moment. Then, with the same expressionless face, he said, "What I want to convey is that all my hope was on my son, because I was counting on him, that he would

come here, benefit from the educational system, become a professional, and come back home and pursue a professional career and help
me and my kids. That was what I had counted on."

I looked at Elizabeth. She had taken Henok's hand.

As Seraw Tekuneh walked slowly back to his grandson, we rested
our case.

Your Honor . . . we will have proof from Mr. Mazzella's own lips that he was bribed; he is continuously being bribed, he has been coached to suborn perjury in this trial. . . . He's being kept under the wing of Morris Dees here. He has no visible means of support. We will bring in witnesses that show that he is being given money, promised things, and that he's carried on a continual reign of terror in the Ashland area. . . . And this has all taken place since he has become an agent of Morris Dees. I must get into this. He is the key witness in this case. Without Dave Mazzella, there is no case.

—Tom Metzger,
October 18, 1990

CHAPTER NINETEEN

October 18, 1990
■
Portland, Oregon

In 1975, I was charged with attempted subornation of perjury in the celebrated North Carolina murder trial of Joan Little, whom I was helping to defend. The accusation was precipitated by my cross-examination of a witness who had given me a statement favorable to our case but had then changed her story on the stand. During a court recess, I had shown the witness her earlier statement, told her I was going to again question her on the contradiction, and then told her to tell the truth as she had in her statement.

When court resumed and I renewed my questioning, the judge stopped the proceedings, asked the witness about my remarks to her during the recess, and then threw me out of the courtroom. Within an hour, the local district attorney had arrested me for a felony that carried a maximum sentence of ten years. The trumped-up charges drew considerable outrage, including an editorial in the *Raleigh News and Observer* that criticized the authorities and described me as a "hapless victim of hometown justice." In this instance, the hometown boys didn't like an outsider coming in and exposing a white male jailer's sexual assault of a black female inmate.

A full week went by before the district attorney finally dropped the charges. Those seven days were among the worst in my life. I worried about my client; now represented by others, she faced the death penalty if convicted. I worried about my mother, my wife and children, and the Center, all of whom faced humiliation if the charges against me stuck. And I worried about myself; the arrest threatened to destroy my good name, my career, and my freedom. Rarely had I felt such fear and, when it was all over, anger.

When, on the morning after we had rested our case, Tom Metzger proclaimed in open court that he had evidence that I had bribed Dave Mazzella, those same emotions revisited me. I knew there was no basis for the accusation. At the same time, however, I realized that Metzger was desperate, and his young followers, whether brainwashed or just loyal, would perjure themselves to save their hero. Metzger claimed to have witnesses, "letters, pictures, and other evidence."

Fortunately, Metzger had delivered his inflammatory accusations outside the jury's presence, during a hearing on totally unrelated motions. Our job now was to invoke the proper objections to keep him from presenting false charges to the panel without first establishing that there was any basis for his wild accusations. I reminded Judge Haggerty that Metzger had already questioned Dave about receiving payments from me and the Center. Dave had adamantly denied being bribed. Metzger had also questioned him thoroughly about the "reign of terror" in Ashland and Medford.

Metzger said he now had witnesses to dispute Dave's testimony about his recent arrests and his recent white supremacist activities, including the alleged incident at the Confetti Club.

Judge Haggerty shook his head. "I can tell you we are not going to get into the newspaper article concerning the Confetti Club." He acknowledged he faced a dilemma in deciding whether or not to allow the impeachment of Mazzella's testimony about recent events in Medford and Ashland because "the jury might find a basis to consider whether Mr. Mazzella was truthful in other parts of his testimony."

Metzger explained that this was not the "thrust" of his inquiry. 'If I present a letter in Mazzella's own handwriting in which he says his buddy Morris Dee has offered to have these Oregon charges dropped and take care of him because Morris Dees has friends in high places, in the government . . . and Dees is such a cool dude, do you believe that will have some bearing on this case?"

"I would suspect," said the judge.

Metzger wheeled and turned to me. "Well, that's what we intend to do."

What the hell had Dave written?

The hearing had produced some good news. Judge Haggerty had previously deferred ruling on the Metzgers' and the ACLU's motions to dismiss certain claims. When we had rested our case on Wednesday afternoon, he had scheduled arguments on the First Amendment issues for this morning.

Those issues had been mooted weeks earlier when we presented our position in a pretrial brief that had dropped any problematic claims. In preparing the original complaint eighteen months earlier, we had alleged that the defendants' behavior was, in the alternative, negligent or reckless, or intentional. We were well aware that the First Amendment protected the Metzgers from liability if their speech had merely been negligent. Case law on liability for reckless speech was ambiguous. But we had never intended to argue that the Metzgers incited the violence resulting in Mulugeta's death through their publications. Indeed, we never argued that the Metzgers incited anyone. Instead, we had always maintained that the Metzgers' agent, Dave Mazzella, pursuant to the Metzgers' instructions, had intentionally encouraged violence.

Metzger objected. "This is a slick move to keep out a really healthy and spirited debate by the ACLU and other people on the Constitutional issues by watering down another part of this suit."

When was Metzger going to understand that this wasn't a free speech case, never had been? The ACLU finally understood . . . almost. Michael Simon, from the Oregon chapter, presented what he described as "curtailed and limited" argument "in light of plaintiff's motions." Disavowing any sympathy for the Metzgers, he offered an eloquent, if irrelevant, analysis of the First Amendment: "It isn't needed to protect socially acceptable, mainstream views. . . . It is needed to protect the extreme, the radical, and, I dare say, even the repugnant."

We agreed. Indeed as Richard Cohen told Judge Haggerty after Simon finished, the plaintiffs and ACLU disagreed on only one point: whether a political organization like WAR or the NAACP was liable for the reckless selection of an agent who commits intentional torts.

Richard argued it was, and Judge Haggerty agreed with his assertion that this was a common-law count based on agency that had nothing to do with the Constitution. Once again Richard had moved us safely through troubled waters.

Elden took the helm an hour later when Tom Metzger called his first witness, Dave Mazzella. When Metzger immediately tried to show Dave a document, Elden argued that we should be allowed to see it before Metzger introduced it to Dave and the jury. Judge Haggerty asked to see it, then excused the panel.

The document was the letter written by Dave that Metzger had referred to during the morning session. Elden and I read it together quickly. On August 29, 1990, from the Jackson County jail, where he was being held on the assault charges, Dave had written a friend named Laura that I would be getting him out of jail on October 5. We weren't troubled by this assertion. We did indeed get him out of jail to come to the trial as a witness.

It was the next paragraph that threw me for a loop: "Morris is so cool. He's probably going to have all of the charges against me thrown out. He's so fucking rich, and he has all kinds of influential friends in the government and law agency."

I had no friends who could get the charges against Dave thrown out, and it would have been unethical to do so under any circumstances. Dave had already testified that I had never promised him anything. The letter was nothing more than the boasting of a kid trying to impress his friends.

Elden rose to argue that the letter and its subject matter should be off-limits. The fact that I might be wealthy or influential was irrelevant, Elden explained, because there was no suggestion that promises had actually been made.

Judge Haggerty adopted a Solomonic posture. Metzger could question Dave about what he had written about me in the letter. He could not, however, introduce the letter itself, most of which, the judge pointed out, was not even remotely relevant to the case.

When the jury returned and Metzger had Dave indentify his signature on the letter and continued his examination, Dave again denied that I had made him any promises or deals. I had merely offered to look into the charges pending against him for the assault in Medford that he alleged someone else had committed.

"Were you impressed about his connections to people in government, law enforcement, big shots?"

"No, I wasn't impressed. I wrote in this letter that he had various connections, and I was hoping with those, they would be able to uncover what really happened in Medford."

Metzger smiled and shook his head. "Oh, what a tangled web we weave."

Had Dave been pushing Bill Albers's American Klan as recently as August?

Dave repeated his earlier testimony: He had not.

How, then, did he explain another letter, dated August 27, 1990, in which he provided Albers's address to friends?

"Several people requested his address because they were interested in him. I had it, so I gave it to them."

And what of the racial symbols and the signature "Racially, Dave Mazzella" at the bottom of the letter? "I thought you were out of this stuff," Metzger said.

Dave reiterated that he had spent time with people in the racist community when things had turned sour and he needed "a sense of security."

Finally, what of the salutation at the beginning of the letter: "Heil, mein bruders"?

"It means 'hello, my brothers,' because they were friends of mine."

"Are you into German culture?" asked an incredulous Metzger.

"I'm part German, yes, a little bit."

"Is that a Nazi greeting?"

"No."

Metzger had done some homework. He displayed a photograph in which Dave and two other young men wore black leather jackets. Dave denied they belonged to an organization.

"Well what kind of un-organization were these people in?"

"We had a little group. It was party clothes. We all just drank and sat around and some other people one day said, 'Let's call it SOS.' " Southern Oregon Skinheads.

Returning to the night of Seraw's murder, Metzger asked Dave if he had directed anyone at the party "to go out and find the nearest nonwhite and hurt them or kill them?"

"No."

How exactly had Metzger taught Dave "the methodology of killing and hurting people"?

Judge Haggerty overruled my objection that this had been asked and answered several times. Again Dave explained that when he would tell Metzger about things he was doing, "You said, 'You're doing a good job. Keep up the good work.'"

After John Metzger chose not to examine Dave, I asked one important question: At the time of his arrest, long before Dave met me or anyone else associated with the case, hadn't he told the Portland police that he worked under Tom Metzger and had committed and encouraged violence?

"Yes."

And finally, Dave Mazzella's ordeal on the witness stand was over . . . for good.

Apparently Dave had written the letter describing me as "so cool" to Metzger's second witness, Laura Jean Dailey of the Medford area. A tight gray-and-black-patterned skirt and a sleeveless black top showed off this tall young woman's striking figure as she walked to the witness stand. Her long bleached-blond hair was parted on the right, revealing a hard, plain face and . . . swastika earrings.

After identifying herself as a member of Southern Oregon Skinheads, Dailey stated that Mazzella had told her "he most likely would get money and a house" out of the case. He had said that he was testifying "for the money." Did the jury believe this? Although Dailey was not particularly credible, on cross-exam I would have to reveal her testimony for the lie it was.

Metzger showed her the photograph of Dave and two skinheads in their leather jackets. She identified the young men as Henry Sullivan and her boyfriend, Leif Bargé, members of SOS. Dave had been the leader, she said. This exhibit was quickly becoming Metzger's favorite. He held it up for the jury to see once again, smiled confidently, and said he had no further questions.

I had several.

Q: Did Mazzella tell you that three days after the murder he told Detectives Nelson and Hefley of his relationship to Mr. Metzger and encouraging violence on his behalf in this community?"

A: No, nothing like that.

Q: Do you believe in the racial beliefs that Mr. Metzger believes in or espouses?

A: Yes, I do.

Q: Well, do you understand that Dave's testimony in this case has potential for hurting Mr. Metzger and his organization?

A: Somewhat, yes.

Q: And you don't want that to happen, do you?

A: Not necessarily.

Metzger's next witness, Leif Bargé, was a strapping young man, six feet four, with short brown hair. Dressed in black, he wore a red cast on his right hand. He testified that he had never met the Metzgers before the trial. A few days earlier, he said, his father had contacted Metzger's wife in Fallbrook and she had put him in touch with Tom.

His credentials were interesting. He belonged to both the Oregon National Guard and SOS, which he had led after Mazzella went to jail. He had visited Dave in jail shortly before the trial. At that time Dave supposedly told Bargé that "if Morris Dees found out he was a skinhead, he wouldn't represent him." Dave also told him, "Tom Metzger had to go under for not helping him . . . when he was in jail. Tom and John totally denied everything ever since the incident happened in Portland."

This wasn't nearly so damning as what Laura Dailey had alleged.

Metzger terminated his questioning without asking Bargé to corroborate his girlfriend's claims. I did.

Had Dave told him, as Laura Dailey alleged, that he expected to get money, a home, or anything else from testifying?

No, said Bargé.

I caught a glimpse of the Metzgers. They looked shocked. I'm certain that they had expected Bargé to protect them, as Laura Dailey had done.

Shane Bukowsky, the final skinhead from Medford, had so little to add that I didn't ask him a single question. Metzger had presented three stooges, none of whom had been able to deliver the goods he had promised earlier in the day.

We had weathered the ACLU and SOS. Now it was time for the NSV.

Metzger had concluded day nine by leading Bonecrusher Straight through a series of self-serving questions. No, Bonecrusher insisted, he had never seen Tom or John teach or encourage violence.

We suspected that Metzger might call witnesses on day ten to do the same. If so, Rick Cooper, the director of the National Socialist Vanguard Association (NSV) and publisher of the *National Socialist Vanguard Report,* would probably be among them. We had not expected Cooper to testify until someone in our group overheard Metzger's thugs mention him after court had adjourned.

Klanwatch's Sara Bullard deserved to be in Portland with us. She had pushed hard to bring this lawsuit and had done much of the research that enabled us to stay one step ahead of the defendants throughout the trial. Knowing we might need more information during the course of the proceedings, we had asked her to stay at the Center, where all our information was housed.

After overhearing the conversation about Cooper on Thursday, we quickly called her and asked for everything she could dig up on the NSV director. By evening, she had rushed out key documents, to arrive the next morning via Federal Express, and had faxed copies to the hotel for our immediate use. She'd struck gold! I stayed up until three in the morning preparing my cross-examination.

Dressed in gray slacks and a Western-style yellow flannel shirt, Cooper took the stand early Friday. He testified predictably. In the sixteen years that he had known Metzger, he had never heard him advocate violence. Had Cooper himself ever promoted violence when dealing with his skinhead friends in the Portland community?

No, he had advocated obeying the law. Indeed, Cooper said, he had tried to avoid potential trouble by mediating differences between rival skinhead groups in the area.

"Have you seen a lot of agent provocateurs who attempt to cause violence for the government's best interests?" asked Metzger.

Yes, said Cooper, adding that it would follow that these same agent provocateurs would infiltrate skinhead groups and thus create violence in the community. I didn't object to this irrelevant testimony; the cross-examination would be a lawyer's dream.

Sara's gems in hand, I began by showing Cooper the October issue of his publication, the *National Socialist Vanguard Report,* just received, thanks to Federal Express. Cooper acknowledged that he had written, at the time when Dave Mazzella arrived in town, that skinheads were moving up to Portland. He had also written: "Likewise, almost immediately skinhead activity increased in Portland with reports of increased assaults on non-whites, racially mixed couples and race traitors."

This was exactly what Mazzella had told the jury. To gain respect and point East Side White Pride in the right direction, he had led them on a reign of terror. How did Cooper get this information so that he could put it in his report?

"Some of it is from the newspapers. Some of it is from personal contact. . . . I get sources all over and I report it."

"Are you telling the jury that you didn't have skinheads, Dave Mazzella and others, reporting to you about all of this violence and you weren't on the phone to Tom Metzger telling him about it so he could put it on his update?"

"Dave Mazzella called me," Cooper said, but he insisted that newspapers were also a source for these reports.

I asked him to read the next sentence of his own article. "These assaults were noted by the police department and tallied, but there was nothing in the news until November thirteenth."

Nothing in the news. Mazzella had obviously been his source.

Cooper said he had no knowledge that Mazzella was an agent of the city of Portland and did not believe he was an agent of the Klan. Metzger had apparently failed to inform Cooper of this last-ditch defense.

Whom did he think Mazzella was representing in Portland?

"I think he was representing himself."

"You do?" I asked. "Why don't you read the next sentence in your report that was written way before this trial and a few weeks before Mr. Seraw's death."

Cooper read: "It should also be noted that both WARskins leaders Dave Mazzella and Mike Barrett from Southern California began recruiting in Portland by distributing large quantities of the WAR newspaper."

I showed him another exhibit listing the WARskins post office box. "That's Tom's address, isn't it?"

"Yes."

Turning back to the *NSV Report,* I asked if the swastika, or Aryan cross, he used as the newspaper's logo was the same one Adolf Hitler used in Germany.

"Sure is," Cooper said proudly.

"Mr. Cooper, have you got some problem with the U.S. government that makes you call it ZOG?"

"Yes, it's a Zionist Occupational Government. It's controlled by the international Jewish bankers used to create wars and revolutions to make a profit."

The words "National Socialist" in NSV were not there by accident. Cooper was a neo-Nazi. ZOG, he said, controlled in part the government in Portland, too.

"Have you about reached your breaking point with this whole thing?"

"Well, I'm very, very angry. Sometimes I wonder how long I can go without breaking."

During a brief recess after Cooper was dismissed, Joe Roy spilled a cup of coffee. As Joe reached for a napkin, a spectator asked him if he was going to clean up the blood on the witness stand.

Tom Metzger rose. "At this time I would like to serve a subpoena on Morris Dees to be a witness in this case."

Judge Haggerty did not even wait for our objection. "Ladies and gentlemen," he told the jury, "we'll have to take a recess here."

When the jury was gone, Metzger explained his reason for subpoenaing me. "I would like to give Mr. Dees the opportunity to clear the air on the charges that we make of bribery, suborning perjury, and other illegal tactics that this attorney has been involved in, not only in this case but in several cases before."

Judge Haggerty reminded Metzger that allegations concerning other cases were off-limits. Elden admitted that such charges had been made by Klansmen on previous occasions. "If anything they are probably badges of honor for Mr. Dees," he said. "But that's not the point. They have nothing to do with this litigation."

"Mr. Dees is not on trial here," agreed the judge. "The court is not going to require him to take the stand."

Metzger grew angry. "I have attempted to open up the doors to evidence during this trial and at every point that door has been locked to us. . . . This is totally germane to the case. It goes to the witch-hunt on Tom Metzger by Morris Dees. And if we don't get him here, we are going to get him somewhere else."

Elden turned angrily. "Is that a threat, Mr. Metzger?"

"I'm talking about in court, Mr. Rosenthal."

Stymied in this last attempt to discredit me, he rested his case.

Metzger had said that his threat referred only to actions in court. During our lunch break, however, Danny said that police intelligence indicated we should all be on guard outside of court. "I know it's been quiet this last week," he said, "but that's the time you really have to be careful." Elizabeth grabbed my hand.

Jim McElroy changed the subject. "I thought for a minute there that you were gonna be a witness, Morris."

"My lawyer told me not to," I said, winking at Elden. He had done a superb job in limiting the scope of inquiry with Metzger's skinhead witnesses and then keeping me off the stand. "Actually, I don't mind if Tom tries to make this a Metzger versus Dees thing. If the jury has to vote, I think they'll vote for me."

"I don't know," Elden replied, smiling. "I think it would be mighty close."

As I stood to begin my closing argument, I saw little Henok and his grandfather sitting on the bench. I walked over to this little boy, who had lost the father he had never known. I clasped both his hands and then hugged him. Then I turned to the jury and said:

Ladies and gentlemen, we have spent two weeks here together trying to get at the truth. . . . This case has important significance not only for Mr. Seraw, who is not here, his son, his father, his uncle, the Metzgers . . . but *this* case is also important for the community, for the state, for the nation. The verdict you are going to render is going to have very far-reaching effects. We hope that verdict will tell Tom Metzger and his organization and all other people who peddle and preach hate and violence in this country that this jury says, No. We are going to stop you right here.

I told the jurors that they had been given a rare look into the inner workings of a hate group, a hate business, and I asked that they use their common sense in judging the evidence. "You heard people talk about 'deadly' not meaning 'deadly'; 'casualty reports' meaning 'I win, you lose.' " John Metzger, I said, "gives new meaning to the word 'mealy-mouth.' " And Tom Metzger "wouldn't tell the truth until he was confronted with prior inconsistent statements, telephone calls, or pieces of film he didn't know existed."

As for Rick Cooper: "I had no idea that the best piece of evidence in the trial was going to come off the witness stand today through one of Tom's witnesses." I held up the *NSV Report,* noting that I'd highlighted in yellow the sections the jurors should read when they retired to reach a verdict.

When trying a case, I explained, I liked to start with evidence that nobody could tamper with. Just four days after the murder, Dave Mazzella had told the Portland police the same thing he told the jury—that he was the Metzgers' man in Portland, that he had instructed the skinheads in the violent ways of WAR. Mieske himself had said that he had never attacked a black person until Dave arrived.

I reminded the jury of the picture Nick Heise had drawn "less than thirty minutes before this child's father's brains were beat out."

Judge Haggerty would instruct the jury about free speech, that it was not absolute, that jurors could look at the words of WAR and the Metzgers as evidence of what they had done or instructed others to do.

Did the jury remember the drawing in the WAR newspaper about inflicting pain with steel-toed boots against "ill-prepared sludge"? I looked at Metzger. "My client is not sludge. Nobody in this room is sludge. Nobody is mud. We are all human beings."

The jury had heard from the man who carried the Metzgers' message to Portland. "If I had a sales manager like Dave Mazzella, I would give him a raise," I said. "This is a fellow who goes off to represent them in a business that he's been sold on to the point he's willing to lay down his life for it."

I showed the jury a large poster-board with a blowup of Metzger's critical admission that Mazzella was an agent who had provoked Mieske and Brewster to commit the violence leading to Mulugeta's death. Whose agent was he? The city's? Chief Walker and District Attorney Schrunk had denied this, and Metzger had offered no proof. Or the Metzgers' and WAR's? John's letter to Ken Death, the record of phone calls, the WAR newspaper itself identifying Dave as vice president of War Youth left little question as to whom Dave was representing.

The jury should not forget that Tom Metzger was making a pretty good living off of this mail-order hate business. John had testified that cash accounted for at least 70 percent of the contributions and payments for books, papers, manuals, and videotapes. Tom had testified that he often took this money from the business account and put it in his own personal account. "I'll be surprised if the other white supremacists don't want to look at his books, too, because at least they claim they are nonprofit," I said.

I moved closer to the jury box and continued:

Juror Johnson said "freedom with responsibility." There are limits to what people can do. . . . In Tom Metzger's America, there would be no Bill Cosby or Jonas Salk or the black man who is the highest-ranking official in our military, General Colin Powell. There wouldn't be the music of Leonard Bernstein. . . . The Aryan, white America that Tom Metzger would like to have is an America that never existed.

He said this skinhead Mieske did "a civic duty." Well, you can do a civic duty when you return a verdict for the plaintiff. Mulugeta Seraw's life will not be like Dr. Martin Luther King's.

But I promise you, if you return a verdict of twelve and a half million dollars of punitive damages and other damages, this case will make history.*

John Metzger would speak before his father. He looked at me and said, "Well, a lot of talk there, Morris. I almost felt like laughing through the whole thing, because, to be perfectly honest, this is a twilight zone trial. I was expecting Rod Sterling to come through the door any minute."

He rambled for another fifteen minutes, demanding, "Where's the beef?" We had piled exhibit upon exhibit, he said, but they proved nothing. "I'm not ashamed for anything I have said or done, because I know I'm right. . . . I never told anyone to go to Portland and do this."

His final remarks were most telling. John told the jury he was the victim of those who for years have heard "this propaganda that people who think of race, especially white racists, are bad. How can I defend myself against people that have that prejudice?"

If Mulugeta Seraw could have spoken, he might have asked that same question.

---

*Elden and I had decided to split our time for closing arguments, with me going first.

The plaintiff has alleged three different bases for holding John Metzger, Tom Metzger, and WAR liable.

First, plaintiff has alleged that those three, through their agents, substantially assisted in or encouraged the conduct that caused Mr. Seraw's death.

Second, plaintiff alleges that Tom Metzger, John Metzger, and WAR were involved in a conspiracy with Kenneth Mieske and Kyle Brewster that led to Mr. Seraw's death.

Third, plaintiff has alleged that Mr. Seraw's death was caused by John Metzger, Tom Metzger, and WAR in recklessly selecting or retaining agents to organize East Side White Pride.

—Judge Ancer Haggerty, instructions to the jury,
October 22, 1990

CHAPTER TWENTY

October 22, 1990
■
Portland, Oregon

In many cases, a jury in a civil suit is merely required to reach a verdict—for the plaintiff or for the defendant. If the decision is for the plaintiff, the jury then assesses damages. Our case was different. The jury would fill out a verdict form that asked five questions about the culpability and intent of each defendant with respect to our various counts. These answers were essential because they would affect our ability to collect a judgment for the next twenty years. The Metzgers could not avoid payment by declaring bankruptcy, for example, if the jury determined that their actions had been intentional rather than reckless or negligent.

During my closing argument, I had led the jurors through the form, question by question. All had listened intently as I explained how we wanted them to answer, and several had taken notes when I suggested the amount of damages to assess against each defendant. Our entire team felt that if the panel had immediately gone off to render their verdict, they would have done exactly as I instructed.

Unfortunately, the jury did not deliberate immediately. After John Metzger concluded his argument late Friday afternoon, Judge Haggerty sent the jury home, announcing that Elden Rosenthal and Tom Metzger would speak on Monday. That was a lot of time in which something bad could happen. We spent a restless weekend in the hotel, watching college and pro football games and hoping there would be no more October surprises on the order of the Confetti Club. Nothing materialized. Perhaps Tom Metzger was too busy preparing for his final hour on center stage.

At nine-thirty on Monday morning, Metzger approached the jury. He held what appeared to be a black metal lunch box. "Ladies and gentlemen, in ancient times in Greece to resolve tribal conflicts people came before leaders and pled their own case, much like I've done and my son has done," he began.

Soon, however, a class of people arose to argue these cases, he explained. They were called rhetoricians, "and these rhetoricians grew into a parasite class we now know as lawyers." He nodded to me and Elden.

"You see this black box," he continued. "It's Morris Dees's and Mr. Rosenthal's view of this case. They put it together. They colored it black. It's evil and sinister. And they began to put their objects into it. Not evidence. Public information. . . . And they got themselves a star witness . . . in reality their only witness."

Without Dave Mazzella, there was no case, argued Metzger. And he proceeded to explain why Mazzella was a liar: Dave had exaggerated everything from the number of times he visited the Metzger house to the number of violent incidents in Portland. More important, he never satisfactorily explained how the Metzgers taught him to hurt or kill. Indeed, he had told the Portland police that the Metzgers did not instruct him in the skinhead ways. "Where is the meeting of the minds here" to suggest a conspiracy? Metzger asked. Where was the agency? Dave had gone to Portland on his own to escape his wife, "probably just to look for girls." WAR had no agents. "WAR is Tom Metzger. That's it."

Metzger wondered, "Where is the smoking gun? . . . Mazzella never testified that, 'hey, after the meeting we decided to go out and get a black man.'"

Could the jury find him not guilty? "I don't think there are four people in this jury that have the guts to find for Tom and John Metzger," he said, and then he warned: "It won't make any difference to me. . . . They say they want to build a ten-million-dollar wall at the Oregon border to keep people like Tom Metzger out. You're whistling past the graveyard." Every day people who agreed with the Metzgers were fleeing California for Oregon to avoid the immigrant "invasion."

He picked up his lunch box. "What is in this case? This black sinister case? Let's look." As he started to open it, the police officers in the courtroom collectively inched forward on their seats. "Nothing," he said. The officers relaxed. Metzger continued:

When you open this box, you are unleashing things that you or I don't know what's going to come out. There is a growing underclass of white people in this country. They are dropping through the grating. They are becoming poorer and poorer. And they don't like what's happening in this country, but they would hope that we still have the right to advocate, to form political parties. They would like for us to reassure them that.

But . . . if you take the easy course of punishing Tom and John Metzger . . . when there is no evidence whatsoever that Tom Metzger will ever change his ways, and the family of Mr. Seraw would only get a pittance, what else would come out of this box? Does it make Tom Metzger bigger? Does it make him a martyr?

Elden Rosenthal, whose relatives had perished in Adolf Hitler's concentration camps, stared at Tom Metzger angrily, then turned to the jury. "I'm proud to be a lawyer in this country with our laws," he said. "I'm going to tell you the difference between a lawyer and a rhetorician. A rhetorician walks back and forth and spins tales out of thin air. A lawyer puts evidence on the witness stand and conforms to the laws of our country. I'm a lawyer."

John Metzger had asked, "Where's the beef?" Elden proceeded to dish up a feast for the jury. When he was through, he reminded his fellow Portlanders that "this case is about cleaning our own house." Metzger had said that a finding of guilty would not stop him. "I don't believe that for a moment," Elden countered. Such a verdict "will stop this kind of exported violence by strangling it financially."

He pointed to the box sitting before Tom Metzger. "That box. That black box. That's Pandora's box. You open that and you let the stuff out, and anything can happen. And it happened on the streets of Portland. . . . Give us the verdict to put this man out of business." Elden sat down. He had been eloquent, powerful, and hometown.

* * *

While the jury deliberated, I shot pool in the police station recreation room with the fellows who had done such a terrific job protecting us for almost three weeks. Shortly before five o'clock, about five hours after the jury had retired, we received a call that a verdict had been reached.

As the jurors filed in, I motioned for Henok to come and sit up on my lap. I had my arms around him when the clerk read the verdict presented by the foreman, Mr. O'Connor. By a vote of 11 to 1, the jury had found all defendants guilty on all counts. They had assessed damages exactly as I had asked: $10 million in punitive damages apportioned as follows:

> Kyle Brewster: $500,000
> Ken Mieske: $500,000
> John Metzger: $1,000,000
> WAR: $3,000,000
> Tom Metzger: $5,000,000

The jury also awarded $2.5 million in damages for Mulugeta's unrealized future earnings and the pain and suffering he felt during the beating. This was to be apportioned evenly among the defendants.*

Elizabeth told me that when the verdict was announced John Metzger blinked uncontrollably and Tom Metzger put his hand to his forehead.

We met the press after the verdict, breaking our self-imposed silence for the first time in two weeks. I said that we would collect every penny we could for Mulugeta's family. "I think we finally peeled off Metzger's public front down to his stuffing his pockets full of money that people sent him in contributions." Metzger needed to be stopped, I explained, because he had been growing more and more dangerous, training with assault rifles and distributing military manuals explaining how to make explosives.

Through a translator, Mulugeta's father said, "When my son first

---

*Oregon's Tort Reform Act of 1987 limits awards for noneconomic losses (i.e., pain and suffering) in civil cases to $500,000.

came to this country, I had the hope he would work here and go back home and help his people. That didn't happen. People from this country who I would like to call my brothers have avenged my son's death for me. This is the happiest I felt since my son died because I know now he didn't die in vain."

Tom Metzger also held a press conference. He said he had expected the verdict and that he would not let it deter him from his mission. "We will continue. . . . Under the Constitution I can advocate violence now and nobody can sue me anymore. I'll be broke, and all the things that I'm accused of that I didn't do, now I'm totally free to do."

This bit of postverdict revisionism might have been dismissed; he would have a most difficult time continuing his hate business. But Metzger's next comments were chilling. He said he and John were going out to "celebrate" the white racist/white separatist movement. Then, raising his voice and narrowing his eyes, he added:

The movement will not be stopped in the puny town of Portland. We're too deep. We're imbedded now. Don't you understand? We're in your colleges, we're in your armies, we're in your police forces, we're in your technical areas, we're in your banks. Where do you think a lot of these skinheads disappeared to? . . . We've planted the seeds. Stopping Tom Metzger is not gonna change what's going to happen in this country.

Epilogue

After uttering these harrowing words, Tom Metzger was unable to post an appeal bond. As a result the Seraw family forced the sale of his home and personal property. The funds are being held in trust pending the outcome of Metzger's appeal.

After the ruling, Tom Metzger received welfare payments for a time. This must have been especially embarrassing for an able-bodied man fully capable of working who was known for criticizing blacks as welfare cheats. He also received a six-month jail sentence for the 1983 burning of a cross in Los Angeles in violation of local fire laws. He served two months before being released to be with his terminally ill wife, who later died of cancer. A condition of his parole prohibits him from engaging in white supremacy activity for three years.

We had long known that Metzger was receiving help from lawyers, and they surfaced for the appeal. Metzger's main defense is again the First Amendment. He vows to appeal all the way to the United States Supreme Court if necessary. The ACLU has declined to get involved.

Bill Moyers produced a two-and-one-half-hour special on the case for public television. On the program a distinguished panel of legal scholars unanimously agreed that Metzger's actions in the Seraw case crossed the line of First Amendment protection. They agreed with our position that you have the right to hate but not to hurt.

Henok, Seraw's precocious and personable young son, could speak no English when he accompanied his grandfather to the United States for the trial. We appeared together on the *Donahue* show six months later. After he told me in nearly perfect English that he was enjoying school, I asked him what he wanted to be when he grew up. "President, maybe," he said. He stayed with Engedaw Berhanu and his wife for over a year before returning to Ethiopia.

Shortly after the Portland trial, I received a warm letter from Engedaw, thanking me for bringing out the truth about his nephew. He noted that in Ethiopia, one who vindicates the death of a loved one is an honored person. "I'm glad to call you my brother," he wrote.

Cathy Bennett lost her courageous six-year battle with cancer. Shortly before her death, she defied her doctors and left the hospital to handle the William Kennedy Smith case. "They truly have an innocent man on trial in Palm Beach," she told me. This talented, caring, and loving young woman began her career with the Wounded Knee trials and played a major part in most of my significant cases. She never charged the Law Center, returning a $10,000 check I sent her and her husband, Robert Hirschhorn, after the Metzger trial.

Dave Mazzella and Ruth were married and now have a son. Dave has lived an exemplary life since the trial. He has a good job and is seeking more education. My faith in Dave has been vindicated. He lives in an undisclosed location, still fearing that his testimony against the Metzgers could bring severe retribution. Dave did a courageous thing testifying against his former friends. He took a lot of criticism from a cynical press, and I'm sure at times he wonders if it was worth the price he has had to pay, living in isolation from his friends and family.

Mark Sommes, the San Diego WAR member FBI agents apprehended for mailing me the anonymous letter threatening harm for "messing with white power" and for suing Metzger, was sentenced to three years in federal prison.

The real hero since the trial has been San Diego attorney Jim McElroy, who took responsibility for collecting the judgment. He has devoted over a thousand hours, free of charge, in California courts, trying to corner the assets of an increasingly secretive and devious

Tom Metzger. After Jim obtained a court order allowing a receiver to open mail coming to WAR's post office box and remove checks, Tom directed that money be sent to a number of out-of-state addresses. Jim and a team of San Diego volunteer lawyers are now closing in on those who have helped the Metzgers avoid paying the judgment.

As I travel the nation speaking to law students, bar associations, and other groups, I am constantly asked why the Seraw family did not share with the Center some of the $12.5 million they received. I explain that the Seraws have not received millions because the Metzgers don't have millions, only a few thousand dollars more than the value of their $125,000 house; the large verdict represented the punitive damages the jury felt this horrible crime merited. Every penny we collect will go to Henok Seraw. Even the cost of collection will be absorbed by the Center and the Anti-Defamation League.

The verdict sent a strong message to white supremacists. It also allows us to force Tom and John Metzger to pay a portion of their income for the next twenty years to the Seraw family. This should cripple their ambitious plans and make their hate-selling business less profitable.

Since the verdict, the Metzgers have made a lot of noise on their telephone hotline but have published very little. Their donations have fallen off drastically, and they find it hard to do business without bank accounts. They do, however, have the right to speak out on racial matters. Tom Metzger is especially articulate and will be sought by opportunistic talk-show hosts. But skinheads and many white supremacists learned from the trial that the Metzgers were in the movement primarily for money, and these people are now seeking other groups to follow. The role Tom Metzger envisioned for himself as the white supremacist leader in America never materialized.

Sadly, though, Tom Metzger's dire warning, after the trial, that stopping him would not stop the movement was correct. Despite our success in destroying this dangerous demagogue, our nation remains torn by racism and racial violence. Last year our Klanwatch division identified 346 white supremacist groups in this country, a 27 percent increase over the number in 1990. But even more alarming than the growth of these groups on society's fringe is the rising tension in mainstream America. Almost daily we read of vicious hate crimes and other activities that violate moral law, if not criminal law. In Crown

Heights, New York, an African American stabs a rabbinical student. In Medford, Oregon, a white man beats to death a black ex-Marine. In Dubuque, Iowa, white citizens organize to resist local government's attempts to integrate the community. In Olivet, Michigan, a brawl erupts between blacks and whites at a tiny college founded by abolitionists as a bastion of racial tolerance.

Middle-class whites, many born after the civil rights movement, say they have not discriminated against blacks and are angry because they feel that blacks, who once cried for equal opportunity, now want a guaranteed slice of the pie. Quotas, they argue, are unfair. Whites also fear crime, drugs, decreased property values, and deterioration of schools if blacks and Hispanics move into their neighborhoods. Realistic or not, these are the feelings I hear expressed. These whites have little patience with or understanding of the three hundred years of slavery, Jim Crow laws, economic deprivation, and second-class citizenship that blacks have endured.

African Americans say that the promised equal opportunity has not materialized. The businesses that open their doors to minority employment have glass ceilings, limiting advancement to lower-level jobs. The Federal Reserve Board's study of bank loans appears to validate blacks' claims of continuing discrimination in economic areas. The 1991 study showed that blacks with credit credentials as strong as those of whites were denied loans at twice the rate whites were. And blacks insist that job preference goals have done little to narrow the gap between the incomes of white and black college graduates.

Other ethnic groups, especially Asians and Hispanics, are making greater strides than blacks, which causes hard feelings in poorer black neighborhoods. Many Jews, once among the primary supporters of blacks in their struggle for civil rights, are now dismayed by the anti-Semitic remarks of some black leaders and the violent attacks by blacks against Jews in places like Crown Heights.

White jurors in Simi Valley, California, demonstrated their fear of blacks by acquitting the four policemen who beat up Rodney King. The Los Angeles riots that followed were a loud wake-up call. Time will tell if America will get out of bed and deal with the serious problems of racism, inner-city blight, and the diminution of the American dream.

Dr. Martin Luther King, in his 1963 "I Have a Dream" speech, said that one day, he dreamed, the sons of slaves and the sons of former slave owners would sit down around the table of brotherhood. Lawsuits are the result of conflicts and bitter feelings; they are necessary to provide a peaceful method of dispute resolution. Until we all sit around the table of brotherhood and explore our differences, courtrooms will remain active and hate groups will flourish. We must learn to love one another, truly care about our neighbors, and put aside blind prejudice.

Our success in lawsuits against the Klan and the Metzgers, and the success of hatemongers-turned-politicians like David Duke, have forced white supremacists to rethink how they conduct their business. Recently, Thom Robb, a long time Klansman, announced that he was creating his own school. He invited white supremacists and separatists to come to Zinc, Arkansas, where they will be taught everything from history to public relations. His hope is to create a whole generation that will, as Tom Metzger suggested, enter politics, business, law enforcement, and the education system.

If the battlefield is moving from the courtroom to the classroom, we at the Southern Poverty Law Center are ready. Since the Metzger trial we have begun a new project, Teaching Tolerance. Twice yearly we send over two hundred thousand teachers a free magazine that explores concepts for teaching tolerance. In addition, our staff has produced a teaching kit on the civil rights movement that contains a text, teacher's guide, and video. Each year we will develop additional free teaching kits on tolerance for students of various ages. The response has been tremendous.

Until the day when we learn to live in peace, we must remain vigilant against racial violence. As I write these closing lines, we are considering filing suit against the Church of the Creator for the murder of a black sailor in Jacksonville, Florida, by one of the group's "ministers." This virulent racist group, based in North Carolina, recruits primarily in prisons.

The sailor, a veteran of the Gulf war, had been "adopted" as a pen pal during the conflict by a fourth-grade class in his hometown of Oklahoma City. He visited the students when he returned and spoke about the need for racial harmony. After his tragic death, one of the students wrote his murderer, asking, "Why did you kill our hero?"

I hope I can learn the answer as we investigate the killer and his hate group. Even more, I hope I can learn how to reach young minds before the Metzgers of the world turn them into caldrons of seething bigotry. America can be a great nation and live up to its ideals of social, racial, and economic justice. No goal is more important to our survival as a free society.

ABOUT THE AUTHORS

MORRIS DEES is the cofounder and chief trial counsel of the Southern Poverty Law Center.

STEVE FIFFER is an author and attorney who holds a B.A. in American studies from Yale and a J.D. from the University of Chicago Law School.